# New York City Mutual Savings Banks, 1819-1861

# New York City Mutual Savings Banks, 1819-1861

ALAN L. OLMSTEAD

The University of North Carolina Press
Chapel Hill

Library of Congress Cataloging in Publication Data

Olmstead, Alan L
  New York City mutual savings banks, 1819-1861.

  Bibliography: p.
  Includes index.
  1. Savings-banks—New York (City)—History.
I. Title.
  HG1923.N7043     332.2′1′097471     75-28114
  ISBN 0-8078-1265-X

To Marilyn

# Contents

Acknowledgments  xiii
1. Historical Background and Trustee Objectives  3
2. The Changing Nature of Mutual Savings Banks  20
3. Mutual Savings Bank Depositors  48
4. Investment Constraints and the Financing of Early American Development  74
5. The Convergence of Mutual Portfolios: Efficiency Considerations and Trustee Objectives  97
6. The Determinants of Mutual Behavior: Commercial Bank Deposits and Call Loans  117
7. The End of an Era and a Look into the Future  147
Appendixes
A. Occupations of Mutual Depositors  155
B. Total Amount on Deposit and Number of Accounts in Each Mutual, 1 January 1820-1861  157
C. Assets of New York City Mutuals on the First of Each Year  162
D. Total Amount on Deposit and Number of Accounts in All New York City Mutuals, 1 January 1820-1861  182
E. Cumulative Assets of All New York City Mutuals, 1 January 1820-1861  184
F. Balances in Commercial Banks on 1 January  187
Notes  195
Bibliography  213
Index  227

# List of Tables

1 New York City Mutual Savings Banks Chartered Before 1860   16
2 Business Hours of New York City Mutual Savings Banks at Five Sample Dates   31
3 New York City Mutual Savings Bank Dividend Rates, 1820-1860   36
4 Mutual Surpluses in January 1860   44
5 New Customers of the Bank for Savings   51
6 New Depositors by Occupational Classes for the Bank for Savings, Greenwich, and Bowery Savings Banks for Sample Years   52
7 Distribution of Deposits, Bank for Savings in the City of New York   54
8 Distribution of Deposits, Greenwich and Bowery Savings Banks   55
9 Average Balance Per Account for Eighteen New York City Mutuals, the Savings Bank of Baltimore, the Provident of Boston, and all Savings Banks in the United States, 1820-1861   56
10 Distribution of Depositors and Accounts by Size of Accounts, Seamen's Bank for Savings, 1 January 1845   58
11 The Number of Large Deposits, Bank for Savings   61
12 Fluctuations in Net Deposits, Seamen's Bank for Savings, 1830-1861   71
13 The Dates When Various Types of Investments by Mutual Savings Banks First Became Legal   75
14 Rate of Growth of Deposits for Bank for Savings, Seamen's, and Bowery, 1846-1850   104
15 Interest Rates on New York Canal Fund Deposits in Commercial Banks   122

16 Estimate of the Bowery's Subsidy to the Butchers' and Drovers'
   Bank   131
17 Percentage of Assets Loaned on Call, Nineteen New York
   Mutual Savings Banks, 1851-1867   139
18 Financial Structure of Knickerbocker Savings Bank at Time of
   Failure in 1854   142
19 Securities Used as Collateral for Call Loans, Broadway Savings
   Institution, January 1853 to April 1855   144

# List of Figures

1 Key Administrative Changes for Twelve Mutuals 28
2 Rate of Change of Deposits for Four Mutuals 67
3 Rate of Change of Deposits for Five Mutuals Founded after 1848 68
4 The Supply and Demand for State Bonds: The Bank 80
5 The Supply and Demand for State Bonds: The Market 80
6 Government Securities as a Percentage of Total Assets of Four Mutual Savings Banks 100
7 Mortgage Loans as a Percentage of Total Assets of Four Mutual Savings Banks 101
8 Total Amount Invested in Government Securities by Four Mutual Savings Banks 102
9 Amount Loaned on Bond and Mortgage by Four Mutual Savings Banks 103
10 Mortgage Loans and Government Bonds as a Percentage of Total Assets of Six Mutual Savings Banks 106
11 Mortgage Loans and Government Bonds as a Percentage of Total Assets of Seven Mutual Savings Banks 107
12 Real Estate Mortgage Market with a Usury Law 111

# Acknowledgments

Many friends and colleagues have assisted in the research and writing of this book. Jeffrey G. Williamson, Ralph Andreano, and Morton Rothstein labored through the early drafts. My debt to them for their insights and encouragement is enormous. Victor Goldberg and C. Daniel Vencill each supplied thoughtful criticisms on several chapters and were unusually tolerant of my frequent requests that they "take a quick look at this section." Invariably they returned the material vastly improved.

In the formative stages I benefited from conversations and criticisms of John Bowman, Rondo Cameron, Donald Hester, Key Kim, Eric Lampard, and Eugene Smolensky. James Sturm not only read and commented on an early draft, but also tracked down loose ends for me in various New York libraries. In the later stages of my writing, Thomas Mayer read the entire manuscript, made valuable suggestions, and answered numerous questions. Elias Tuma relieved me of some of my teaching responsibilities at a critical time so that I could concentrate on research and writing.

I am grateful to Marguerite Crown and Sally Lu Lake for their editorial criticisms, secretarial assistance, and perseverance at the end.

I would also like to thank the editors of the *Business History Review* and the *Journal of Economic History* for permission to reuse material previously published in those journals. Specifically, parts of Chapter 3 first appeared in the *Business History Review* and parts of Chapters 4 and 5 first appeared in the *Journal of Economic History*.

This book would not have been possible without the sincere interest of the officers of several New York City mutual savings banks who allowed me access to their banks' records and provided me with research facilities. I am indebted to Alfred S. Mills, Chairman of the Board of the New York Bank for Savings, Edmund F. Wagner, Trustee Emeritus Chairman of the Board of the Seamen's Bank for Savings, Clinton W. Bell, Senior Vice-President and Treasurer (retired) of the Seamen's Bank for Savings, Eleanor C. Waters, Vice-President of the Seamen's Bank for Savings, Robert J. LaFrentz, Senior Vice-President and Comptroller of the Seamen's Bank for Savings, William H. Soth, Secretary (retired) of the Bowery Savings Bank, Le Roy Van

Dine, Assistant Vice-President and Secretary (retired) of the Dry Dock Savings Bank, Francis J. Ludemann, Chairman of the Board (deceased) of the Manhattan Savings Bank, L. Emory Boyden, Vice-President (retired) of the Manhattan Savings Bank, E. Harold Kimbark, Senior Vice-President and Treasurer of the Broadway Savings Bank, Helen M. DeLuise, Vice-President (retired) of the East River Savings Bank, and Joseph G. Reily, Senior Vice-President and Secretary of the Emigrant Savings Bank.

I would like to express special gratitude to Anna M. Flaherty, Vice-President (retired) of the New York Bank for Savings, and Mildred M. Berg, Corporate Secretary of the Seamen's Bank for Savings. Their assistance and friendship have been invaluable.

Finally, I would like to thank my wife, Marilyn, for her tolerance, encouragement, many skills, and most of all for enduring all those anecdotes about the provident poor.

# New York City Mutual Savings Banks, 1819-1861

CHAPTER **1**

# Historical Background and Trustee Objectives

## Introduction

Study of the history of capitalism reveals that it is a rare business enterprise that lacks a capital stock or a profit account, is founded and managed by men who expressed no desire for monetary rewards, and lacks owner-entrepreneurs. Mutual savings banks are just such rarities. It has almost become axiomatic that the quest for profit not only is the fundamental rationale for economic activity but also provides the best guarantee for economic survival: in capitalist economies where the invisible hand ruthlessly weeds out weak and incompetently managed firms, the lure of personal reward attracts the bright and aggressive managers needed for success. Firms that do not adhere to the straight and narrow, that place charitable ideals ahead of their striving for profits, must accept a higher risk of failure. According to the conventional wisdom, philanthropic firms without owner-entrepreneurs are more sluggish and less efficient than their profit-seeking counterparts, guided by men whose personal fortunes are at stake. It is thus with some curiosity that we find mutual institutions flourishing in the rapidly changing, dog-eat-dog environment where the likes of Jay Gould and Daniel Drew stalked their financial prey.

More than twenty mutual savings banks were founded in the New York City area in the forty-two years preceding the American Civil War (1819-1861). For the first two decades of this period the story of these banks centers on the activities of one institution—the Bank for Savings in the City of New York. This bank, which received its first deposits on 3 July 1819, was the product of the philanthropic zeal of several of New York's most prominent citizens. Initially the bank was only open six hours a week and transacted its business in a basement room of what was popularly known as the Old Alms House, which the city fathers provided rent-free. While operating in these humble quarters on a part-time basis with a voluntary management, the Bank for Savings rapidly emerged as one of the

3

financial behemoths of the time. Within two years of its opening it had become the single most important financier of the Erie Canal and within a decade it bore a similar relationship to the internal improvement projects of Ohio and New York City.

Compared to other important savings banks, the Bank for Savings' early growth was phenomenal. The Savings Bank of Baltimore, which was the subject of Payne and Davis's path-breaking study, took eleven years to accumulate deposits equal to the amount held by the Bank for Savings at the end of its first full year of operation.[1] In 1825 there were fifteen savings banks in the United States, yet the Bank for Savings held 56 percent of all savings bank deposits. By 1835, when fifty-two savings banks were in existence, it still accounted for 34 percent of all deposits and 42 percent of all customers. At this later date the size of this one New York enterprise measured in terms of total assets and the number of depositors was roughly equal to the combined strength of all twenty-two savings banks in Massachusetts.[2] By 1861 another New York institution, the Bowery Savings Bank, surpassed the Bank for Savings as the nation's largest mutual. At that time each of these banks commanded deposits in excess of $10 million, and a third New York mutual, the Seamen's Bank for Savings, was approaching that mark.

Since the 1820s New York City has been the hub of mutual savings banking activity. As of 1969 nine of the ten largest mutual savings banks in the nation, with combined assets in excess of $14 billion, were located in New York City.[3] Most of these institutions trace their origins back to the antebellum years. Notwithstanding the absolute size and importance of mutual savings banks today, their heyday was in the antebellum era, for never since has their relative stature or impact on the economy been equaled. In 1860 their combined assets were more than six times those of the next most important type of non-bank financial intermediary, life insurance companies.[4] Even more impressive was the size of some of the individual banks; in 1860, three New York City mutuals (the Bank for Savings, the Bowery, and the Seamen's) ranked among the ten largest business organizations in the country.[5] New York's mutual savings banks had a considerable effect on local and regional economies. They were the single most important source of funds for many municipal and state governments, they dominated the local mortgage market, they were an important source of deposits for commercial banks, and many were active in the call-loan market. Mutuals also affected the savings habits of a large number of New Yorkers; in 1860 the number of mutual savings bank accounts approximately equaled one-fourth of the city's total population. Additionally, many of these institutions attracted the support of some of the city's most prominent businessmen and politicians. Indeed, it would be difficult to find among the annals of business history a more distinguished group of individuals than that associated with the founding of the Bank for Savings.

Given the historical importance and organizational novelty of mutual savings banks, there has been inadequate investigation into their origins. What were the trustees' objectives? Were bank operating procedures consistent with achieving these stated objectives? How did these objectives and procedures evolve in response to a changing legal environment and to a rapid growth in business? Who were their depositors? How did mutuals influence local and regional development? How did they interact with each other and with the commercial banking sector? Answers to these questions will help fill the void in our knowledge of New York City mutuals and will offer a firmer foundation for evaluating mutuals organized in other cities. The answers will also provide some insights into the behavior of commercial banks in New York and will give us a better understanding of the more general process of the accumulation and allocation of financial capital during a critical period in American economic development. The first step in this quest is to give a brief account of the evolution of the savings bank movement.

## The European Antecedents

Savings banks date back to the second half of the eighteenth century, when several small savings institutions were formed in Germany and Switzerland. Little is known about these organizations except that they accepted small deposits and catered to the working class. Many probably were not savings banks in the sense that we know them today, but were annuity schemes that did not allow withdrawals until members reached a certain age. By the end of the eighteenth century the notion that savings banks could significantly benefit the lower classes and play a leading role in society's crusade against pauperism gained popularity among leading British social thinkers, including Jeremy Bentham, David Hume, Robert Torrens, Thomas Malthus, and David Ricardo. In 1797, as part of his overall program for the management of paupers, Bentham proposed that a national system of "Frugality Banks" be attached to "Industry Houses" and church vestries, and Malthus in his *Essay on the Principle of Population* advocated a network of country banks to serve the laboring poor.[6]

In this sternly individualistic age the British upper class saw society plagued by pauperism and longed for a solution that would satisfy immediate humanitarian needs without fanning the fire of poverty by rewarding idleness. To this dilemma savings banks offered an appealing answer. Whereas indiscriminant alms-giving would promote corruption, reward laziness, and weaken family ties, savings banks would encourage public order, thrift, sobriety, virtue, industry, and prosperity. With such noble goals in mind several philanthropic groups, usually in association with churches or friendly societies, instituted modest savings and annuity schemes for the poor between 1790 and 1810. Notwithstanding the existence of these programs, the Reverend Henry Duncan is generally credited with founding the first modern, self-supporting savings bank at Ruthwell, Scotland, in 1810. From there the idea began to spread and by the end of 1815 approximately twenty-six savings banks had been founded in Scotland and England. These pioneer institutions experimented with various organizations and procedures, thereby providing models for others to copy. And copy they did, for the next three years witnessed one of the most rapid spontaneous social movements in British history, as savings bank enthusiasts spread their gospel with an almost missionary-like zeal. By the end of 1818 there were 465 savings banks in the British Isles. It was on the crest of this expansionary wave that the savings bank movement came to the United States.[7]

**The Savings Bank Movement in New York: The Legal Environment**

The first known reference to a savings bank in New York (and in the United States) is attributed to John Pintard, who advanced the idea of forming a "Savings Association" in 1809, but it was not until the spring of 1816 that serious efforts to establish a bank began.[8] In a letter dated 3 April 1816 Pintard remarked that he was aiding in the promotion of a new association "to induce habits of economy by receiving the savings of labourers & domestics & putting them out to interest. . . ."[9] At approximately the same time Thomas Eddy, who like Pintard was a successful New York insurance and stock dealer, became interested in organizing a savings bank. Since the turn of the century Eddy had been corresponding with Patrick Colquhoun, a London magistrate who in 1806 had proposed a national system of savings banks to be overseen and guaranteed by the Crown. Eddy probably had been aware of this and other proposals afloat in Britain for some time, but a letter dated 19 April 1816, in which Colquhoun described the great success of the savings bank movement in Britain and enclosed a detailed outline of the organizational structure of a bank recently opened, is credited with spurring Eddy to take action.[10]

The first public meeting to organize a savings bank was held on 25 November 1816. Events moved swiftly and in less than a week two more meetings took place at which the proposed bank's form began to take shape. A meeting held on 27 November 1816 resulted in a public statement entitled "A Bank for the Poor," which described the origins and success of similar institutions in England and Scotland and offered a vague outline of the bank's philanthropic intent, its mode of management, and the scope of its investments. At the third meeting held on 29 November 1816 and presided over by Eddy, a detailed constitution for "The Savings Bank of New York" was formally adopted. The document named thirty "Directors" including such political notables as DeWitt Clinton, Cadwallader Colden, Peter A. Jay, Richard Varick, and Brockholst Livingston.[11] At the next meeting, held on 10 December 1816, the board of directors appointed committees to locate a suitable home for the bank, to draft an address to the public, and to report on the expediency of applying to the state legislature for a corporate charter. On 17 December 1816 a draft of the proposed "Act of Incorporation" was presented and plans were laid to apply for a charter. The board also decided to advertise that the bank would open for business on 4 January 1817.[12]

Since the directors could not have hoped to have secured a charter on such short notice (the legislature was adjourned until 21 January 1817), we must presume that they intended to commence operations without one. Such a procedure would not have been unusual; the Philadelphia Saving Fund Society opened on 2 December 1816 but was not incorporated until 25 February 1819, and the Savings Bank of Baltimore opened on 16 March 1818 but was not incorporated until 30 January 1819.[13] For unspecified reasons the directors of the proposed New York enterprise had a change of heart and in late December decided to postpone opening until they acquired a charter. As events transpired this proved to be a fateful decision; the legislature refused to grant a charter. Whereas attempts to organize savings banks in most states engendered little legislative opposition, in New York similar efforts became enmeshed in political difficulties. Previous accounts of the early failure have treated it as an unfortunate or quaint episode that delayed the establishment of a savings bank in New York by two and one-half years but otherwise had little lasting significance. But a re-examination shows that during the struggle to obtain a charter, the bank's constitution was amended in ways that profoundly affected the development of mutual savings banks in New York state.

As the story of mutual savings banks in New York City unfolds, it will become evident that they evolved quite differently from their counterparts in other large seaboard cities, and that much of this difference can be attributed to the legal environment of New York. When the Bank for Savings in the City of New York finally commenced operation in 1819, its charter stipulated that all funds be invested in debt issued by the government of the United States or New York state.[14] This was much more binding than the legal constraints found in Massachusetts or Pennsylvania, and a far cry from the free enterprise, "go for broke" spirit of the laws regulating savings banks in Maryland. In subsequent chapters the legal environment and its effect on bank policy will be analyzed in considerable detail, but an understanding of its original level is intertwined with the account of the attempts to establish a bank in New York.

The constitution adopted on 29 November 1816 contrasted sharply in several important respects with the charter finally granted on 26 March 1819. The most important difference concerned investments. The 1816 document stipulated that "all monies deposited in the Bank, except such sums as it may be deemed necessary to reserve for immediate purposes, shall be invested in Government securities of the United States, of this State, of the Corporation of the city of New-York, *or in such other funds as the Directors may deem expedient.*"[15] This open-ended declaration was similar to that enacted on behalf of the Philadelphia Saving Fund Society and probably would have been no more binding than the charters of the Savings Bank of Baltimore and the Provident Institution for Savings in the Town of Boston, both of which gave almost unlimited discretion to the banks' trustees.[16] Another important feature of the 1816 constitution is found in article four, which reads in part: "The Directors shall appoint a Cashier, and such other persons as they may deem necessary to be employed in the Bank. . . ."[17] The term "cashier" as well as the general administrative structure envisioned in the plan of 1816 were adopted from the parlance and organization used by commercial banks, where the cashier was typically the managing officer in charge of day-to-day affairs. This choice of terms and structure was undoubtedly a tactical error because the record of the bill of incorporation indicates that many legislators who were opposed to incorporating banks of discount failed to comprehend the special character and purpose of savings banks. A bill to incorporate "The Savings Bank of the City of New York" was introduced into the Assembly on 3 February 1817 and referred to a select committee for consideration. On 11 March 1817 the committee reported the bill back to the Assembly but with the unfavorable evaluation that it doubted the bank could succeed because the operating expenses would be too great. As an alternative the committee recommended that one of the existing commercial banks in New York allow one of its " 'clerks to transact the business for a small extra allowance.' " On 31 March 1817 the Assembly considered the bill and returned it to another select committee. Two days later this committee reported that it had made sundry amendments to the bill and recommended that it be passed into law. There is no record of the amendments made except that the title was altered to "An Act *to incorporate an association by the name of the saving corporation of the city of New York.*"[18] This attempt to distinguish the savings bank from a commercial bank by substituting the word "corporation" for "bank" in the name failed to win sufficient support and the bill died without a recorded vote. Reflecting on these events two years later, the directors of the savings bank attributed their failure to a lack of understanding of the principles and functions of a savings bank and to widespread objections against incorporating more commercial banks.[19] There is good reason to accept their knowledgeable assessment, and it probably was to prevent similar confusion that three of the four savings banks incorporated prior to the Bank for Savings (1819) did not include the word "bank" in their names. It is also significant that two of these banks operated for a considerable period of time before applying for acts of incorporation, thereby accumulating goodwill and demonstrating their significant differences from commercial banks before votes were ever taken.

The directors' tactical errors combined with the ignorance of some legislators contributed to the failure of 1817 and may help explain the strict legal environment finally established in New York in 1819, but a more fundamental explanation of these events rests in the state's political history. In the period in question New York was a relatively difficult state in which to obtain banking privileges. Hammond notes that between 1810 and 1812 the New York legislature chartered ten commercial banks which "relative to what other states were doing was conservative."[20] For the remainder of the decade only thirteen banks were chartered in the state and only one of these was in New York City. Few issues incited more political turbulence than the business of chartering banks. Special interest groups, both those seeking a new charter and those with charters in hand trying to protect their privileges, spared few tricks as they scurried to line up votes. Memories of the deception employed to charter the Manhattan Company and the no-holds-barred fight to charter the Bank of America gave ample reason for legislators to doubt the stated intentions of the savings bank's directors.[21] A seemingly minor event may have further aroused legislative suspicions. On 10 March 1817, the day before the bill to incorporate the savings bank was first reported out of committee, a rival group petitioned for a charter for a bank named "The New York Interest Bank." Although we know little about this petition or its backers, Keyes has surmised "that some sharp-eyed financier, cognizant of the movement in favor of a Savings Bank . . . , saw in the scheme plausible grounds upon which to secure a private charter for a new banking corporation." A year later in March 1818 another unsuccessful attempt was made to incorporate a commercial bank disguised as a philanthropic savings bank. The petitioners cloaked their request for note issuing and discounting privileges with lengthy accounts of their benevolent intentions to help widows and orphans, honest and fair tradesmen, and to "beget habits of economy, of calculation, and of foresight in all classes of the community." The fact that one of the names attached to this petition, that of Dennis McCarthy, would also be listed among the incorporating trustees of the Bank for Savings in 1819 may have in part given rise to the close scrutiny its petition was to receive.[22]

The dejected promoters of the defeated New York Savings Bank decided to pursue their goal by working through a new association, The Society for the Prevention of Pauperism. Several of the savings bank's supporters, including Pintard, Eddy, John Griscom, Brockholst Livingston, and Zachariah Lewis, took the lead in founding this group in December 1817. The society's first step was to assign a committee of eight (which included the five men named above) to write a report on the subject of pauperism. This paper, reportedly drafted by Griscom, analyzed the causes of pauperism and recommended a multi-front attack to stamp it out. Griscom calculated that nine-tenths of the city's poor were responsible for their state of affairs and thus "artificial" paupers. Among the causes of poverty he listed ignorance, idleness, intemperance, extravagance, imprudent marriages, lotteries, prostitution, and charitable organizations which in spite of sincere intentions rewarded laziness and sapped independence. The report called for brigades of volunteers to go into every household to inquire into the condition of the poor and to offer practical and moral advice to them; it recommended churches be opened in working-class districts; it demanded stricter supervision of public relief to weed out the able-bodied; and it proposed tighter restrictions on the sale of liquor and on gambling. But the heart of this plan, which would strike at the very roots of poverty, was a savings bank.[23]

To further its goals the society undertook a campaign to educate the public and the state legislature on the merits of savings banks. To this end it distributed information on the success of banks in Boston, Philadelphia, Baltimore, and Salem, and in December it sponsored a meeting with several members of the state legislature at which Pintard explained the nature of a savings bank in order "to obviate any plausible objections that might arise."[24] Help also came from other quarters, for in 1817 DeWitt Clinton, one of the would-be directors of the 1816 venture, was elected governor of New York. In his first annual message to the legislature in 1818, Clinton explicitly called for the establishment of savings banks as part of a larger plan to "prevent or alleviate the evils of pauperism."[25] But even with the society's educational campaign and with Clinton's endorsement, the bill to incorporate the Bank for Savings in the City of New York encountered considerable opposition and passed only after several amendments were made. Keyes has reproduced the entire legislative record of this bill from the date it was introduced on 19 January 1819 to the date it finally passed on 26 March 1819. In all, there were fourteen entries in the Assembly and Senate journals as the bill passed in and out of several committees and bounced back and forth between the two houses. The record indicates that the bill was closely scrutinized, that it was amended on several occasions, and that there were major disagreements between various legislative factions. But the record offers little direct evidence as to the nature of the amendments or the disagreements.[26]

A search of the Bank for Savings' minutes, the records of the Society for the Prevention of Pauperism, and of newspapers in New York City and Albany failed to uncover an early, unamended copy of the petition or other relevant details and thus we do not know whether the trustees actually requested more liberal investment guidelines. The bank's supporters were aware of the far less severe (or nonexistent) investment constraints regulating mutuals in Boston, Philadelphia, and Baltimore and seemingly would have desired to secure similar provisions for their own institution. But the fact that no commentary on this subject exists in the bank's records suggests that the trustees were not too concerned by the stricter guidelines at the time they were imposed. This lack of concern is understandable, because the trustees had no idea of the impending success of their enterprise. Prior to the bank's opening John Pintard hoped that it might receive $52,000 the first year.[27] In actuality, this figure was surpassed in less than two months, and at the end of six months the bank held about $155,000 in deposits. As a result of underestimating the growth in deposits the trustees did not anticipate the problems they would encounter trying to invest in the few markets legally open. In fact, in December 1816 they naively thought that it might be possible to make an arrangement "with the City Corporation, to receive all . . . deposits on Interest."[28]

Though the precise origins of the strict investment constraints in New York remain a mystery, little doubt remains as to their general causes. The savings bank movement became entangled with the general opposition found in New York to incorporating commercial banks. Even after supporters of the movement had waged a three-year campaign to distinguish savings banks from commercial banks, the New York legislature took special precautions to restrict the new institution. It is unclear whether legislators were motivated primarily by a concern for the profits of existing commercial banks or for the safety of the savings bank's depositors, but whatever their rationale, this initial legal environment shaped bank policy for many years.

## The Issue of Trustee Objectives

Given this early history of mutual savings banks, most of the literature on mutuals has argued that these institutions were founded for philanthropic purposes by men who desired only to help the poorer classes of society. Indeed, the preceding discussion has made such an assertion. Although pervasive, this view has never been scrutinized. For purposes of analysis it would be useful to juxtapose this traditional belief that mutuals were philanthropic institutions against the alternative hypothesis that the mutuals were organized and managed in order to yield a profit to their trustees. This second hypothesis attributes conventional profit motives to mutual trustees (the same motives that presumably impelled their private business ventures). Because of the nature of mutuals, neither hypothesis can be easily associated with one explicitly defined set of operating procedures.

The problem is complicated by the fact that mutuals were complex organizations with many and often competing objectives. All mutuals had to rank their priorities, and these rankings changed over time and differed between banks. How a mutual ranked its priorities depended in part on its trustees' objectives. A basic and unavoidable conflict that each mutual confronted no matter what its trustees' goals was how much emphasis to place on safety relative to the nominal rate of return on its portfolio. More philanthropic banks could be expected to have been more concerned with safety and thus have settled for a lower rate of interest on investments than would a "profiteering" mutual.

A mutual's ability to satisfy its goals was inhibited by a complex set of exogenous constraints, the most important of which were legal restrictions on investment decisions. Since these constraints did not apply uniformly to all firms and changed over time, a simple model of mutual behavior would not adequately capture their effects. Even market forces did not affect all firms equally. Because of the relative size of their holdings, some of the larger mutuals had to consider the impact of their actions on market prices. Precipitant selling of one type of security could drastically depress both the market price a bank received and the value of the issues remaining in its portfolio. Changes in legal investment constraints not only made it easier for mutuals to satisfy their goals and allocate resources more efficiently, but also resulted in the restructuring of some firms' priorities. For example, the legalization of mortgage loans and call loans undoubtedly enticed many individuals to become mutual trustees in order to obtain credit. This in turn led to a fundamental reordering of some mutuals' priorities and to a basic change in bank operating procedures. A closer examination of the motives expressed by early trustees as well as the potential sources of profiteering will help establish a framework for the following chapters.

## THE PHILANTHROPIC MOTIVE

When the Bank for Savings in the City of New York opened in July 1819, similar institutions were already doing business in Boston, Salem, Philadelphia, and Baltimore. According to all accounts the founding trustees viewed their creations as a powerful moral force designed to reform and uplift the poor. One of the early directors of the Savings Bank of Baltimore expressed this feeling in 1819 when he noted that: " 'there are on the books of the Institution some pleasing instances of the rapid increase in small sums regularly deposited by persons who, persevering in economy and sobriety, are enabled weekly to save a part of their earnings, and thus secure for themselves and families a resource in sickness and old age. How different must be the hopes and future prospects of the poor wretches who spend a like proportion of their earnings in grog shops to the utter ruin of themselves, and the misery of their families; besides forfeiting all claim to the mercy of an offended Deity.' "[29]

A wealth of contemporary evidence found in letters, diaries, newspapers, and minutes of the Bank for Savings in the City of New York indicates that its founders likewise saw their bank was a mechanism for effecting a broad range of economic and social changes. But even the founders of the Bank for Savings were not without ulterior motives, because many of the bank's supporters expected that an immediate and practical result would be a decline in pauperism and thus a reduction in the tax rate. " 'The number of poor are increasing on us beyond all calculation,' Thomas Eddy wrote in February 1817, observing in astonishment that there were fifteen thousand persons in the city who were 'receiving public bounty.' " Eddy, who became one of the bank's most active trustees, expressed little sentimentality in his approach to the problem of poverty. In a letter to De Witt Clinton in 1817 Eddy stated that he was " 'tired of assisting [the poor] in their distress and it appears to me more wise, to fix on every possible plan to prevent their poverty and misery by means of employment and establishing savings banks and to do all in our power to discourage the use of spiritous liquors.' "[30]

While some trustees undoubtedly hoped for lower taxes as an end in itself, others desired to increase government expenditures on projects with which they were associated; they realized that this could be achieved more easily if expenditures could be cut elsewhere in the budget. For example, in 1817, John Pintard, the driving force behind the savings bank movement in New York City, contemplated going to Albany in order to secure patronage from the legislature for the New York Historical Society. But he lamented that even with the support of Governor Clinton, any chance of aid was slight because "the difficulty is where to find the resources" in a budget oppressed by "expenses of the late war & the appropriations for carrying on the great Canal. . . ." Pintard continued that he had "hit on a plan wh[ich] it is not reasonable to disclose for fear of opposition. A wide survey is about being taken of the state of pauperism in our city to see if we cannot check in some degree the growth of the present system of relieving the poor. . . ."[31] His plan was to create a savings bank. In this one letter Pintard connected the founding of the Bank for Savings with the financial problems of New York state and of the State Historical Society. It is interesting that he thought that the significant contribution would come from the proposed bank's effect on reducing the poor rolls, not from funds the bank would invest in various projects.

The following year, in 1818, Pintard was so concerned about the abuse of gambling and drinking that he decided to undertake a study of "political economy" in order to be more able to discharge his duties to society. At the same time he wrote that the most important group he belonged to was the Society for the Prevention of Pauperism, an organization he joined in order to lobby for a savings bank. Shortly after the Bank for Savings opened in 1819, Pintard boasted that three-fourths of the monies to be deposited would be "rescued from dram shops [and] frippery." After a decade of service to the Bank for Savings, Pintard was not the least bit disillusioned with the results of his work, as shown by the claim that "this Instit[ution] is working wonders with that class [low Irish], [and] Temperance is increasing among them. . . ."[32]

Many New Yorkers firmly believed that a savings bank would lower the incident of pauperism and thus keep taxes down. The popular view was that many persons on relief were victims of seasonal unemployment. They earned enough money during the peak employment season to tide them over during periods of unemployment, but mismanaged their affairs. A savings bank would help these individuals to resist the temptation of hard spirits, gambling, and licentiousness, and allow them to equate their income and consumption streams through periods of employment and unemployment. Pintard expressed this opinion in 1817: "There is little absolute cause for mendicity in a country that affords such demand for labour as the U[nite]d States. Our city is surcharged with indigent foreigners, who finding employm[en]t in the summer at high wages, become imprudent & extravagant & pennyless by midwinter. To let them perish is impossible & to support them in iddleness [sic] is cherishing the growth of an oppressive evil."[33]

The founders of other New York City mutuals expressed motives similar to those expressed by the Bank for Savings' trustees. The Seamen's Bank for Savings, founded in 1829, was the city's second mutual. The organizers of this enterprise were led by a group of the Bank for Savings' trustees who were discouraged by the small number of seamen among their bank's depositors and concluded that a mutual was needed near the docks. For five years the Seamen's accepted deposits only "from Seamen and those connected with a seafaring Life."[34] Through interlocking boards of directors the Seamen's Bank for Savings was closely associated with seamen's charities such as the Society for Promotion of the Gospel among Seamen in the Port of New York and the Seamen's Fund and Retreat. This latter organization and the Marine Merchants' Association frequently extended financial assistance to help defray the bank's operating expenses during its formative years.[35] These connections offer an indication of the broad philanthropic goals of the bank's founders.

Many other mutuals ostensibly catered to a specific area of the city or group of citizens, but none went as far as the Seamen's and actually refused deposits from "outsiders." Table 1 lists all of the mutual savings banks founded in New York City before 1860. In many cases the names of these mutuals indicate the group they were founded to help. For example, the Dry Dock Savings Institution (1848) was intended to serve dockworkers, seamen, and mechanics who labored on what were then the Upper East Side docks.[36] In a circular announcing the opening of the East River Savings Institution in 1848, its trustees declared: " 'The design of this Institution originated in the belief, that in this section of the City, it would afford advantages to a numerous class of citizens residing in its vicinity, among whom are Laborers, Mechanics, and Domestics, desirous of safely investing their surplus earnings, and who for want of time and opportunity, are unable to avail themselves of the privileges afforded by similar institutions more remotely situated.' "[37] The Emigrant Industrial Savings Bank (1850) and the German Savings Bank (1859) were founded by persons of Irish and German descent.[38]

Many declarations of purpose similar to those narrated above exist for most of the mutuals listed in Table 1, but the credibility of these claims remains to be questioned. If a mutual's goals changed over time, or if the mutual were organized for profit instead of for charity, its trustees would not have advertised their true intentions. To the contrary, one would expect their public pronouncements to convey the most noble objectives in an effort to take advantage of the goodwill sown and cultivated by other mutuals. The questions which remain to be asked are: How would a philanthropic mutual behave? How would a profiteering mutual behave, and specifically, how might its trustees profit?

Table 1    New York City Mutual Savings Banks Chartered Before 1860[a]

| Bank | Date Opened |
|---|---|
| Bank for Savings in the City of New York[b,c] | 3 July 1819 |
| Seamen's Bank for Savings[c] | 11 May 1829 |
| Greenwich Savings Bank | 1 July 1833 |
| Bowery Savings Bank[c] | 2 June 1834 |
| East River Savings Institution[c] | 22 May 1848 |
| Dry Dock Savings Institution[c] | 10 June 1848 |
| Institution for Savings of Merchants' Clerks | 1 July 1848 |
| Emigrant Industrial Savings Bank[c] | 13 September 1850 |
| Manhattan Savings Institution[c] | 26 March 1851 |
| Broadway Savings Institution[c] | 1 October 1851 |
| Irving Savings Institution | 23 December 1851 |
| Knickerbocker Savings Institution[d] | not known |
| Mechanics' and Traders' Savings Institution[d] | 26 May 1852 |
| Mariners' Savings Institution[c,e] | 14 April 1853 |
| Sixpenny Savings Bank | 1853 |
| Rose Hill Savings Bank[b] | 26 June 1854 |
| Bloomingdale Savings Bank[d] | 4 September 1854 |
| Union Dime Savings Institution | 18 May 1859 |
| German Savings Bank | 1 July 1859 |

Source: Emerson W. Keyes, *A History of Savings Banks in the United States*, 2:174-264; and Emerson W. Keyes, *Special Report on Savings Banks*, pp. 238-96.

[a] Five other mutuals, founded in Brooklyn and Queens during this period, are not included.

[b] In 1963 the Bank for Savings in the City of New York merged with the New York Savings Bank (originally named the Rose Hill Savings Bank) and adopted its present name, The New York Bank for Savings.

[c] Banks that made data available to the author.

[d] These banks failed.

[e] The Mariners' changed its name to the Metropolitan Savings Bank in 1865. In 1942 it merged with the Manhattan Savings Bank.

Economic theory tells us relatively little about how a philanthropic savings bank should behave.[39] Presumably it should attempt to maximize its depositors' interest or well-being, but this vague notion only begs the question. The banks' own records offer only vague statements of purpose. Typically such statements include an expression of the trustees' desire to "guarantee" the safety of the poor's savings and at the same time offer a modest rate of return as a reward to the thrifty. In actuality the trustees were aware that they could reduce risk to the small investor, but that they could never eliminate it. Given the expressions of concern for security of the poor's savings, one would expect a philanthropic mutual to be more risk averse in its portfolio management than a profiteering organization would be. Presumably philanthropic trustees, after weighing risks, should have attempted to maximize the rate of return on their portfolio in order that more profits could be passed on to depositors in the form of dividends or accumulated in a surplus account to provide added security.

## THE PROFIT MOTIVE

It is not immediately evident how the trustees of a savings bank might exploit it for their own profit. They probably would not attempt to maximize the mutual's profits (as measured by a mutual's surplus account) because its surplus could not legally be divided among its trustees. One would instead expect profiteering trustees to allocate any potential surplus to themselves, friends, or business associates by paying high salaries, giving low-interest loans, or making low-interest deposits in "friendly" commercial banks. Transfers of these types could easily be disguised and therefore overlooked even in cases where abundant data are available.

For a number of reasons one would expect the profiteering motive to have been relatively weak in 1819 when the first New York City mutual was organized. Its founders had no idea of the impending success of their venture and therefore little awareness of its potential for profit. One would expect men interested in lucre to look elsewhere, since even if the bank's future growth had been expected, the opportunity to profit from it was limited by legal restrictions. Until the 1830s about the only possible avenue of profiteering for trustees would have been to make low-interest deposits in a "friendly" commercial bank. As constraints were lowered over time, the possibilities for gain increased. Most important was the legalization of mortgage loans in the 1830s; prior to this change New York mutuals could not loan directly to individuals or to private firms. Although a trustee could not take out a mortgage loan himself, he was in a position to provide funds to friends, relatives, and business associates; in addition, he could deny credit to competitors. A new dimension was created in the early 1850s when some mutuals started making call loans. These short-term loans, which required less collateral than mortgage loans and were often used for speculation in the stock market, introduced a new opportunity for trustee profiteering and a new element of risk to mutual portfolios.

One would expect to find some men taking advantage of these opportunities. The financial history of the antebellum years was rampant with commercial bank scandals, and millions of dollars were made and lost as a result of corners on the stock market. Public regulatory commissions, even when they existed, were notoriously ineffective. The works of Gustavus Myers are filled with descriptions of shady transactions and illegal behavior.[40] Why should the Jacob Littles, Daniel Drews, and the hundreds of less successful (and thus less well-known) manipulators exclude savings banks from their field of operations? Emerson Keyes, who firmly believed mutuals had done wonders in uplifting the morals and improving the economic situation of the lower classes, was especially harsh in his description of the misuse of "these most benevolent institutions." Keyes described efforts by unscrupulous politicians to add the names of political cronies to the board of trustees of new mutuals applying for charters. One legislator unsuccessfully attempted to exchange the entire board of trustees named in a bill pending before committee with favorites of his own.[41] Although most of the abuses that Keyes described were exposed after the Civil War and after the institutions in question had failed, the opportunities for abuse were also rife during the prewar era. But was the profit motive limited to a few mutuals or was it widespread? How early did it appear?

In 1853, the state legislature prohibited any trustee of mutuals thereafter incorporated from being a director of a commercial bank in which the mutual made deposits.[42] The passage of this act suggests broad concern about trustee conduct as early as 1853. But was this concern justified? Was it the result of past abuses? New York mutuals had been keeping deposits in commercial banks since 1819, and after 1833 many mutuals were founded by the directors of a particular commercial bank. Interlocking directorates were the rule rather than the exception. The following quotation from a letter Emerson Keyes received from Thomas Jeremiah, who was the president of the Bowery Savings Bank from 1858 to 1872, offers a candid admission of how interlocking directorates linked savings banks with commercial banks. The letter also offers a hint that the profit motive appeared at a relatively early date. " 'The measure of establishing a savings bank in the Bowery, to be called the Bowery Savings Bank, originated with the directors of the Butchers' and Drovers' Bank, and while the great object for which such institutions was intended may have received a proper degree of attention, yet the prevailing idea was undoubtedly the prospect of some collateral advantages. The relation of these two institutions will be apparent from the fact that nine out of the thirteen directors of the Butchers' and Drovers' Bank were among the original incorporators of the Bowery Savings Bank.' "[43] What did Jeremiah mean by "collateral advantages"? He could have meant that there were economies of scale: the savings bank could and did use the same building as the commercial bank with little added cost. But the context of the paragraph suggests he meant that the directors of the Butchers' and Drovers' Bank, while giving proper attention to philanthropic considerations, were primarily interested in the benefits that a savings bank would pass on to their commercial bank.

This need not imply that the savings bank was mismanaged (the advantages could have been in the form of referrals, economies of scale, and economies of information), but it does indicate that the philanthropic motive was not the only reason for founding the mutual.

# CHAPTER 2

# The Changing Nature of Mutual Savings Banks

## Introduction

Most early mutual savings banks commenced operations on a part-time basis, managed by trustees who volunteered their time and expertise. Their personal involvement and their refusal of monetary payment for their services has deeply impressed most outside observers, who have cited such behavior as evidence of the trustees' philanthropic intentions. Payne and Davis express this view in the comparative study of the Savings Bank of Baltimore and the Provident of Boston: "The administrative organization that was first adopted by the two institutions reflected the charitable interest of their founders, but the problems that accompanied success and growth could not be met with this early structure. Instead, professional managements—operating the institutions as businesses rather than charitable enterprises—were needed, and the administrators of both banks gradually evolved in this way." These authors further argue that the evolution in administrative structure of these two banks was typical of changes in the administration of other mutuals founded in the second decade of the nineteenth century.[1] Since trustee contributions have been used as a key index of philanthropy, a number of questions should be asked. How much work did a bank's trustees actually perform? How rapidly did trustees relinquish their obligations to employees? Were there significant differences in trustee responsibilities between banks? Were administrative changes simply a necessary response to the pressures that developed with success and growth or were these changes also accompanied by significant shifts in bank behavior and trustee philosophy?

Answers to these questions require a detailed comparison of the administrations of several mutuals and an inquiry into their dividend policies, their hours of business, and their advertising policies. The hypothesis underlying this discussion is that the stronger the philanthropic spirit, the less a bank's trustees would feel pressure to turn over manual tasks and the reins of management to paid employees, and the less the trustees would feel compelled to compete with other mutuals for deposits. This hypothesis has its roots firmly embedded in the historical literature on mutual savings banks.

## The Administration of the Bank for Savings

The governing body designated in the bank's Act of Incorporation was its board of managers, consisting of twenty-eight members. The charter required the board to elect from among its members a president and three vice-presidents, and it stipulated that no board member receive directly or indirectly any pay or emolument for his services. The bank's original bylaws provided for the election of a secretary and a treasurer from the board and for two permanent committees, which were responsible for the successful operation of the bank. The monthly attending committee, consisting of three members, was to supervise the bank during its business hours. The funding committee, also with three members, was charged with the bank's investment portfolio. The members of this latter committee were exempted from having to serve on the attending committee and from other duties. Both committees were to keep minutes and make reports to the board at its regular meetings. The trustees also chose attorneys from among their members to represent the bank in legal matters. Cadwallader Colden and Peter Jay usually served in this capacity until their resignations from the board in 1832 and 1838, respectively.[2]

In the first few years of business clerks, tellers, and porters employed by neighboring commercial banks (which were directed by some of the Bank for Savings' trustees) volunteered their services to the mutual. The trustees took turns serving on the attending committee, which managed the bank during the five to six hours a week during which it was open for business. These trustees personally received deposits, paid drafts, and transferred the day's receipts to a local commercial bank for safekeeping.[3] The trustees hoped that by rotating the responsibility they could all become familiar with the depositors on a personal basis and therefore be in a position to offer them advice on moral as well as financial matters.[4]

As the bank's assets and its number of depositors grew, the simple organization described above became inadequate. Although the bank was open for business only six hours a week, it required far more than six hours of managerial input. John Pintard repeatedly noted that the three hours when the bank was open on Saturday generally obliged him to work six hours on the attending committee that evening. (He usually arrived about four in the afternoon and seldom left the bank before ten or eleven at night.)[5] Within a few months of the bank's opening it had grown beyond Pintard's wildest expectations;

the work was wearing down some of the trustees so that he had to attend to their duties as well as his own.[6] Although the bank continued to grow at a rate that exceeded the expectations of its trustees, resulting in heavy demands on them, they did not rapidly transfer their responsibility to paid employees. Several steps were taken to economize on the trustees' time and to introduce more efficient procedures, but given the growth of the bank the actual amount of work required of the trustees may have increased as time passed.

The bank's bylaws of 1831 show that few fundamental changes in the trustees' duties had occurred since its founding in 1819. One change reduced the size of the attending committee from three members to only one. This was an action which several other mutuals would later take to economize on their trustees' time.[7] As the bank prospered the trustees gradually hired additional employees and transferred some of their managerial functions to the accountant, who was the highest ranking employee. In 1826 the trustees decided to open the bank from 9 A.M. to 2 P.M. daily so that depositors could leave their passbooks to have interest entered. No other business was transacted during this time of the day, and the attending committee was not required to be present. During these non-business hours the accountant was responsible for the general supervision of the bank and of the other employees. This procedure reduced the peak-load problem which accompanied the evening rush, and allowed the staff to perform the time-consuming task of entering interest into passbooks during slack daytime hours. These hours were also devoted to copying and checking the bank's books. In general, every hour that the bank was open required three or four hours of work by the staff to keep the books in order.

Managing the bank's investment portfolio demanded financial expertise and a considerable amount of drudgery, as the following excerpt from one of John Pintard's letters illustrates. "I have again to go [to] the Phoenix Bank to examine the Certificates of Alabama Stock purchased yest[erday]. I have been at work all the morn[ing] from 10 to 12. There are 50 Certificates of $1000 each & 100 of $500 each, total $100,000, with 3 transfers to each & another in a transfer book, all which are to be singly examined, no small task for my old eyes. . . ."[8] In 1834 the bank's charter was amended to permit making loans secured by real estate. This provision eventually led to increased labor because the trustees personally had to inspect all property, negotiate loans, and often handle the legal matters associated with searching titles and inspecting deeds. Beginning in the early 1840s, the board employed the law firm headed by George W. Strong to represent the bank in all legal matters, but since two of this firm's partners, George W. Strong and Marshall Bidwell, were also trustees they did not accept any payment for their services. The third member of the firm, George T. Strong, was paid for his services until 1858, when he too was elected to the board.[9]

Not until 1851 did the trustees make a significant change in the structure of the bank's administration, at which time they voted to fill the position of treasurer with a paid employee who was not a member of the board. The bank's bylaws of 1857 explicitly listed the treasurer's duties and give an indication of the burden that the trustees had carried until 1851. The treasurer was required to "receive all moneys payable to the Bank, collect the interest and dividends on its stocks and other securities, and deposit all moneys . . . in the [commercial] Bank designated by the Board, . . . [and] he shall make the payments authorized by the Board." His other duties included keeping "faithful account of all moneys . . . deposited and drawn on account of this Bank," making monthly and yearly reports to the trustees showing all transactions; and keeping "charge of the deeds, stock certificates, bonds, mortgages, and . . . other papers relating to the property of the Bank . . . ."[10] Furthermore, the treasurer was to live and have an office in the bank and have general supervision of the banking room. The primary responsibility of the treasurer was to work with the funding committee and with the bond and mortgage committee in managing the bank's investments. He also assumed some of the managerial duties which before 1851 had been the responsibility of the attending committee and the other officers. The specific timing of this change in the bank's management was determined by the death of one and resignation of another trustee who had performed most of the tasks transferred to employees. In 1851 the bank's president, Philip Hone, died and Caleb O. Halstead, who had served as treasurer since 1843, resigned from the board.[11] The bank's assets had almost doubled since these men had taken office and were about $7 million at the time of their departure.

Similar circumstances led to the next fundamental structural change in the bank's administration in 1861. In 1860 Najah Taylor, the bank's president since 1851 and the last of the original trustees, died in office at the age of ninety. Taylor had been an active supporter of mutuals since 1819. He was the first president of the Seamen's Bank for Savings and served on that bank's board of trustees until 1852. In 1851 he tried to resign from the board of the Bank for Savings because of his advanced age (he was eighty-one), but his fellow trustees refused to accept his resignation and shortly thereafter unanimously elected him president. Retired from private business, Taylor devoted much of his energy to the bank. His death marked the end of an era and was closely followed by the transfer of many of the duties he and other trustees had performed to a new salaried officer—the comptroller.[12] One of the bank's most active trustees, James De Peyster Ogden, resigned from the board to accept this new position. Ogden took over the actual day-to-day management of the bank under the general direction of the president and the board of managers. One trustee, George T. Strong, noted that this change marked "the close of the system on which the business of the Bank for Savings has been done for more than forty years . . . ." Strong felt the change was long overdue and was happy to be freed from work which he felt could just as easily be performed by employees. "The new system will make the duties of "attending trustee" practically nothing. At present, he is bound to do nothing but sign checks, and it will soon be found that that office can be executed more conveniently and with equal safety by the functionaries of the bank. I am very glad to be relieved from the annual fortnight of drudgery, and especially from the handling of pass books, many of which look and smell as if smallpox and malignant dysentery were concentrated in the filth of their covers. . . ."[13]

As an aside, the only known account written by one of the bank's depositors corroborates Strong's description of the stench in the bankroom. Massett's narrative, "A Full and True Account of My First and Last Deposit in A Savings Bank," also gives us our only glimpse of a depositor's view of the trustees:

> I arrived at the portals of the institution, trembling from head to foot with the frightful responsibility of my position, and with shaky fingers, counting over and over again, the greasy pieces of paper, taking my place among files of chambermaids, cooks, waiters, carmen, mechanics, young and old, fat and thin, clean and dirty.
> I think it was about four o'clock before my time came.
> Arrived at the hole and looking through some wire grating, I beheld an elderly gentleman with a very bald head, seated on a very high stool, having on the top of his very red nose a pair of the largest kind of spectacles.
> I managed to get off the fact, that I wished to open an account there, to which he replied, in a very gruff and disagreeable voice,—
> "Well, sir! what's the amount?" To which I hesitatingly replied, "$16 sir."
> Gruntingly, "$16? that all?" (Here an audible titter from two or three of the clerks, and instantly caught up by the whole row of depositors, made me so nervous that I nearly fainted, and I'd have given all the world if I'd been *out*side instead of *in!*)

After worrying for two days that the bank would burn down and his money would be lost, Massett summoned all his courage, fabricated a story, and resolved to close his account:

I found myself at the dreaded hole with the wire round it.

To the interrogatory, "What is it, Sir?"

I feebly replied that I had a little "account to settle" with him!

Now whether the old cock thought I was going to punch him in the eye or throw something at him through the little hole, I know not, but he involuntarily drew back, saying,

"I don't understand you, Sir!"

"Well, Sir," said I, "the fact is, Sir, I deposited some money here the other day (all this time the people were crowding and pressing in, the heat was intense, and I in a perfect vapor bath of excitement), and in consequence of a large death in our small family, Sir, I have to go to sea."

"See what, Sir? I don't comprehend you, Sir!"

"No, no, Sir! I mean a sea voyage, Sir. I want the money for an outfit, Sir; to pay my passage to Rhode Island, Sir; where the ship is, Sir."

Oh Lord. I was nearly fainting, but I then intended to "stick it out."

With a look of perfect contempt at me over his specks, that haunted me for years afterwards, he fumbled over the leaves of his big book with the clasps, came to the unfortunate letter "M," and with pointed finger at the wretched item (I saw from the top my name in large letters occupying the two entire sheets), gave a "click" with the pen, went to the drawer, and counting out the sixteen dollars, added, with a sneer, that there was just *one cent interest due me!*

Then, with a look of intense disgust at me and my red face, he very impertinently, I thought, suggested, that the *next time* I made a deposit in a banking house I should have *something* to put in it![14]

There is no way of knowing how many other depositors were similarly intimidated.

By 1861 much of the administration of the Bank for Savings had been turned over to its professional staff. The bank's trustees still supervised general policy and actively participated in making investment decisions. This basic structure was not changed until 1885, when the president started receiving a salary and actively took over the management of the bank.[15] The philosophy of the early trustees remained a strong force in determining the decisions of their successors forty years later, and only after the scale of operation and associated burdens increased far beyond the wildest dreams of the bank's founders did the board yield and begin transferring the reins of management. This persistence can best be explained by the high regard the trustees felt for the bank, its work, and its traditions. Twenty-two years after the bank was founded, Philip Hone wrote in the privacy of his diary:

I was elected yesterday president of the Bank for Savings . . . .
I cannot but feel gratified at having been elevated by the unani-
mous vote of my associates to the honourable station of president
of the greatest associated institution in the United States, —greatest
in the influence which it exerts over the community; greatest
in the amount of business which it transacts, and by which it
is drawn into intimate contact with the people; and greatest (I
think I may from experience assert) in the good which it has
already done and all it may hereafter (with the continuance of
the blessings of Almightly God) be the means of doing.[16]

Hone's opinion should not be taken lightly, for he was an active
and knowledgeable citizen. In addition to being a former mayor of
New York City, he was on the board of three insurance companies,
the president of the American Exchange Bank, a trustee of Columbia
College, and a trustee of a half-dozen other benevolent institutions.

In 1858 George T. Strong was elected to the board of the Bank
for Savings. He, like Hone almost twenty years earlier, candidly
expressed the honor and responsibility he associated with a trusteeship.

Notified by James DePeyster Ogden this morning that I was elected
trustee or director of the Bank for Savings, the Bleecker Street
bank (formerly of Chambers Street) of which my father was many
years a prominent officer. It is the oldest and the most important
of our institutions of that class, holds many millions of deposits,
and is controlled by a very highly "respectable" board—Ogden,
Lord, Bidwell, Najah Taylor, Suydam, Kennedy, and others. The
appointment titillates my Pharisaism so agreeably that I am
disposed to accept it, though acceptance involves much time and
work and anxiety in times like those of a year ago and cuts me
off from a share in the profits of our professional business for
the bank, heretofore divided between Charles E. Strong and
myself, Bidwell having been a trustee for a long time past. But
Rabbi Strong is such a self-sacrificing, philanthropic Rabbi! If
I accept, I shall try to do the work according to my capacity,
such as it is, but what folly to select me for this responsible
place! I could name forty men of my age and standing who would
fill it better . . . .[17]

Such unsolicited testimonials emphasize the inadequacy of the profit-
maximizing motive in explaining Strong's participation as a trustee,
for the reward he sought was not financial, but the higher prize of
the respect of his peers.[18]

### The Administration of Other Mutuals

In the foregoing discussion three key changes in the Bank for Savings'
administration stand out. The first occurred when the board decided

to fill the treasurer's offices with an employee in 1851. The second occurred in 1861 when the comptroller took over the management of the bank. The third change took place when the president started receiving a salary in 1885.

It remains to compare the experience of the Bank for Savings with that of other mutuals. How did the responsibilities of the various banks' trustees differ at the time the banks were organized? How many years passed after a bank was formed and how large were its deposits before its trustees transferred some of their duties to paid personnel, created new managerial positions, and accepted salaries themselves? An investigation into these questions shows that there were marked differences in administrative procedures and philosophy between the older and the younger banks; the older institutions generally maintained their original structure, which emphasized trustee contributions, far longer than the younger banks.

Figure 1 summarizes the key changes in several banks' administrations. When the banks were first organized there were significant differences in the tasks allocated to employees and thus differing wage payments to hired inputs. The magnitude of these differences is not fully evident in Figure 1, which lists the title of the paid offices at the time of organization but does not specify their responsibilities. The secretaries of the East River, Dry Dock, Manhattan, and Mariners' and the accountant of the Bowery were responsible for the duties performed by the accountant and secretary, and in many cases all or part of those duties performed by the treasurer of the Bank for Savings.[19]

Another point not evident from Figure 1 is that, as was the case for the Bank for Savings, the specific timing of many administrative changes was determined by the death or retirement of important trustees. Often an active trustee would continue to carry out duties that had been defined several years earlier when the bank was much smaller and the tasks much less demanding. With the departure of such a trustee the board would reorganize the administration, perhaps realizing that it would have been hard put to find another member who would have voluntarily assumed the old position.

The most significant change in the administration of the Seamen's Bank for Savings came when its trustees decided to hire a cashier in February 1851, just one month after the death of the bank's president Benjamin Strong.[20] The board of the Bowery voted in 1858 to compensate its new president, Thomas Jeremiah, with a yearly salary of $3,000. His predecessor, James Mills, had been eligible for compensation during his last year in office, but he refused to consider the matter, declaring that he would retire rather than receive payment. Mills died in office.[21] Similarly, the board of the Dry Dock Savings

**Figure 1** Key Administrative Changes for Twelve Mutuals

The scale along the top of the figure gives the "age" of the bank at the date of key changes, i.e., years from incorporation to date of change. The numbers underneath each bank's time-line gives the approximate amount in millions of dollars due depositors at various years.

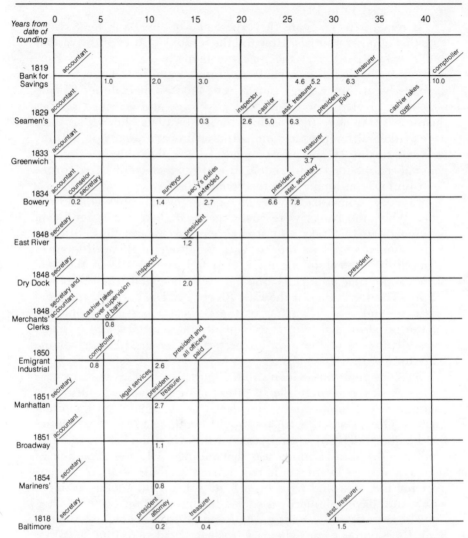

Sources: Compiled from the minute books of the Bank for Savings, Seamen's, Bowery, Dry Dock, Manhattan, Broadway and Mariners' savings banks; Peter L. Payne and Lance E. Davis, *The Savings Bank of Baltimore*, pp. 46–49; Emerson W. Keyes, *A History of Savings Banks in the State of New York*, p. 173; James H. Collins, *Ninety Years of the Greenwich Savings Bank*, pp., 21–22, 66–67; Andrew Mills, *That's My Bank*, pp. 123–24; Dorcas Elisabeth Campbell, *The First Hundred Years*, pp. 25–26, 31, 37, 40–49, 60, 63; Bennett, comp., "A Chronological History of the Emigrant Industrial Savings Bank," in the archives of the Emigrant Savings Bank, pp. 1–4; Charles E. Knowles, *History of the Bank for Savings in the City of New York*, pp. 179–90.

Institution had offered compensation to its president, Andrew Mills, but he refused and continued serving voluntarily until his death in 1879. The resignation of the president of the East River Savings Institution in 1862 because of ill health resulted in the reorganization of the bank's administration. William H. Slocum, who took over on a full-time salaried basis, assumed responsibility for the day-to-day affairs of the bank (the secretary had previously been in charge of most of the bank's business).[22]

It would be useful to compare the evolution of these New York mutuals with that of the Savings Bank of Baltimore, since Payne and Davis have suggested it was representative of early American mutuals.[23] The key administrative changes in the evolution of the Baltimore bank are included in Figure 1 and indicate that its experience was not very similar to its early New York counterparts. In fact, its trustees relinquished their administrative burdens much more rapidly than did any of the New York banks founded before 1850. In 1827, when the Baltimore bank's deposits had not yet reached $200,000, its board voted to pay the bank's president a yearly salary of $500. In noting this change, Payne and Davis observe that "the presidency was becoming too much of a burden for anyone to take without compensation."[24] They also argue that

> the establishment of these salaried posts [the president, the treasurer (1832), the assistant treasurer (1847), and the attorney (1828)], resulting from a growing recognition by the board of the need for full-time professional management, marks the beginning of a steady transference of the Bank's administration from the board of directors to its officers. As long as the Bank was surrounded by an aura of charity it was closely managed by its founders and their successors, but the great success achieved by these men resulted in an inevitable supersession of their own management. As the Bank received the funds of an ever-growing number of depositors, it became apparent that its affairs could no longer be properly administered by directors who could not afford to devote their whole attention to it.[25]

The other mutual which Payne and Davis suggest was typical of savings banks founded early in the ninteenth century was the Provident Institution for Savings in the Town of Boston, but compared to its New York counterparts this mutual also evolved rather rapidly from "benevolence to business." Payne and Davis noted that by 1830 paid employees had taken over the day-to-day administration of the Provident, and by 1840 the paid "officers had become so accustomed to making investment decisions that the board found it necessary to issue a special order to limit new loans and renewals to those they had specifically approved."[26]

Evidently the trustees of many New York mutuals were more dedicated than their counterparts in Boston and Baltimore; even though several New York City mutuals conducted a much larger volume of business, their officers continued to serve without remuneration for decades after the Baltimore and Boston institutions began paying their officers. Payne and Davis's argument that this and other changes in the Baltimore bank's administration were needed to insure competent and professional management should not be generalized to apply to all mutuals. The larger New York enterprises were never plagued by a lack of expertise. All of these institutions had commercial bankers and insurance company directors on their boards, and generally their leading officers had an impressive list of financial ties.

### Changes in Bank Operating Procedures

Little detailed information about the administration of New York's other prewar mutuals is available, but information on all the banks' dividend policies, hours of business, and locations can be gleaned from newspaper advertisements and city directories. This information shows that in the 1850s there was a movement away from the operating procedures that had characterized the industry for over thirty years. These policy changes were usually introduced by new, relatively small entrants into the industry and were not a result of older mutuals' adjusting in an effort to handle an ever-growing volume of business. The new policies were indicative of the more businesslike and less philanthropic administrative philosophies of the newer institutions. Whereas all the older institutions started out as part-time operations open a few hours a week, most of the banks organized after 1850 rapidly adopted full-time hours and introduced policies designed to compete with other mutuals for deposits. These new policies were at first strongly resisted by many of the industry's older firms.

MUTUAL BUSINESS HOURS

An examination of mutual hours is useful because few other indices better contrast the early mutuals' gradual movement from part-time to full-time institutions with the rapid changes which occurred in the 1850s among the newer mutuals. A lengthening of business hours was often marked by a transferral of trustee responsibility to paid managers, because as hours increased it became more difficult for trustees to manage a bank properly in their spare time.[27] Thus one would expect institutions with a tradition of trustee management to resist adopting longer business hours. An investigation into the particular hours of the day a mutual was open can offer considerable insight into its trustees' objectives. Presumably, those mutuals most interested in serving the poor and with a large amount of trustee inputs would choose to open during the evenings or the lunch hour because those were times when workers could do business and when trustees could be absent from their own business establishment.

Table 2 lists the hours of each mutual by decade. Data on the business hours are available for six of the seven banks opened before 1850. Not one of these six was initially open more than six hours a week, and five of the six were only open two or three days a week during the late afternoon and evening. This time of the day was popular because it was relatively easy for the trustees to be in attendance and more convenient for working-class depositors. The Seamen's Bank for Savings was open daily (Monday through Saturday) during the lunch hour, which offered similar conveniences.

These six banks maintained their part-time hours even after

Table 2    Business Hours of New York City Mutual Savings Banks at Five Sample Dates[a]

| | Date Opened | Total Hours per Week | | | | |
|---|---|---|---|---|---|---|
| | | 1820 | 1830 | 1840 | 1850 | 1860 |
| Bank for Savings | 1819 | 5 | 7/37[b] | 8/38[b] | 12/42[b] | 12/42[b] |
| Seamen's | 1829 | | 6 | 6 | 24 | 24 |
| Greenwich | 1833 | | | 4 | 6 | 30 |
| Bowery | 1834 | | | 6 | 6 | 30 |
| East River | 1848 | | | | 6 | 26 |
| Dry Dock | 1848 | | | | 6 | 15 |
| Merchants' Clerks | 1848 | | | | 10 | 30 |
| Emigrant Industrial | 1850 | | | | 42 | 42 |
| Manhattan | 1851 | | | | | 60 |
| Broadway | 1851 | | | | | 32 |
| Irving | 1851 | | | | | 30 |
| Mechanics' and Traders' | 1852 | | | | | 54 |
| Mariners' | 1853 | | | | | 39 |
| Sixpenny | 1853 | | | | | 66 |
| Rose Hill | 1854 | | | | | 36 |
| Bloomingdale | 1854 | | | | | 36 |
| Union Dime | 1859 | | | | | 42 |
| German | 1859 | | | | | 42 |

Sources: Compiled from the minute books of the Bank for Savings, Seamen's, Bowery, Dry Dock, Manhattan, Broadway, and Mariners' savings banks; Dorcas Elisabeth Campbell, *The First Hundred Years*, pp. 40, 49; *New York Herald*, 1841–1861; *New York Times*, 1851–1861; *New York Tribune*, 1841–1861; *Longworth's American Almanac, New York Register, and City Directory*, 1827–1842; *Doggett's New York City Directory*, 1842–1851; *Rode's New-York City Directory*, 1850; *Trow's New-York City Directory*, 1853–1864.

[a]The Knickerbocker Savings Bank failed and is not listed.

[b]The Bank for Savings' hours are listed in the numerator and total hours in the denominator (see text p. 22).

crowded banking floors became a regular occurrence. The Bank for
Savings reduced its hours from six to five a week in 1819, and not
until July 1825, after deposits reached $1.5 million, was the bank
opened an extra two hours a week on Friday, for females only. This
marked the beginning of a tradition that would be adopted by several
other mutuals and in many cases continued into the twentieth century.
The popularity of special hours and windows for women only illustrates
one of the burdens of simultaneously catering to a working-class
population and to some of the city's fine ladies. Paintings and
descriptions of mutual waiting rooms indicate that barroom vulgarities
were not limited to dram houses. The Bank for Savings' trustees,
more gentlemen than egalitarians, were unable to reform some of
their male customers' chewing and swearing habits, so they decided
to protect the dignity of the bank's female clientele by introducing
the special day. In 1826 the trustees opened the bank from 9A.M.
to 2 P.M. daily so that depositors could leave their passbooks to have
interest entered.[28] In 1847 the bank was opened daily from 4 to 6
P.M., and it continued to keep these hours into the 1860s.

The other mutuals founded before 1850 were also slow in moving
from being open on a part-time to a full-time basis. The Seamen's
kept a six-hour week for over ten years. Both the Greenwich and
the Bowery maintained six-hour weeks into the mid-1850s, and increased their hours only after their deposits had exceeded $2 million
and $4 million, respectively. The East River and Dry Dock retained
a six-hour week for about five and ten years, respectively. There is
no information on the original hours kept by the seventh bank, The
Institution for the Savings of Merchants' Clerks (founded in 1848),
but it appeared to follow the same pattern as the Dry Dock and East
River. In 1854 it increased its hours from ten to thirty a week. This
was accompanied by a complete reorganization of the bank's administration and the creation of a new officer, the cashier, who was charged
with the general supervision of the bank's affairs.[29]

Starting in 1850 there was a basic shift in the banking hours
of newly formed mutuals, indicating a difference in philosophy and
administration of many of these banks. The banks founded in the
1850s tended to adopt hours equal to or exceeding those of the older
and larger banks. The Knickerbocker and Rose Hill savings banks
commenced operation with a sixty- and fifty-four-hour week, respectively. (The hours of the Rose Hill were later reduced to those given
in Table 2.) Within a few years of opening, the Emigrant Industrial
adopted a forty-two-hour week, the Broadway a thirty-hour week,
and the Manhattan a sixty-hour week. By 1860 the seven mutuals
organized before 1850 averaged about twenty-four hours per week
(or twenty-eight if the Bank for Savings' morning hours are included).

Those mutuals founded between 1850 and 1860 averaged almost forty-four hours per week.

The short hours kept by the early mutuals reflect the nature of their trustees' duties. There was a limit to the amount of time most trustees were willing to contribute to managing a bank, and an increase in business hours clearly meant an added burden for them. As a result, the lengthening of hours was often accompanied by the hiring of more employees and by a basic shift in bank management to a system relying much less on the voluntary inputs of the banks' trustees and much more on full-time, professional administrators. The longer hours kept by the newer banks reflect their more aggressive attitude toward attracting business and in most cases indicate their boards' greater willingness to relegate the day-to-day management to functionaries of the banks.

Many of these mutuals initially shared offices with commercial banks or insurance companies. In these cases a special window or room would be rented and labeled as "the savings bank," with a clerk or accountant of the commercial bank charged with tending the savings bank as well as carrying out his duties in the commercial bank. As the savings bank grew this employee would be hired on a full-time basis by the savings bank. This arrangement offered significant economies of scale, particularly regarding managerial inputs, which could be supplied with little additional effort or inconvenience by those trustees who were associated with the commercial bank. But to take advantage of these economies it was necessary for the two banks to keep similar hours. The hours of all commercial banks were from 10 A.M. to 3 P.M. daily. Thus, in some cases the newer mutuals' longer hours may simply reflect greater willingness to take advantage of commercial bank facilities. However, the alliance between commercial and savings banks in itself represented a change in mutual behavior.

The founding trustees of both the Bank for Savings and the Seamen's Bank for Savings were careful to avoid identifying the savings banks with commercial banks. The trustees were aware that there was much distrust of commercial banks, and they reasoned that the city's poor and middle classes would be less likely to deposit their savings if the mutuals were closely associated with banks of discount. One of the best examples of this effort to separate mutuals from banks of discount in the public mind occurred during the worst days of the Panic of 1837, when the trustees of the Bank for Savings placed advertisements in local newspapers proclaiming that the savings bank did not "have any stock, concern or interest in any banking institution whatever . . . ." The trustees' efforts evidently met with some success, for some of the most vociferous critics of the commercial banking community came to the aid of the savings bank. In the eyes of the fiery James Gordon Bennett, publisher of the *New York Herald,* the "harlots of paper money" were little better than the "thieves, burglars, robbers or the banditti of Spain or Italy." Bennett, who accused the banking community of bringing on the panic and advocated that "a great public meeting be called to prepare indictments against all the corrupt broken bank managers of New York," came to the defense of the Bank for Savings. The *Herald* advised "that the money of the depositors is entirely safe, and that they need be under no anxiety respecting their funds, but remain quiet, and await better times."[30]

This tradition of strict separation was broken first in 1833 and again in 1834, when the Greenwich and Bowery savings banks were founded. Both of these enterprises were closely identified with banks of discount. Chapter 6 discusses these and other ties between commercial banks and savings banks in more detail.

The records of the Broadway Savings Institution offer an excellent example of the relationship between a bank's hours and its trustees' motivation. In 1851 the Broadway Savings Institution commenced business in the office of the Broadway Bank, but the two banks kept different hours; the savings bank, following the tradition of almost all mutuals opened before it, was open from 5 to 8 P.M. three nights a week.[31] On 8 August 1854 a special committee reported that the mutual should start opening during the day since its trustees were also officers of the Broadway Bank and could easily oversee both operations. The board responded favorably and starting in October 1854 the savings bank was open from 10 A.M. to 2 P.M. and during its regular evening hours. In 1858 the evening hours were reduced to two hours one night a week. Both this administrative change and the shift to daytime hours reflect a basic difference between this mutual and many others in trustee conception of the functions of a mutual. The same committee that recommended adoption of the daytime hours also reported that "a considerable amount of Profits results from the use of money deposited and withdrawn at periods when under the rules it is not entitled to draw interest. Funds are frequently placed in Savings Banks for the sake of security while waiting opportunities for investment, and deposits of this kind naturally occur more frequently during business hours in daytime than at night."[32] These recommendations demonstrate how changing a bank's hours could indicate the degree of professional management as well as reflect a change in the basic goals of the institution's directors. The committee wanted to institute policies that would attract relatively large, short-run business deposits in the hope that these deposits would not remain dormant long enough to qualify for interest payments. This policy was in sharp contrast to both the original purposes stated in this bank's charter and the policies of some of the older savings institutions.[33] The often-stated and generally followed policy of the Bank for Savings was to encourage stable accounts and to discourage short-run deposits of the type the Broadway was seeking. The Bank for Savings' board had come to the conclusion that servicing the latter type of account, besides being outside the legitimate role of a savings bank founded to assist the poor, represented a potential hazard to the banks' other depositors. The board reasoned that businessmen were most apt to liquidate their accounts during periods of general business unrest marked by falling bond prices and rising interest rates. Heavy withdrawals during such periods forced the bank to sell bonds at unfavorable prices or deplete its cash reserves (or prevented the bank from taking full advantage of the favorable market for securities). The different attitude toward business accounts also reflected the different types of investments the two banks were willing to make. This in turn indicates the relative weight each board placed on the liquidity and safety of its portfolio. The Broadway's board was relatively active in lending money on call to individuals, but the Bank for Savings' directors were highly critical of this practice for safety reasons and refused to make any call loans.

MUTUAL DIVIDEND POLICY

Table 3 lists the dividend rates paid by most New York City mutuals from 1820 through 1860. Under each bank is listed the interest rate it paid and the basis upon which the rate was determined. For example, from 1820 through 1831 the Bank for Savings paid 5 percent on all sums. In 1832 it started paying 5 percent on accounts with sums of $500 and less and 4 percent on the entire account if the balance was in excess of $500.[34]

In all cases the higher interest rate was paid on small sums. This procedure was introduced by the Bank for Savings to discourage large accounts and was voluntarily adopted by most New York mutuals founded before 1853. Banks formed after 1853 were affected by a general law which required that "the rate of interest on all deposits of five hundred dollars and under, shall be one percent per annum greater than shall be allowed on any sum exceeding five hundred dollars."[35] This law occasionally conflicted with specific charter provisions and probably was not strongly enforced. It was also subject to conflicting interpretations as to whether the lower rate applied to the entire balance or just that part over $500. In any case, at some inconvenience and cost a depositor could certainly circumvent the intent of the split interest policy by opening accounts in several banks. A key consideration was how strict the trustees of each bank were

**Table 3**   New York City Mutual Savings Bank Dividend Rates, 1820-1860

| Date | Bank for Savings % | Basis | Seamen's % | Basis | Greenwich % | Basis | Bowery % | Basis |
|---|---|---|---|---|---|---|---|---|
| 1/1820-7/1829 | 5 | all[a] | | | | | | |
| 1/1830 | 5 | all[a] | 5 | all | | | | |
| 7/1830 | 5 | all[a] | 5 | all | | | | |
| 1/1831 | 5 | all[a] | 5 | all | | | | |
| 7/1831 | 5 | all[a] | 5 | all | | | | |
| 1/1832 | 5/4 | $500[b] | 5 | all | | | | |
| 7/1832 | 5/4 | $500[b] | 5 | all | | | | |
| 1/1833 | 5/4 | $500[b] | 5 | all | | | | |
| 7/1833 | 5/4 | $500[b] | 5/4 | $500 | | | | |
| 1/1834 | 5/4 | $500[b] | 5/4 | $500 | 5/4 | $500 | | |
| 7/1834 | 5/4 | $500[b] | 5/4 | $500 | 5/4 | $500 | | |
| 1/1835 | 5/4 | $500[b] | 5/4 | $500 | 5/4 | $500 | 5/4 | $500 |
| 7/1835 | 5/4 | $500[b] | 5/4 | $500 | 5/4 | $500 | 5/4 | $500 |
| 1/1836 | 5/4 | $500[b] | 5 | all | 5/4 | $500 | 5/4 | $500 |
| 7/1836 | 5/4 | $500[b] | 5 | all | 5/4 | $500 | 5/4 | $500 |
| 1/1837 | 5/4 | $500[b] | 5 | all | 5/4 | $500 | 5/4 | $500 |
| 7/1837 | 5/4 | $500[b] | 5 | all | 5/4 | $500 | 5/4 | $500 |
| 1/1838 | 5/4 | $500[b] | 5 | all | 5/4 | $500 | 5/4 | $500 |
| 7/1838 | 5/4 | $500[b] | 5 | all | 5/4 | $500 | 5/4 | $500 |
| 1/1839 | 5/4 | $500[b] | 5 | all | 5/4 | $500 | 5/4 | $500 |
| 7/1839 | 5/4 | $500[b] | 5 | all | 5/4 | $500 | 5/4 | $500 |
| 1/1840 | 5/4 | $500[b] | 6 | all | 5/4 | $500 | 5/4 | $500 |
| 7/1840 | 5/4 | $500[b] | 6 | all | 5/4 | $500 | 5/4 | $500 |
| 1/1841 | 5/4 | $500[b] | 6 | all | 5/4 | $500 | 5/4 | $500 |
| 7/1841 | 5/4 | $500[b] | 6 | all | 5/4 | $500 | 5/4 | $500 |
| 1/1842 | 5/4 | $500[b] | 6 | all | 5/4 | $500 | 5/4 | $500 |
| 7/1842 | 5/4 | $500[b] | 6 | all | 5/4 | $500 | 5/4 | $500 |
| 1/1843 | 5/4 | $500[b] | 6 | all | 5/4 | $500 | 5/4 | $500 |
| 7/1843 | 5/4 | $500[b] | 6 | all | 5/4 | $500 | 5/4 | $500 |
| 1/1844 | 5/4 | $500[b] | 6 | all | 5/4 | $500 | 5/4 | $500 |
| 7/1844 | 5/4 | $500[b] | 6 | all | 5/4 | $500 | 5/4 | $500 |
| 1/1845 | 5/4 | $500[b] | 6/5 | $1,000 | 5/4 | $500 | 5/4 | $500 |
| 7/1845 | 5/4 | $500[b] | 6/5 | $1,000 | 5/4 | $500 | 5/4 | $500 |
| 1/1846 | 5/4 | $500[b] | 6/5 | $1,000 | 5/4 | $500 | 5/4 | $500 |
| 7/1846 | 5/4 | $500[b] | 6/5 | $1,000 | 5/4 | $500 | 5/4 | $500 |

Sources: Compiled from the minute books of the Bank for Savings, Seamen's, Bowery, Dry Dock, Manhattan, Broadway, and Mariners' savings banks; Dorcas Elisabeth Campbell, *The First Hundred Years*, p. 101; Andrew Mills, *That's My Bank*, p. 109; *New York Herald*, 1841-1861; *New York Times*, 1851-1861; *New York Tribune*, 1841-1861; *Longworth's American Almanac, New York Register, and City Directory*, 1827-1842; *Doggett's New York City Directory*, 1842-1851; *Rode's New York City Directory*, 1850; *Thow's New York City Directory*, 1853-1864.

[a]5% on all sums.

[b]5% on all accounts of $500 and less, 4% on all accounts over $500.

[c]6% on all accounts of $500 and less, 5% on all accounts between $500 and $1,000, 4% on all accounts over $1,000.

[d]Advertisements may have only listed maximum rate; this bank may have paid 6/5/4-$500/$1,000 for the entire period.

Table 3   (Continued)

| Date | Bank for Savings % | Basis | Seamen's % | Basis | Greenwich % | Basis | Bowery % | Basis |
|---|---|---|---|---|---|---|---|---|
| 1/1847 | 5/4 | $500[b] | 6/5 | $1,000 | 5/4 | $500 | 5/4 | $500 |
| 7/1847 | 5/4 | $500[b] | 6/5 | $1,000 | 5/4 | $500 | 5/4 | $500 |
| 1/1848 | 5/4 | $500[b] | 6/5 | $1,000 | 5/4 | $500 | 5/4 | $500 |
| 7/1848 | 5/4 | $500[b] | 6/5 | $1,000 | 5/4 | $500 | 5/4 | $500 |
| 1/1849 | 5/4 | $500[b] | 6/5 | $1,000 | 6/5 | $500 | 6/5 | $500 |
| 7/1849 | 5/4 | $500[b] | 6/5 | $1,000 | 6/5 | $500 | 6/5 | $500 |
| 1/1850 | 5/4 | $500[b] | 6/5 | $1,000 | 6/5 | $500 | 6/5 | $500 |
| 7/1850 | 5/4 | $500[b] | 6/5 | $1,000 | 6/5 | $500 | 6/5 | $500 |
| 1/1851 | 5/4 | $500 | 6/5 | $500 | 5/4 | $500 | 5/4 | $500 |
| 7/1851 | 5/4 | $500 | 6/5 | $500 | 5/4 | $500 | 5/4 | $500 |
| 1/1852 | 5/4 | $500 | 6/5 | $500 | 5/4 | $500 | 5/4 | $500 |
| 7/1852 | 10/8 | $500 | 6/5 | $500 | 5/4 | $500 | 5/4 | $500 |
| 1/1853 | 5/4 | $500 | 6/5 | $500 | 5/4 | $500 | 5/4 | $500 |
| 7/1853 | 5/4 | $500 | 6/5 | $500 | 5/4 | $500 | 5/4 | $500 |
| 1/1854 | 5/4 | $500 | 6/5 | $500 | 5/4 | $500 | 5/4 | $500 |
| 7/1854 | 5/4 | $500 | 6/5 | $500 | 5/4 | $500 | 7.5/6 | $500 |
| 1/1855 | 5/4 | $500 | 6/5 | $500 | 5/4 | $500 | 5/4 | $500 |
| 7/1855 | 10/8 | $500 | 6/5 | $500 | 5/4 | $500 | 7.5/6 | $500 |
| 1/1856 | 5/4 | $500 | 6/5 | $500 | 5/4 | $500 | 5/4 | $500 |
| 7/1856 | 5/4 | $500 | 6/5 | $500 | 5/4 | $500 | 7.5/6 | $500 |
| 1/1857 | 5/4 | $500 | 6/5 | $500 | 5/4 | $500 | 5/4 | $500 |
| 7/1857 | 5/4 | $500 | 6/5 | $500 | 5/4 | $500 | 5/4 | $500 |
| 1/1858 | 5/4 | $500 | 6/5 | $500 | 5/4 | $500 | 7.5/6 | $500 |
| 7/1858 | 10/8 | $500 | 6/5 | $500 | 5/4 | $500 | 5/4 | $500 |
| 1/1859 | 5/4 | $500 | 6/5 | $500 | 5/4 | $500 | 7.5/6 | $500 |
| 7/1859 | 5/4 | $500 | 6/5 | $500 | 5/4 | $500 | 5/4 | $500 |
| 1/1860 | 10/8 | $500 | 6/5 | $500 | 5/4 | $500 | 5/4 | $500 |
| 7/1860 | 5/4 | $500 | 6/5 | $500 | 5/4 | $500 | 5/4 | $500 |

| Date | East River % | Basis | Dry Dock % | Basis | Merchants' Clerks % | Basis | Emigrant Industrial % | Basis |
|---|---|---|---|---|---|---|---|---|
| 1/1849 | 5 | all | 6 | all | 6 | all | | |
| 7/1849 | 5 to | $500 | 6/5 | $500 | 6/5 | $500 | | |
| 1/1850 | 5/4 | $500 | 6/5 | $500 | 6/5 | $1,000 | | |
| 7/1850 | 5/4 | $500 | 6/5 | $500 | 6/5 | $1,000 | | |
| 1/1851 | 5/4 | $500 | 6/5 | $500 | 6/5 | $1,000 | | |
| 7/1851 | 5/4 | $500 | 5/4 | $1,000 | 6/5 | $1,000 | | |
| 1/1852 | 5/4 | $500 | 5/4 | $1,000 | 6/5 | $1,000 | 6/5 | $500 |
| 7/1852 | 5/4 | $500 | 6/5 | $500 | 6/5 | $500 | 6/5 | $500 |
| 1/1853 | 5/4 | $500 | 6/5 | $500 | 6/5 | $500 | 6/5 | $500 |
| 7/1853 | 5/4 | $500 | 6/5 | $500 | 6/5 | $500 | 6/5 | $500 |
| 1/1854 | 5/4 | $500 | 6/5 | $1,000 | 6/5 | $500 | 6/5 | $500 |
| 7/1854 | 5/4 | $500 | 6/5 | $1,000 | 6/5 | $500 | 6/5 | $500 |
| 1/1855 | 5/4 | $500 | 6/5 | $1,000 | 6/5 | $500 | 6/5 | $500 |
| 7/1855 | 5/4 | $500 | 6/5 | $1,000 | 6/5 | $500 | 6/5 | $500 |
| 1/1856 | 5/4 | $500 | 6/5 | $1,000 | 6/5 | $500 | 6/5 | $500 |

**Table 3**   (Continued)

| 7/1856 | 6/5 | $500 | 6/5 | $1,000 | 6/5 | $500 | 6/5 | $500 |
|---|---|---|---|---|---|---|---|---|
| 1/1857 | 6/5 | $500 | 6/5 | $1,000 | 6/5 | $500 | 6/5 | $500 |
| 7/1857 | 6/5 | $500 | 6/5 | $1,000 | 6/5 | $500 | 6/5 | $500 |
| 1/1858 | 6/5 | $500 | 6/5 | $1,000 | 6/5 | $500 | 6/5 | $500 |
| 7/1858 | 6/5 | $500 | 6/5 | $1,000 | 6/5 | $500 | 6/5 | $500 |
| 1/1859 | 6/5 | $500 | 6/5 | $1,000 | 6/5 | $500 | 6/5 | $500 |
| 7/1859 | 6/5 | $500 | 6/5 | $1,000 | 6/5 | $500 | 6/5 | $500 |
| 1/1860 | 6/5 | $500 | 6/5 | $1,000 | 6/5 | $500 | 6/5 | $500 |
| 7/1860 | 6/5 | $500 | 6/5 | $1,000 | 6/5 | $500 | 6/5 | $500 |

| Date | Manhattan | | Broadway | | Irving | | Mechanics' & Traders | |
|---|---|---|---|---|---|---|---|---|
| | % | Basis | % | Basis | % | Basis | % | Basis |
| 1/1852 | 6/5/4 | $500/$1,000[c] | | | | | | |
| 7/1852 | 6/5/4 | $500/$1,000[c] | 6/5 | $500 | 6 to | $500[d] | 6 | all |
| 1/1853 | 6/5/4 | $500/$1,000[c] | 6/5 | $500 | 6 to | $500[d] | 6/5 | $500 |
| 7/1853 | 6/5/4 | $500/$1,000[c] | 6/5 | $500 | 6 to | $500[d] | 6/5 | $500 |
| 1/1854 | 6/5/4 | $500/$1,000[c] | 6/5 | $500 | 6 to | $500[d] | 6/5 | $500 |
| 7/1854 | 6/5 | $500 | 6/5 | $500 | 6 to | $500[d] | 6/5 | $500 |
| 1/1855 | 6/5 | $500 | 6/5 | $500 | 6 to | $500[d] | 6/5 | $500 |
| 7/1855 | 6/5 | $500 | 6/5 | $500 | 6 to | $500[d] | 6/5 | $500 |
| 1/1856 | 6/5 | $500 | 6/5 | $500 | 6 to | $500[d] | 6/5 | $500 |
| 7/1856 | 6/5 | $500 | 6/5 | $500 | 6 to | $500[d] | 6/5 | $500 |
| 1/1857 | 6/5 | $500 | 6/5 | $500 | 6/5/4 | $500/$1,000 | 6/5 | $500 |
| 7/1857 | 6/5 | $500 | 6/5 | $500 | 6 to | $500 | 6/5 | $500 |
| 1/1858 | 6/5 | $500 | 6/5 | $500 | 6 to | $500 | 6/5 | $500 |
| 7/1858 | 6/5 | $500 | 6/5 | $500 | 6 to | $500 | 6/5 | $500 |
| 1/1859 | 6/5 | $500 | 6/5 | $500 | 6 to | $500 | 6/5 | $500 |
| 7/1859 | 6/5 | $500 | 6/5 | $500 | 6 to | $500 | 6/5 | $500 |
| 1/1860 | 6/5 | $500 | 6/5 | $500 | 6/5/4 | $500/$1,000 | 6/5 | $500 |
| 7/1860 | 6/5 | $500 | 6/5 | $500 | 6/5/4 | $500/$1,000 | 6/5 | $500 |

| Date | Mariners' | | Sixpenny | | Union Dime | | Blooming-dale | |
|---|---|---|---|---|---|---|---|---|
| | % | Basis | % | Basis | % | Basis | % | Basis |
| 1/1854 | 6 | all | | | | | | |
| 7/1854 | 6/5 | $500 | | | | | | |
| 1/1855 | 6/5 | $500 | | | | | | |
| 7/1855 | 6/5 | $500 | | | | | | |
| 1/1856 | 6/5 | $500 | | | | | | |
| 7/1856 | 6/5 | $500 | | | | | | |
| 1/1857 | 6/5 | $500 | 6 | all | | | | |
| 7/1857 | 6/5 | $500 | 6 | all | | | | |
| 1/1858 | 6/5 | $500 | 6 | all | | | | |
| 7/1858 | 6/5 | $500 | 6 | all | | | | |
| 1/1859 | 6/5 | $500 | 6 | all | | | | |
| 7/1859 | 6/5 | $500 | 6 | all | 6/5 | $500 | 6/5 | $1,000 |
| 1/1860 | 6/5 | $500 | 6 | all | 6/5 | $500 | 6/5 | $1,000 |
| 7/1861 | 6/5 | $500 | 6 | all | 6/5 | $500 | 6/5 | $1,000 |

in enforcing this provision, for it could also be avoided by opening several accounts in the names of family members or under false names. Chapter 3 covers trustee policy pertaining to this issue.

With some exceptions to be mentioned later, all New York City mutuals calculated interest payments in a similar manner. Interest was credited and compounded on 1 January and 1 July but was not paid or entered into passbooks until the middle of these two months.[36] Six months' interest was paid on all sums on deposit for six months prior to 1 January, and 1 July. Three months' interest was paid on all sums deposited on or after 1 January (or 1 July) but before 1 October (or 1 April). No interest was allowed on sums not on deposit for three months prior to 1 January or 1 July, nor on sums of less than $5, nor on fractions of a dollar. These stipulations meant that there were always some funds which the banks had use of but which were ineligible to receive interest. Not until the 1850s did some New York City mutuals begin to announce interest rates for future periods. The policy adopted by the Bank for Savings in 1819 was to declare dividends every January and July for the past six-month period. This is an important point, for it meant that, unlike today, savers had no assurance what rate they would receive at the time they made a deposit. Thus savings accounts were like most other investments in that the rate of return was not guaranteed in advance.

Several aspects of Table 3 deserve comment. The first is the relative stability of mutual interest rates over a forty-year period marked by several panics and booms and two protracted depressions. The Bank for Savings paid the same rate on accounts of $500 and less for the entire period, with the exception of four years when it declared extra dividends.

Second, the Seamen's Bank for Savings consistently paid the highest rate in the city. From 1836 to 1849 it paid a higher rate than any other bank, and for all other years it was among the highest. The interest differential on sums of $500 and less never exceeded 1 percent, but in the 1840s the Seamen's paid 2 percent more than the other mutuals on accounts over $500.

Third, if savings banks were becoming more competitive as their number increased, one would expect interest rates to converge. In fact, all the banks founded after 1848 paid almost identical rates for every year. Of the banks founded in or before 1848, the East River paid a lower than normal rate until 1856, and starting in 1858 the Greenwich lowered its rate below the popular rate of 6 percent on accounts up to $500 and 5 percent on larger accounts. This similarity in the interest rates paid by the newer mutuals was an indication of each bank's awareness of and responsiveness to the policies of its competitors. The following chapter shows that mutual depositors were marginally responsive to interest differentials, and banks paying lower rates grew more slowly than those paying higher rates. When banks increased their rates, their growth vis à vis that of other mutuals and their own past performance improved.

The Bank for Savings and the Bowery maintained their lower base rates but declared several extra dividends which nearly equalized the average rate they paid with that paid by other mutuals. From 1852 through 1860, including these extra dividends, the Bank for Savings paid an average rate of interest of 6.1 percent on accounts under $500 and 4.9 percent on larger accounts. From July 1854 through 1860 the Bowery paid an average rate of 6.0 percent on accounts under $500 and 4.8 percent on accounts over that amount.[37]

The rationale for these extra dividends and the procedure the banks followed in declaring them offers considerable insight into the nature of these two institutions. In 1852 the New York State Assembly passed a bill that would have effectively confiscated all savings banks' surpluses; a Senate committee amended the proposed legislation to limit the surplus of any savings bank to 5 percent, but that offered little comfort to the trustees of the Bank for Savings, who had recently calculated that the bank's surplus was 12.5 percent. This legislation was not enacted, but similar bills were considered throughout the 1850s. This action was based on the popular misconception that the surplus in savings banks represented the lapsed legacies of thousands of poor who had died without heirs and had left "'unclaimed millions of deposits which no living being claims save the trustee. . . .'"[38] As late as the 1870s some legislators were of the opinion that the "surplus would some time exceed the deposits, and eventually absorb the entire property of the State . . . ."[39]

Faced with the possibility of such unfavorable legislation, the trustees of the Bank for Savings and the Bowery Savings Bank could either have raised the dividend rates paid to depositors or lowered interest rates to borrowers. If the trustees were profiteering, the threat to the mutuals' surpluses offered an excellent excuse to negotiate a lower interest rate on loans and commercial bank deposits. (Chapters 5 and 6 will examine whether such transfers occurred.) But both boards decided to pass on parts of their surpluses to their depositors, and they both debated whether this should be done by declaring large extra dividends or by permanently raising their interest rates. Both mutuals decided to declare extra dividends because they feared that they would attract too much money from other mutuals if they raised their rate on a permanent basis. Neither bank advertised its intent to pay an extra dividend, nor did either encourage any special publicity at the time the dividends were declared. In all cases the announcement of the extra dividends appeared in the newspaper advertisements that these banks regularly ran for about a week in mid-January and mid-July to announce their interest rates for the past six months. The boards probably felt that depositors of other banks would be less likely to transfer their savings since there was no assurance that any extra dividends would be paid in the future; furthermore, a depositor would have had to sacrifice three months' interest in order to have made such a transfer.

While these two older institutions were managing their dividends so as to discourage their own growth, most of the younger banks were actively soliciting deposits. The increased competition which first appeared in about 1850 took two forms. First, many of the new banks started advertising in several newspapers on a daily basis the interest rate they would pay in the future. Although this was an important innovation that undoubtedly created a more efficient savings market through the lowering of information barriers, it was looked upon disdainfully by the trustees of the older banks. Since in theory mutual dividends were to be a proportion of past profits, many mutual trustees considered it improper to promise a particular dividend rate for six months in the future. They reasoned that in the advent of a sharp decline in the value of the bank's assets, paying a relatively high rate announced during better times could endanger the bank's liquidity. Records indicate that the decision by some banks to advertise rates in advance was often in direct response to similar policies by other banks. For example, the finance committee of the Manhattan Savings Institution reported on 19 December 1854 that "because several other banks are advertising their dividend the committee has decided to do the same."[40]

Another device used by most banks founded after 1848 to entice customers away from older institutions was to advertise a grace period.[41] This was a period extending up to fifteen days into a new dividend period during which deposits would draw interest from the beginning of the period. Younger banks were paying rates as high or higher than the older banks, and they were conveniently located for many of the older banks' customers. But without a grace period depositors would have had to sacrifice three months' interest if they decided to change banks. The introduction of grace periods eliminated this impediment to depositor mobility. Contemporary observers were well aware of the general increase in the use of aggressive practices employed to attract funds from other mutuals. In 1862 the superintendent of banking for New York state lamented the increase in competition, which had started over a decade earlier. "Institutions which are just commencing business, not infrequently promise, in advance, a high rate of interest on deposits, and, thus seek to divert business from institutions of established reputations to those of more doubtful character."[42]

The boards of the Bank for Savings, the Seamen's, and the Bowery took a dim view of the practices of many of the newer mutuals, and they all refused to respond with similar inducements during the prewar era.[43] The attitude of most of the trustees of these banks had traditionally been to encourage the founding of new mutuals. Many of the Bank for Savings' trustees were founders of the Seamen's, and the board of the older bank made a special point of passing a resolution "approbating the project least [sic] it might be objected that it was a rival institution." John Pintard, who was active in the administration of both of these banks, expressed what was the common attitude of these banks' early trustees. "So far from Jealousy, I wish there was a Savings Bank in every Ward, so advantageous do they prove to the humbler classes. . . ." The Bank for Savings' trustees expressed similar sympathies when the Greenwich was founded in 1833. The next year when the Bowery opened, the trustees of the Bank for Savings sent their accountant, Daniel C. Tylee, to help organize the new bank's affairs.[44]

The less competitive attitude of the more established banks was most in evidence during the several monetary panics that plagued the prewar era. During these periods of great stress even the largest mutuals were hit by runs, and many of their trustees suffered losses in their private businesses. Yet, in 1837 the trustees of the Bank for Savings made life-saving loans to mutuals that were on the verge of collapse. Similar rescues were made in 1854 and 1857 by the Bank for Savings and the Seamen's Bank for Savings.[45] It is significant that no records of similar transactions can be found during the heavy runs that accompanied the outbreak of the Civil War. The older banks may not have been ready to compete actively for deposits, but they were no longer willing to come to the aid of the more aggressive and weaker institutions.

## Mutual Surplus Accounts

The attitudes of the older banks, particularly the Bank for Savings, differed from those of the newer mutuals with regard to the accumulation of surplus, as well as to most other policies. The primary result of accumulating a surplus was to decrease risk: the greater the surplus, the less vulnerable the bank was to short-run fluctuations in financial markets. This decrease in risk might be desired by trustees for three reasons. First, they might have reasoned that their customers desired less risk, and therefore they were catering to their customers' demands.[46] Second, trustees might have been imposing their own values concerning risk aversion on "the humbler classes." Many trustees did feel a deep personal responsibility for the safety of their depositors' savings and, by their own testimony, experienced much anguish at the thought of depositors' losing their savings during monetary panics. Third, a large surplus made the task of management easier; with less risk of failure there was less pressure on trustees to manage a bank's portfolio efficiently.[47]

The Bank for Savings began accumulating a surplus in 1819, though its charter did not explicitly authorize it to do so. In 1831 the bank's trustees succeeded in obtaining a charter amendment that permitted a surplus equal to 3 percent of the bank's deposits. In 1835 and 1836 the trustees devoted a considerable amount of time and effort to consideration of a policy on surplus. Their reports filled several pages of the bank's minute books. After a thorough evaluation of the bank's portfolio, the board concluded that a "three per cent surplus is altogether inadequate to meet the effect of a commercial revolution and much more so that of a war." The board further declared that it should strive to build a surplus equal to 10 percent of the bank's deposits.[48] Upon request, the legislature increased the bank's limit to 10 percent in 1836.[49] The bank's minutes indicate that the trustees' principal concern was to decrease risk to savers. On several occasions in later years the board reaffirmed its belief that 10 percent was an optimal surplus.[50]

The records of other mutuals reveal much less about their trustees' intentions or policies, but it is evident that no other bank placed as much emphasis on the accumulation of a surplus as did the Bank for Savings. The first mention of a surplus in the minutes of the Bowery Savings Bank was in March of 1848, when the board decided not to raise the dividend rate because its surplus was not large enough to guarantee payment in times of panic. At that time the board did not state what it considered to be an adequate surplus. In November of the same year the board reversed its previous decision and decided to raise its dividend rate in January 1849 on the grounds that the bank had experienced "excessive profits" during the last four years. In January 1849 the Bowery's surplus was approximately 8 percent of its deposits. In 1859 the bank's executive committee recommended that no more extra dividends be paid until the bank's surplus was built up to 7 percent of assets. This was the first explicit statement in this bank's records regarding what was considered a proper surplus.[51]

The trustees of the Seamen's Bank for Savings never expressed a policy concerning what level of surplus the bank should strive to maintain. The first mention of the bank's surplus in the board minutes appeared in 1852 when the trustees decided to send a lobbyist to Albany to work against legislation that would confiscate mutual surpluses. In 1853 the board noted that its surplus was less than 2 percent of deposits and that it was needed as a safeguard to the bank's customers.[52] This percentage was evidently considered to be adequate, for there was no apparent effort to increase the bank's surplus. The minutes of the Dry Dock, Manhattan, Mariners', and Broadway savings banks do not mention the banks' surpluses, let alone explicitly state how much of a surplus their trustees considered to be adequate. None of these banks accumulated much of a surplus during this period, as is shown in Table 4.[53]

By 1860 only three of the fourteen banks organized during or after 1848 had accumulated surpluses of more than 1 percent, and six banks actually had negative surpluses. The four oldest mutuals all had substantial surpluses in 1860, but the Bank for Savings' and Bowery's surplus-to-asset ratios had declined by about 4 percent and 2 percent, respectively, during the 1850s. The Seamen's and Greenwich's surplus-to-asset ratio remained relatively stable over this decade.

These findings are difficult to interpret because several hypotheses could explain the difficulty the newer banks had accumulating a surplus and the inability of some older mutuals to maintain theirs. First, the threat of state confiscation was influential in the older banks' decision to cut their surplus ratios, but this probably was not a major concern of the newer mutuals.[54] Second, the discussion of bank operating procedure earlier in this chapter suggests that as the number

Table 4   Mutual Surpluses in January 1860

| Bank | Amount of Surplus (Assets - Deposits) | Surplus as a Percentage of Total Assets |
|---|---|---|
| Bank for Savings | $695,862 | 6.8 |
| Seamen's | 249,457 | 2.9 |
| Greenwich | 107,216[a] | 2.6 |
| Bowery | 447,391 | 4.5 |
| East River | 24,785 | 2.4 |
| Dry Dock | 943 | 0.0 |
| Merchants' Clerks | −4,552[a] | negative |
| Emigrant Industrial | 29,220 | 1.3 |
| Manhattan | 17,823 | 0.7 |
| Broadway | 17,900 | 1.7 |
| Irving | −570[a] | negative |
| Mechanics' and Traders' | −2,588[a] | negative |
| Mariners' | −2,424[a] | negative |
| Sixpenny | 0[a] | 0.0 |
| Rose Hill | 945[a] | 0.8 |
| Third Avenue | negative | negative |
| Union Dime | 0[a] | 0.0 |
| German | −2,546[a] | negative |

[a]Estimated by adjusting amount due depositors upward by 2% to account for interest which had accrued to depositors; see n. 74.

of mutuals increased and new policies appeared, the competition for deposits became keener. If so, it would have become harder for mutuals to build a surplus. Third, there might have been a change in trustee objectives; the previous analysis suggests that many of the newer banks' trustees may have been less philanthropically motivated and more concerned with "collateral advantages" than were the trustees of the older banks. If there were a change in objectives, trustees would have been less risk averse and thus less interested in surplus accumulation. More importantly, if they were profiteering, one would expect them to pass any potential surplus on to cronies in the form of low-interest loans. It is probable that all three of the above explanations apply: the state did exert pressure, competition for deposits did increase, and some trustees did profiteer.

## Changes in Mutual Behavior: Causes

The banks formed later in the period were more competitive for several reasons. Some were most likely formed for no other reason than to yield a profit to their trustees, who were also officers of commercial banks and insurance companies. In Chapter 6 an examination of mutual investment portfolios will show some mutuals were satellites of commercial organizations. Other mutuals, organized by men at least partly motivated by benevolent considerations, were entering a more competitive market than had existed prior to the 1850s.[55] Because these banks were not able to offer the reputation for security of the more established institutions, they were forced to adopt the policies of the newer, more competitive, entries.

The ascent to power by managers in the new banks further increased the competition for deposits. Although the boards of trustees still made the important policy decisions concerning interest rates and banking hours, managers had substantial authority. A manager could be lenient in accepting large deposits from relatively wealthy individuals and lax in allowing savers to split their accounts in order to receive the higher rate paid on smaller balances. Furthermore, board decisons probably became more and more dependent on information supplied by employees. In some cases, e.g., the Mariners' Savings Institution, it is clear that trustee participation was minimal.

The Mariners' opened in April 1853. The bank's name and early statements of objectives indicate that it was organized by a group of socially dedicated businessmen who were primarily interested in aiding seamen. If this were the case, one would expect the philanthropic zeal of its board to have been strongest during the first years of business, for this would have been the period when the founding spirit was still fresh. Yet in 1853 and again in 1855 for lack of a quorum the board did not meet for as long as four months in a row.[56] There can be little doubt that at least during these periods the bank's policies were being determined by the few trustees who were closely connected with the Hanover Insurance Company and the Hanover Bank, and by the savings bank's paid secretary, with little supervision from the board as a whole.

The salaries of management in all the banks studied were dependent on the bank's deposits. Again the Mariners' Savings Institution provides an example. The salary schedule in 1855 provided for automatic increases when the bank's deposits reached successive plateaus. The secretary's salary was to increase by $500 per year every time deposits climbed by $50,000 (later changed to $100,000).[57] Thus there was a strong incentive for employees to maximize deposit growth, and as more and more responsibility was passed on to functionaries the likelihood of their doing so increased.[58]

Another distinction between many of the newer banks and the older institutions that might explain the marked difference in their evolution from "benevolence to business" is found in the composition of their boards of trustees. Generally the boards of the newer mutuals were drawn from the ranks of prosperous businessmen in the bank's neighborhood. In contrast, the boards of many of the older institutions, especially those of the Bank for Savings and the Seamen's, were made up of independently wealthy individuals who devoted much of their time to public service. Furthermore, the newer institutions did not have any time-honored traditions standing in the way of a change-over from trustee to employee management.

When woven together, the different threads of evidence presented in this chapter form a fairly consistent pattern. There were significant differences in policy—in the burdens assumed by trustees, business hours, dividend policy, and advertising programs—which reflected a basic difference in trustee objectives. Philanthropic motivation was indeed highly instrumental in explaining the behavior of several banks. As a general rule the earlier a bank was founded the stronger was the philanthropic spirit of its trustees and the longer this spirit affected policy. Conversely, banks formed later in the period tended to become more aggressive as their trustees rather quickly came to rely on professional managers and adopted policies that the older mutuals had shunned for decades. Many of the older mutuals retained their traditional policies even when doing so adversely affected deposit growth.

The persistence of the older mutuals in maintaining their traditional emphasis on trustee managment and the accompanying adherence to their less aggressive policies offers an excellent example of the importance of what Neil Chamberlain terms "corporate personality" in determining a firm's behavior. Chamberlain describes a variety of personality types or strategies that are available to a firm:

> Rather than use the awkward expression, "corporate personality," we shall refer to these differing behavioral patterns of business firms as their "strategy sets." Some firms tend to be risk-taking and innovative; others are cautious and imitative. Some adopt a strategy set that seeks to identify their own activities with the public interest; others adopt a more aloof and disengaged stance that stresses their freedom from any broader social responsibility than the efficient provision of goods and services. Some firms limit their interests to a single industry, with managers who think of themselves as "steel" men or "oil" men; other firms emphasize diversification and fluidity of capital movement. Some firms develop paternalistic attitudes with respect to their employees and stockholders; others deal with one or both groups objectively, matter-of-factly.[59]

The policies of specific mutuals were to a significant extent a product of the bank's history and its trustees' philosophy. Barring powerful exogenous shocks, a mutual's strategy would be fairly stable over time. The oldest mutuals, which were founded by men who had a strong philanthropic commitment, affirmed that commitment long after most of the founders had passed on and after newer firms had adopted new methods and goals. Each mutual tended to recruit men oriented toward its way of doing business, and prospective trustees tended to join mutuals with which they felt comfortable. This process of self-selection was most evident in the case of the Bank for Savings. Its minute books indicate that its board generally devoted more time and consideration to making new appointments than did other mutuals. Likewise, the decision to accept a trusteeship was not taken lightly, for it involved much responsibility and labor.

An imperfect market or product differentiation or both were necessary conditions for these differences in "corporate personality" to coexist. In a perfectly competitive market non-optimizing firms would be driven to the wall and punished with losses or failure, but market imperfections permitted non-maximizing behavior to exist. Many of the issues raised in this chapter will appear again, and the differences in "corporate personality" already evident will become more pronounced in subsequent chapters.

CHAPTER 3

# Mutual Savings Bank Depositors

Who were the anonymous individuals whose savings were so instrumental in the success of the Erie Canal, the Croton Water Works, and the numerous other public and private economic ventures along the North Atlantic seaboard? Were the millions of dollars entrusted to mutual savings banks really, as so often claimed, the exclusive property of an army of laborers, domestics, and other poor souls occupying the bottom rungs of the economic ladder? If so, the success of mutuals not only suggests the existence of a phenomenally frugal and relatively prosperous urban proletariat, but also represents an historical free-market alternative to various forced savings schemes designed to finance social overhead capital.

This chapter addresses these issues by examining the variety of occupations of mutual customers. Next it analyzes the issue of how deposits were distributed by size and discusses who owned the larger accounts. The third part of the chapter describes the efforts mutual trustees made to limit account size and to restrict wealthy people from using the banks. The final section explores how mutual depositors responded to competitive incentives and particularly how they responded to the differentials and changes in interest rates treated in the previous chapter. In all, this account will correct some false impressions concerning the sources of mutual deposits and concerning the banks' influence on the aggregate level of savings and investment. It will also offer a glimpse of some of the banks' administrative problems and procedures and it will provide a clearer insight into the role of mutuals as philanthropic institutions. Before analyzing the data, it would be useful to review briefly the positions of previous writers and to trace out some of the implications that follow from their conclusions.

The hypothesis widely accepted by scholars who have studied early American mutuals was first formulated by Emerson Keyes in 1876. He wrote that savings banks soon "became the resort not only of the indigent poor, whose meager savings they had been instituted primarily to preserve and protect, but of industrious and thrifty toilers. . . ."[1] Recent scholars have added little to Keyes's conclusion. Fritz Redlich took an identical position, and Payne and Davis concluded that "whether this [Keyes's] hypothesis is true, or whether, merely more people of the same class [i.e., indigent poor] began to deposit their funds in the bank cannot be proved. . . ."[2] In their 1958 article Payne and Davis offer a somewhat more sober account. "The founders of the banks, wishing to inspire confidence, first opened their doors to all, rich and poor alike, but from the start the intention was ultimately to restrict the depositors to the 'frugal poor.' As both banks were an almost instantaneous success . . . , they soon moved to restrict their depositors." Payne and Davis then describe how the banks successfully employed various discriminatory practices to ferret out depositors who were not of the "industrious or laboring, poor."[3] This general portrayal of mutual depositors as poor, even indigent laborers has found its way into a diverse number of publications.[4] An accurate description of mutual depositors is needed to correct the historical record, but more importantly, such a description is required to evaluate the performance of mutuals as philanthropic organizations, for their claim to eleemosynary status has always rested heavily on the presumed socioeconomic characteristics of their customers. It is entirely possible that, as was the case with the English trustee savings banks, American mutuals were a boon to the middle classes rather than to "the poor."

Perhaps more than anything else we need an accurate description of mutual depositors in order to assess properly the impact these institutions had on the aggregate level of savings, on financial markets, and on the nation's economic development. It follows from the accepted descriptions of depositors that a substantial proportion of the funds accumulated by savings banks constituted a net addition to the economy's supply of financial capital, because in the first half of the nineteenth century few alternative investment opportunities were open to laborers possessing small blocks of savings and little market information. If one accepts the traditional description of mutual customers, the emergence of mutuals allowed "the poor" to transfer savings, which they previously had hoarded, into productive activities; mutuals also stimulated the laborers to increase their savings ratios by offering the combined incentives of interest and security. In either case mutual deposits represented funds which, in the absence of mutuals, would not have been invested. But the greater the percentage of savings bank depositors who were wealthier individuals and businessmen with a wider set of investment opportunities open to them, the lower the percentage of mutual holdings which can be viewed as additions to total investment.

## A Socioeconomic Analysis of Mutual Depositors

Data on the socioeconomic status of mutual customers, although relatively abundant and accessible, have until now escaped analysis. In their annual reports the trustees of the Bank for Savings, the Bowery Savings Bank, and the Greenwich Savings Bank published detailed lists itemizing the occupations and social characteristics (the number of minors, widows, single women, orphans, and trustees—described as deposits in trust for children, orphans, apprentices, etc.) of all *new* depositors.[5] The data for the Bank for Savings are the most complete. Because it was the first mutual in New York, one would be most likely to observe a change from "indigent poor" to "steady workers" among its depositors if in fact such a change actually occurred. Another justification for focusing on this one bank is that its trustees were particulary active in restricting wealthy individuals from opening accounts, so, if some middle- and upper-class depositors are found among its customers, it is even more likely that similar people saved in other mutuals.

In 1819 about half of the Bank for Savings' depositors were from society's middle and upper classes, while only about one-fourth were unskilled workers.[6] By far the largest group of depositors was children, who constituted 37 percent of all depositors in 1819. The bank's records indicate that these minors were generally the sons and daughters of upper- and middle-class parents who presumably were giving their children practical instruction in the virtues of thriftiness.[7]

About 7 percent of the 1,527 people who opened accounts the first year were professionals, artists, or property owners. Among this group were twelve merchants, five doctors, three druggists, two lawyers, seven shipmasters, three gentlemen, six students, one dentist, four clergymen, and numerous shopkeepers, innkeepers, and others who derived at least part of their income from property. There were also a large number of skilled workers, some of whom were talented craftsmen and probably owned their own shops, including jewelers, gunsmiths, watchmakers, and the like.

Over a ten-year period there was a decline in the proportion of children among new depositors and an increase in the proportion of skilled and unskilled workers. Table 5 shows the proportion of domestics and of unskilled workers found among the bank's new customers between 1819 and 1847. The large number of domestics reflects their general ubiquity in the urban labor market as well as their conditions of employment. Since domestic employment was relatively steady and since board and room were often supplied, servants could put aside much of their cash income. Furthermore, many employers exerted pressure on their domestics to open accounts.

**Table 5**   New Customers of the Bank for Savings

| Year | Percentage Domestics | Percentage Unskilled Laborers (Domestics Included) |
|------|------|------|
| 1819 | 15 | 24 |
| 1820 | ... | ... |
| 1821 | ... | ... |
| 1822 | 13 | 23 |
| 1823 | 16 | 28 |
| 1824 | 12 | 30 |
| 1825 | 9 | 24 |
| 1826 | 10 | 29 |
| 1827 | 12 | 34 |
| 1828 | 16 | 42 |
| 1829 | 20 | 43 |
| 1830 | 20 | 40 |
| 1831 | ... | ... |
| 1832 | 18 | 41 |
| 1833 | 19 | 42 |
| 1834 | 22 | 45 |
| 1835 | 19 | 44 |
| 1836 | 18 | 43 |
| 1837 | 27 | 48 |
| 1838 | 28 | 50 |
| 1839 | 31 | 51 |
| 1840 | 27 | 49 |
| 1841 | 23 | 46 |
| 1842 | 29 | 49 |
| 1843 | 29 | 50 |
| 1844 | 26 | 45 |
| 1845 | ... | ... |
| 1846 | ... | ... |
| 1847 | 22 | 45 |

Source: Compiled from *Annual Reports of the Trustees of the Bank for Savings* in *New York State Assembly Journal*, 1820, 1823-1829, and *New York State Senate Documents*, 1830, 1833-1842, 1844-1845, 1848, and *New York State Assembly Documents*, 1831, 1843.

Note: See Appendix A for a list of the specific occupations in each category.

An interesting example of the type of inducement used to stimulate servants to "put aside their meager earnings" is found in the letters of John Pintard. The Society for the Encouragement of Faithful Domestic Servants in New York offered substantial rewards to frugal domestics. Pintard took great pride in the fact that his cook Tamer Felmenter received a "$20 premium, a Bible and certificate and $5.53 being 1 per cent on her Saving Bank Book."[8]

A comparison of the Bowery and the Greenwich savings banks with the Bank for Savings (see Table 6) indicates that the two newer banks had proportionately fewer unskilled laborers among their customers. The percentage of skilled laborers in the two younger institu-

Table 6   New Depositors by Occupational Classes for the Bank for
Savings, Greenwich, and Bowery Savings Banks for Sample Years

| | Percentage Unskilled | | | Percentage Skilled | | | Percentage Merchant and Professional | | |
|---|---|---|---|---|---|---|---|---|---|
| Year | Bank for Savings | Green-wich | Bowery | Bank for Savings | Green-wich | Bowery | Bank for Savings | Green-wich | Bowery |
| 1833 | 42 | 19 | ... | 36 | 46 | ... | 11 | 13 | ... |
| 1835 | 44 | 26 | 16 | 38 | 51 | 50 | 10 | 11 | 11 |
| 1838 | 50 | 26 | 23 | 34 | 42 | 45 | 10 | 14 | 12 |
| 1844 | 45 | 20 | ‾18 | 36 | 46 | 44 | 14 | 18 | 13 |

Sources: Compiled from the *Annual Reports of the Trustees of the Bank for Savings; Annual Reports of the Trustees of the Bowery Savings Bank;* and *Annual Reports of the Greenwich Savings Bank,* all in *New York State Senate Documents,* 1834, 1836, 1839, 1845.

tions was higher than in the Bank for Savings, and the percentage of merchants, landowners, and the like was about the same for all three banks. This evidence suggests that although a majority of mutual depositors were working people, many customers did not fit that description. Furthermore, among those savers listed as "workers" were many skilled craftsmen who may have owned shops and could more properly be termed petite bourgeoisie than classified "provident poor." To arrive at a better understanding of the importance of middle- and upper-class depositors we need to know how balances were distributed among various classes of customers.

## The Distribution of Accounts by Size

The available data on the distribution of accounts by size suggest that, even in those mutuals that actively expelled wealthy depositors, a substantial proportion of total deposits belonged to a relatively few customers who were skilled craftsmen and professionals. The only evidence that specifically ties depositor account size to occupations is for the Bank for Savings in 1824. In that year the bank's trustees directed a special committee to compile a list of all persons who held "exceptionally large balances." In December of 1824, the committee reported that there were 330 customers with balances exceeding $500, which, when summed, represented about $360,000. This meant that about 3.5 percent of the bank's customers held claims to over 27 percent of the bank's funds. The report also noted that 166 of these depositors had balances exceeding $1,000, which accounted for almost 20 percent of the total amount on deposit. The committee was of the opinion that the size of these accounts (over $500) was ample proof "that the depositors are not of the poor and labouring class for whose benefit the institution was intended."[9]

A detailed check of the occupations of these 330 customers reveals that very few of these customers were unskilled workers. About 4 percent were domestics, 9 percent unskilled laborers (including domestics), and 28 percent skilled laborers and tradesmen. Adding the above indicates that about 37 percent of these large accounts belonged to people who could be classified as working men and women. The remaining 63 percent of these large accounts were owned by children (10 percent) of middle- and upper-class families, widows or the wives of fairly substantial citizens (19 percent), and professionals and merchants (33 percent).[10] From a slightly different perspective these figures indicate that, of the bank's customers who were domestics or unskilled laborers, about one in a hundred was among the privileged 330, while almost one out of ten of the professional-merchant class was in this group.

Table 7 presents another set of data covering a longer time period which corroborates and extends the impression given above. The Bank for Savings' annual reports included a breakdown, by size, of all the deposits made during any given year.[11] These reports indicate that from 1819 through 1860 the bottom 50 percent of the deposits made accounted for about 10 percent of the amount received, whereas the top 10 percent of the deposits accounted for at least 40 percent of the amount received. In most years deposits of $100 or more accounted for at least 50 percent of the bank's receipts. In 1849, $50 was about one-fourth the annual wage earnings in the woolen industry and one-sixth of that in the iron industry, yet deposits of $50 and more accounted for about 75 percent of the additional funds accumulated by the bank. A look at Table 8 shows similar results for the Greenwich and Bowery savings banks.

A comparison of the average size of accounts in various mutuals gives reason to believe that wealthy individuals also frequented other institutions. Table 9 indicates that in most years for which there are data the average balance in the Bank for Savings was below the national average, and it generally was $50 to $100 below that for the Savings Bank of Baltimore and the other established New York City banks.[12]

The Seamen's Bank for Savings generally had one of the highest average balances in the nation and is the only New York bank for which it was possible to compute the distribution of its accounts by size.[13] Table 10 reveals that although small savers were numerically important, they held claim to a relatively small amount of the bank's total deposits. Persons with balances of $200 or less accounted for almost 65 percent of the bank's customers, but they held title to only about 16 percent of its funds. At the other end of the scale were an elite 6 percent of the bank's clientele, all of whom held balances of at least $1,000 and as a group owned 36 percent of all the money on deposit.

**Table 7** Distribution of Deposits, Bank for Savings in the City of New York

| Year | Top 10% (% of Money Received)[a] | Bottom 50% (% of Money Received)[b] |
|---|---|---|
| 1819 | 56 | 3 |
| 1820 | 56 | 5 |
| 1821 | 47 | 6 |
| 1822 | 47 | 7 |
| 1823 | 48 | 7 |
| 1824 | 46 | 8 |
| 1825 | 48 | 9 |
| 1826 | 47 | 9 |
| 1827 | 44 | 10 |
| 1828 | 43 | 11 |
| 1829 | 43 | 11 |
| 1830 | 46 | 11 |
| 1831 | 43 | 11 |
| 1832 | 42 | 11 |
| 1833 | 44 | 11 |
| 1834 | 44 | 11 |
| 1835 | 40 | 12 |
| 1836 | 40 | 13 |
| 1837 | 42 | 11 |
| 1838 | 42 | 11 |
| 1839 | 40 | 12 |
| 1840 | 42 | 12 |
| 1841 | 45 | 11 |
| 1842 | 43 | 11 |
| 1843 | 44 | 11 |
| 1844 | 42 | 12 |
| 1845 | . . . | . . . |
| 1846 | . . . | . . . |
| 1847 | 41 | 12 |
| 1850 | 42 | 12 |
| 1855 | 43 | 11 |
| 1860 | 44 | 12 |

Source: Compiled from the *Annual Reports of the Trustees of the Bank for Savings* in New York State Assembly Journal, 1820-1829; *New York State Assembly Documents*, 1831, 1843, *New York State Senate Documents*, 1830, 1832-1842, 1844-1845, 1848; *Annual Reports of the Trustees of the Bank for Savings*, 1851, 1856, and 1861 in the archives of the New York Bank for Savings.

[a] In 1819, 10% of the deposits made accounted for 56% of the money received.

[b] In 1819, 50% of the deposits made accounted for 3% of the money received.

A look at contemporary wage levels indicates the ownership of these larger accounts. In 1850 an unskilled laborer in New York City earned about $.90 a day while a skilled carpenter made approximately $1.38. Both of these occupational groups were subject to seasonal unemployment, and thus their annual income could vary substantially. Able-bodied seamen, who were also subject to regular periods of unemployment, earned about $15 a month. Female domestics were paid about $1.05 per week with room and board.[14] Given the prevailing wage rates and the correlation between large accounts and upper-class occupations for the Bank for Savings' depositors, it seems likely that most of the larger balances listed in Table 10 belonged to craftsmen, professionals, merchants, and the like, rather than to working-class depositors.

The general conclusions reached in these first two sections on the nature of savings bank depositors and the distributions of deposits are similar to those obtained by Albert Fishlow in his study of the English trustee savings banks. Fishlow pointed out that relatively affluent individuals took advantage of the trustee banks because they

**Table 8** Distribution of Deposits, Greenwich and Bowery Savings Banks

| | Greenwich Savings Bank | | Bowery Savings Bank | |
|---|---|---|---|---|
| Year | Top 10% (% of Money Received)[a] | Bottom 50% (% of Money Received)[b] | Top 10% (% of Money Received)[a] | Bottom 50% (% of Money Received)[b] |
| 1833 | 48 | 8 | . . . | . . . |
| 1835 | 52 | 9 | 55 | 11 |
| 1840 | 49 | 13 | 43 | 10 |
| 1844 | 42 | 10 | . . . | . . . |
| 1847 | . . . | . . . | 43 | 11 |

Source: Compiled from the *Annual Reports of the Trustees of the Greenwich Savings Bank,* and the *Annual Reports of the Trustees of the Bowery Savings Bank* in *New York State Senate Documents,* 1834, 1836, 1841, 1845, and *New York State Assembly Documents,* 1848.
[a] In 1833, 10% of the deposits made accounted for 48% of the money received.
[b] In 1833, 50% of the deposits made accounted for 8% of the money received.

paid a rate of interest that was at least twice that paid by commercial banks and from 1819 to 1824 higher than the yield on Consols.[15] The American mutuals, unlike their English counterparts, were not subsidized by the government, but they were still able to attract funds from many investors who had high preferences for security and liquidity. There is little doubt that more businessmen and upper-class citizens would have deposited in mutuals had it not been for policies introduced to discriminate against large accounts.

## Trustee Policy Toward Large Accounts

A wide gap often separated trustee statements and actual bank policy concerning large accounts, and the enforcement of policies discriminating against wealthy customers varied significantly between banks and over time. It might seem that a mutual could encourage large

Table 9   Average Balance Per Account for Eighteen New York City Mutuals, the Savings Bank of Baltimore, the Provident of Boston, and All Savings Banks in the United States, 1820-1861 [a]

| Year (Jan. 1) | United States | Bank for Savings | Baltimore | Provident | Seamen's | Greenwich | Bowery |
|---|---|---|---|---|---|---|---|
| 1820 | ... | $100 | $ 78 | $142 | | | |
| 1821 | $132 [b] | 154 | 100 | 119 | | | |
| 1822 | ... | 160 | ... | 127 | | | |
| 1823 | ... | 160 | ... | 91 | | | |
| 1824 | ... | 155 | ... | 123 | | | |
| 1825 | ... | 154 | ... | 128 | | | |
| 1826 | 150 | 147 | ... | 132 | | | |
| 1827 | ... | 152 | ... | 129 | | | |
| 1828 | ... | 152 | 184 | 136 | | | |
| 1829 | ... | 143 | 185 | 137 | | | |
| 1830 | ... | 140 | 187 | 134 | $216 | | |
| 1831 | 183 | 142 | 202 | 136 | ... | | |
| 1832 | ... | 147 | 208 | 144 | ... | | |
| 1833 | ... | 142 | 229 | 153 | ... | | |
| 1834 | ... | 142 | 237 | 149 | ... | $152 | |
| 1835 | ... | 137 | 253 | 149 | ... | 169 | $123 |
| 1836 | 177 | 143 | 266 | 152 | ... | 175 | 140 |
| 1837 | ... | 134 | 278 | 152 | ... | 172 | 164 |
| 1838 | ... | 113 | 284 | 154 | ... | 158 | 159 |
| 1839 | ... | 117 | 291 | 152 | 173 | 173 | 182 |
| 1840 | ... | 118 | 275 | 152 | 200 | 188 | 176 |
| 1841 | 179 | 124 | 282 | 156 | 220 | 212 | 194 |
| 1842 | ... | 132 | 276 | 159 | 233 | 234 | 196 |
| 1843 | ... | 125 | 252 | 156 | 219 | 223 | 190 |
| 1844 | ... | 132 | 260 | 156 | 257 | 252 | 198 |
| 1845 | ... | 143 | 254 | 157 | 273 | 258 | 205 |
| 1846 | 169 | 151 | 237 | 160 | ... | 258 | 210 |
| 1847 | 172 | 151 | 235 | 161 | ... | 251 | 206 |
| 1848 | 168 | 155 | 231 | 169 | ... | 258 | 207 |
| 1849 | 166 | 152 | 229 | 162 | 287 | 251 | 198 |
| 1850 | 166 | 151 | 237 | 162 | 317 | 268 | 206 |
| 1851 | 173 | 156 | 238 | 164 | 335 | 276 | 215 |
| 1852 | 182 | 160 | 239 | 171 | 322 | 288 | 217 |
| 1853 | 193 | 164 | 243 | 185 | 323 | 291 | 215 |
| 1854 | 198 | 168 | 250 | 186 | 316 | 286 | 209 |
| 1855 | 196 | 164 | 248 | 187 | 313 | 280 | 212 |
| 1856 | 195 | 169 | 248 | 190 | 309 | 276 | 212 |
| 1857 | 196 | 173 | 253 | 198 | 316 | 267 | 215 |
| 1858 | 201 | 174 | 259 | 207 | 308 | 267 | 219 |
| 1859 | 201 | 179 | 262 | 227 | 316 | 257 | 221 |
| 1860 | 207 | 187 | 272 | 212 | 325 | 253 | 230 |
| 1861 | 215 | 192 | 286 | 218 | 335 | 249 | 234 |

Sources: Appendix B; Emerson W. Keyes, A History of Savings Banks in the United States 2: 176-260 and opposite p. 532; and Lance E. Davis and Peter L. Payne, "From Benevolence to Business: The Story of Two Savings Banks," Business History Review 22 (1958): 390.

**Table 9**  (Continued)

| Year (Jan. 1) | East River | Dry Dock | Merchants' Clerks | Emigrant Industrial | Manhattan |
|---|---|---|---|---|---|
| 1849 | $113 | $ 96 | ... | | |
| 1850 | 123 | 161 | ... | | |
| 1851 | 181 | 187 | ... | $132 | |
| 1852 | 180 | 215 | ... | 170 | $225 |
| 1853 | 189 | 215 | ... | 209 | 241 |
| 1854 | 199 | 238 | $263 | 222 | 244 |
| 1855 | 174 | 244 | 219 | 223 | 238 |
| 1856 | 164 | 244 | 237 | 233 | 241 |
| 1857 | 178 | 258 | 236 | 239 | 241 |
| 1858 | 174 | 263 | 227 | 237 | 228 |
| 1859 | 192 | 271 | 246 | 244 | 231 |
| 1860 | 211 | 265 | 254 | 256 | 238 |
| 1861 | 222 | 285 | 260 | 260 | 246 |

| Year (Jan. 1) | Broadway | Irving | Mechanics' Traders' | Mariners' | Sixpenny |
|---|---|---|---|---|---|
| 1849 | | | | | |
| 1850 | | | | | |
| 1851 | | | | | |
| 1852 | $175 | $607 | | | |
| 1853 | 180 | 348 | $208 | | |
| 1854 | 260 | 257 | 200 | $170 | |
| 1855 | 248 | 242 | 177 | 179 | $ 27 |
| 1856 | 238 | 228 | 176 | 236 | 21 |
| 1857 | 247 | 228 | 179 | 183 | 17 |
| 1858 | 224 | 216 | 170 | 192 | 15 |
| 1859 | 246 | 225 | 185 | 212 | 16 |
| 1860 | 259 | 234 | 208 | 233 | 17 |
| 1861 | 271 | 243 | 195 | 243 | 20 |

| Year (Jan. 1) | Rose Hill | Bloomingdale | Union Dime | German |
|---|---|---|---|---|
| 1849 | | | | |
| 1850 | | | | |
| 1851 | | | | |
| 1852 | | | | |
| 1853 | | | | |
| 1854 | | | | |
| 1855 | $ 87 | $ 55 | | |
| 1856 | 196 | 51 | | |
| 1857 | 146 | 69 | | |
| 1858 | 218 | 24 | | |
| 1859 | 261 | 206 | | |
| 1860 | 232 | 162 | $ 58 | $ 55 |
| 1861 | 214 | 200 | 84 | 129 |

[a]Amounts rounded to the nearest dollar. The national data include a few stock savings banks.

[b]The data shown in Keyes are for 31 December rather than 1 January.

Table 10    Distribution of Depositors and Accounts by Size of Accounts,
Seamen's Bank for Savings, 1 January 1845

| Account Size in Dollars | Percentage Distribution | | Accumulative Percentage Distribution | |
|---|---|---|---|---|
| | Depositors | Deposits | Depositors | Deposits |
| 0-10 | 9.4 | .1 | 9.4 | .1 |
| 10-50 | 19.8 | 2.1 | 29.1 | 2.2 |
| 50-100 | 15.6 | 4.0 | 44.7 | 6.2 |
| 100-200 | 19.8 | 9.8 | 64.5 | 16.2 |
| 200-500 | 19.7 | 23.0 | 84.2 | 39.0 |
| 500-1000 | 9.9 | 25.1 | 94.0 | 64.1 |
| over 1000 | 5.9 | 35.9 | 100.0 | 100.0 |

Source: Compiled from Report Book no. 2, July 1839 through January 1845, Seamen's Bank

accounts and remain true to its originally stated purpose of serving
the poor as long as a clear subsidy for the poor existed. But the
trustees of the Bank for Savings argued that wealthy depositors often
speculated at the bank's expense by making deposits when alternative
interest rates were low and withdrawing their savings when more
profitable investments became available. This forced the bank to invest
the funds of the large depositors when unfavorable market conditions
prevailed and deprived the bank of the opportunity to invest when
higher interest rates could be earned. The bank's trustees were
particularly galled by wealthy customers who made large withdrawals
during monetary panics in order to take advantage of the temporarily
soaring interest rates being paid in the call-loan market.[16] Heavy
withdrawals during periods of panic placed a severe strain on the
bank, forcing it to sell bonds at drastically reduced prices. The trustees
also claimed that accepting large deposits added to their own work;
they did not want to volunteer their time and energy to assist persons
fully capable of investing without the aid of a mutual savings bank.
Finally, even if large accounts were not undesirable because of their
cyclical instability, they forced the bank to make less secure and
less profitable investments on the margin; this increased the risk and
decreased the rate of return to all the bank's customers.[17]

Usually all mutuals tended to be more lenient in accepting large
deposits when their trustees had no problem finding what they
considered to be "good" investments. A study of several sets of minute
books reveals that it was generally a bank's funding committee that
suggested placing an upper limit on accounts. The recommendation
was almost always accompanied by a statement that, because of market
conditions, the committee could find few "secure, yet profitable"
investment opportunities. Thus, a bank's policy on limiting the size

of accounts reflected to a considerable degree the type of investments its funding committee was willing to make.

New York mutuals used several techniques to limit the size of accounts. First, most charters stipulated an absolute limit on account sizes. These limits varied from $1,000 to $5,000 and reflected the attitude of the state legislature more than the policies of the various boards of trustees. Several banks established size limitations lower than those listed in their charters, but as will be shown below, these were not uniformly enforced. In some cases, banks refused to accept additional money from persons with large accounts or even asked these people to withdraw some of their funds.

A second method used to discourage large accounts was to introduce a split interest policy under which larger accounts received a lower interest rate than was paid on smaller balances. As was the case with charter limits on account size, this often represented legislative dictates instead of trustee policy because all the banks founded after 1853 were required to pay 1 percent more on sums under $500 than on sums over that amount.[18] This legislation represented an effort to tax wealthier depositors in order to subsidize the poorer savers for whom the banks were supposedly intended.

Both the maximum limit placed on accounts and the split interest rate policy encouraged savers to divide their savings among several accounts in one bank or among several banks. There were many cases of one person's opening several large accounts in trust for members of his family. A third method employed to prevent wealthy persons from using the banks was to prohibit or closely regulate trust accounts. As was the case with the maximum limit placed on account size, prohibitions against trust accounts were not always vigorously enforced, for bank ledgers and report books reveal the existence of numerous trust accounts during periods when boards of directors were stipulating firm prohibitions against such accounts. A detailed look at several banks' internal histories reveals frequent contradictions between enunciated policies and actual practices. This in-depth inquiry also shows how easy it was for other writers, relying solely on trustee proclamations, to conclude that mutuals indeed restricted their services to the working-class poor.

The Bank for Savings' trustees employed all three of the techniques described above to restrict wealthy individuals from depositing. The bank's charter did not stipulate a limit on account sizes, but it did limit the bank to collecting earnings of "Tradesmen, Mechanicks, Labourers, Minors, Servants, and others. . . ."[19] Although there was no official limit on accounts, the trustees soon found it necessary to turn away wealthy depositors. John Pintard pointed out that the main reason for turning away deposits was the bank's inability to find suitable investments. On 10 November 1819, only one month after the bank received its first deposit, the trustees petitioned the legislature to broaden their investment horizons to include New York City bonds and real estate mortgages.[20] When the legislature turned down the application for mortgage loans, Pintard was furious. He noted that "the high price of Stocks paralyze us so much that we are obliged [to refuse] every thing like a large deposit. The wise-acres in our Legislature refused our application to be permitted to loan on Bond and Mortgage and we are now literally suffering." A year later, on 2 July 1821, he noted that during the previous six months the trustees had refused at least $50,000 in deposits "owing to the high price of Stocks."[21]

In 1824 the trustees were still bothered by large accounts. The special committee established to investigate the problem recommended that no further deposits ought to be received from these accounts and that measures should be taken forthwith to induce many of them to withdraw a part or the whole of their deposits. . . ."[22] In May 1825, Pintard observed that accounts were limited to $500, although the directors "regarded more in the character & circumstances of the Depositors than the sum, making the most liberal construction in favor or ministers, Widow & Orphans," but even with this policy the trustees were finding it difficult to "keep down the weekly receipts."[23]

Two years later, on 16 May 1827, Pintard stated the trustees were considering "closing the accounts of a great number of our heavy depositors w[hich] is contrary to my judgement. . . ." He evidently did not have his way, for the next week he wrote that "our institution is too flourishing, & we shall be obliged to close or curtail all acc[oun]ts above $1,000, owing as well to the difficulty of funding out deposits, as apprehensions of some of our timid Trustees who tremble for their responsibility."[24] The bank's minute books show that the accountant was ordered "to refuse all monies offered excepting the small earnings of the poor and labouring classes. . . ."[25]

An examination of the bank's annual reports and ledgers shows that through 1827 the trustees were not as forceful in their actions to prohibit large accounts as their statements indicate. Their policy was at best inconsistent. On one hand, the ledgers show that in 1825 the trustees closed about a third of the accounts over $500 and persuaded several other customers to make substantial withdrawals. But at the same time many new large accounts were opened, and many wealthy depositors were allowed to build up balances. For example, in 1826 Edward Smith, a pilot, made a single deposit of $2,676 and by 1832 his balance exceeded $6,000. Smith, who was by no means alone, could hardly be classified as a fitting exception to the bank's stated policy of allowing large accounts only if owned by widows and frugal laborers.[26] The bank's annual report for 1825 lists 102 deposits made during that year of amounts in excess of $500. Twenty-five of these exceeded $1,000, four were over $2,000, and one was in excess of $3,000. These deposits were all made at a time when Pintard claimed that the limit on accounts was $500.

Starting in 1828 the bank's trustees became more forceful in backing their words with action, causing a sharp downturn in the number of large deposits (see Table 11). In each of the next two years (1829 and 1830) only one deposit larger than $1,000 was accepted, and the ledgers show that many large accounts were closed.[27] An immediate result of this action was a fall of $11 in the average size of accounts between 1827 and 1830.

The purge of large depositors continued, and by 1831 the bank supposedly had closed almost all accounts exceeding $1,000 except those belonging to "the humbler classes for whom this Bank was intended. . . ."[28] On 14 December 1831 the directors amended the bank's bylaws so that one person could not deposit more than $1,000 "unless the Attending Committee shall be satisfied that the depositor is incapable of investing his or her money to advantage." On 1 January 1832 the trustees took a major step to discourage large deposits by instituting a discriminatory interest rate: all sums below $500 received 5 percent while all accounts with sums above $500 received only 4 percent. The trustees hoped that this lower interest rate would remove "the temptation to speculate at the expense of the Bank by depositing money when Stocks are high and withdrawing it when they are low."[29]

Table 11    The Number of Large Deposits, Bank for Savings

| Year | Number of Deposits over $500 | Number of Deposits over $1,000 |
|---|---|---|
| 1819 | 42 | 9 |
| 1820 | . . . | . . . |
| 1821 | 54 | 6 |
| 1822 | 60 | 7 |
| 1823 | 86 | 10 |
| 1824 | 55 | 10 |
| 1825 | 102 | 25 |
| 1826 | 118 | 21 |
| 1827 | 90 | 13 |
| 1828 | 48 | 3 |
| 1829 | 59 | 1 |
| 1830 | 68 | 1 |

Sources: Compiled from the *Annual Reports of the Trustees of the Bank for Savings* in *New York State Assembly Journal*, 1820-1829, *New York State Senate Documents*, 1830; *New York State Assembly Documents*, 1831.

There is other evidence that the trustees were finally enforcing their edicts more consistently. The minutes contain several cases of the trustees' voting to close accounts or directing the accountant to investigate particular depositors. When he discovered a wealthy depositor he was generally ordered to close the account. This initiated a game of cat and mouse as some depositors tried to avoid being closed out by splitting their accounts. A case in point was Henry Gilmore, who was found to have two accounts under different names totaling $1,174. The trustees ordered both of his accounts closed, but undoubtedly many depositors with split accounts were overlooked. It is also revealing that the entire board was voting on whether or not to allow particular individuals to exceed the $1,000 limit; previously this decision had been left to the discretion of the attending committee. [30]

In 1837, 1849, and again in 1857 the trustees reaffirmed their policy of refusing deposits after an account reached $1,000 except in the hardship cases of "deserving persons, widows, and single women . . . who . . . have a settled aversion to an account in any other Savings Institution in the City." In 1857 the trustees had a major debate in which six out of eighteen trustees indicated that they favored lowering the maximum balance from $1,000 to $500. [31] The trustees gave three reasons to justify their actions. The underlying theme behind all three reasons was a desire to serve poorer depositors first and foremost. The trustees did not like working to assist their more prosperous customers. They thought that wealthy depositors forced the bank to make less profitable investments on the margin, and they accused these same depositors of making heavy withdrawals during panics. The claim that wealthier savers placed an undue strain on the bank by transferring out of deposits into cash in times of panic was well founded, for during the worst days of the Panic of 1837, the average size of withdrawals ($216) greatly exceeded the bank's average balance per account ($133). [32]

Of the four oldest New York City mutuals, the Seamen's was the most lenient in allowing the deposits of wealthy persons. From 1836 to 1845, while the Bank for Savings, the Greenwich, and the Bowery were all discriminating against large accounts with their interest policies, the Seamen's paid the same interest rate on all account sizes. In 1845 the Seamen's had three accounts over $5,000, the largest of which was $6,536. The only statement concerning account sizes found in the Seamen's minute books appeared in 1853, at a time when the state legislature was considering limiting accounts to $1,000. The Seamen's trustees noted that they could not comply with such a regulation because "the deposits of many Ship Masters and Seafaring men, exceed the sum of $1,000 and . . . many of these depositors are absent in distant parts of the world, and frequently not heard from in many years."[33]

The board of the Bowery Savings Bank on several occasions considered placing more strict limits on accounts, but the majority of the trustees generally opposed doing so. The subject of restricting account sizes was always raised in years of financial crises (1839, 1848, and 1857) and at about the same times that the Bank for Savings' board was debating the issue.[34] As was the case with the Bank for Savings, the Bowery's board was motivated by its experience during recent periods of unusually high short-term interest rates when many of the bank's wealthy depositors transferred their savings into more lucrative investments. In two of the above periods (1837–1839 and 1857), the high short-term interest rates were accompanied by severe financial panics. These panics were marked by runs that eventually forced all New York City commercial banks to suspend specie payments. During these crises, large withdrawals were especially harmful. The other period (1848–1849), when both boards considered limiting accounts, followed a year marked by commercial unrest and extraordinarily high interest rates.[35]

On 11 November 1839 the trustees of the Bowery Savings Bank resolved that after 1 January 1840 "no person should make a deposit or have an account larger than $1,000," but this did not affect existing accounts of that size. In 1848 a resolution was presented that would have prohibited any person from holding more than $1,000 either "directly or indirectly" (i.e., in trust accounts). The resolution was rejected at the next meeting of the board, apparently with no debate. Not until 1857 did the Bowery's trustees again consider limiting accounts to $1,000. During the Panic of 1857, a committee was established to consider the "desirability of accepting large accounts." On 9 December 1857 this committee reported that "to receive large sums on deposit, subject to be withdrawn at a moment's notice, they [the trustees] depart from their primary objective, impose heavy burdens upon their managing committee, and endanger the character of such Institutions. The Committee assumes, as a fact, that he or she who has evinced ability sufficient to accumulate from five hundred to a thousand dollars, is fully competent to place that money in security without aid of a Savings Bank. Trust companies and mortgages both afford ample modes of investment." The committee recommended that after 1 January 1858 the bank should discontinue paying dividends on any amount over $1,000.[36] This recommendation was not adopted, and after the panic ended the board gave little more thought to limiting accounts to $1,000. Thus, on the three occasions that the issue was raised, the board decided against limiting account sizes twice. Other mutuals generally were not any more persistent in limiting accounts than was the Bowery.

The Dry Dock in its first year of business turned down a request to deposit $8,000. At that time the Dry Dock's board established a maximum account size of $2,000, but in 1852 this limit was officially discarded.[37] Normally the trustees of this bank and the Manhattan, Emigrant Industrial, Mariners', Broadway, and Seamen's made little effort to limit account sizes except in the case of particularly large deposits.[38] As mentioned in Chapter 2, the Broadway's trustees actively solicited large deposits from businessmen. There is no reason to suspect that other banks formed in the 1850s were any more restrictive than those listed above.[39]

An exception was the Sixpenny Savings Bank, founded in 1853. Although there is little information available on this bank, it truly seems to have been a poor man's institution; Table 9 shows its average balance per account was generally less than $20. This bank attracted a large number of depositors, and by 1860 it had about 8,000 open accounts. The bank's name may indicate the reason it attracted small amounts from a large number of persons. Usually most mutuals only accepted deposits in whole dollars and did not pay interest on sums of less than $5. This policy dates back to 1819 and was preserved to minimize the tellers' and bookkeepers' labors. It is likely that the Sixpenny accepted deposits of a few cents and that poor persons responded by opening accounts.

The analysis of trustee policy toward large accounts offers some insights into bank objectives and performance. More than any other mutual in New York, with the possible exception of the Sixpenny, the Bank for Savings tried to restrict its depositors to workers, widows, and others of limited means. Its more persistent policy in part reflects the bank's greater emphasis on safety, which in turn may indicate a greater commitment to philanthropy. Although its trustees were not as forceful as they might have been, they did close numerous accounts and prohibit many persons from using the bank. If the Bank for Savings had been more lenient in regulating large accounts, it would not have been surpassed in the total amount due depositors by the Bowery Savings Bank in 1859. At the time when the amount on deposit in the two banks was almost equal, the Bank for Savings served almost ten thousand more customers than did the Bowery (51,040 compared to 41,692).

Attitudes formulated during the prewar era shaped policy for decades, because the Bank for Savings' trustees continued to limit large accounts well into the Gilded Age. In 1868, when the Bowery held twenty-one accounts exceeding $5,000 each and totaling $175,000, the Bank for Savings held only two accounts of this size totaling $13,272. The trustees did not consider these two accounts in violation of the bank's principles since over $11,000 of this sum represented accumulated interest.[40] In 1873 national figures show that 81 percent of all savings bank customers owned about 40 percent of the total amount on deposit, while the remaining 19 percent of the depositors owned about 60 percent of all deposits.[41] At that time the average size of an account in the Bank for Savings was $278, the national average was $367, and the Bowery's average was $491. Furthermore, the Bank for Savings continued to pay lower interest rates on deposits over $500 until 1881; the Bowery started paying the highest rate on all deposits up to $2,000 in 1869.[42]

A second point deserving emphasis is that on several occasions a deposit of $500 was defined as an amount that could easily be invested without the aid of a savings bank. The trustees of the Bank for Savings first expressed this view in 1824, and they repeated it several times. The Bowery's trustees were of a similar opinion in 1857, and they suggested mortgage loans or trust company deposits as possible alternatives. In 1865 the state superintendent of banking, George W. Schuyler, observed that "it cannot be questioned that many of the depositors in Savings Banks are persons fully capable of investing and guarding their money without the intervention of an agency designed peculiarly for the poor and unsophisticated of the laboring classes."[43] Schuyler thought that persons with $500 generally were neither poor nor unsophisticated and could find other investments. This contemporary estimate of $500 may have been high for many self-employed individuals who, in the absence of mutuals, could have invested in their own businesses.

New York savings banks were not the only mutuals to restrict depositors. The observation of such restrictions in part explains why previous writers concluded that mutual depositors were indeed limited to the "poor and laboring classes." Payne and Davis in their study of the Savings Bank of Baltimore were impressed by efforts to limit account sizes and exclude wealthy persons. The directors of the Baltimore savings bank established "a maximum limit on the amount anyone could deposit in a particular week," and on five different occasions they scrutinized the bank's customers, returning more than $200,000. After observing such policies, it was easy to conclude that "in keeping with its original object, the Bank restricted its depositors to the frugal poor."[44] It is probable, however, that the Savings Bank of Baltimore had a relatively large number of depositors who were neither poor nor nearly as frugal as the traditional accounts imply. From 1827 through 1861, the average balance per account in the Savings Bank of Baltimore was substantially larger than the average in the Bank for Savings, and in eleven of these years the difference exceeded $100. In fact, the average balance in the Baltimore Bank generally exceeded that in any New York City mutual except the Seamen's Bank for Savings.

Professor Redlich was also misled both by trustee efforts to close accounts and by trustee claims that were not backed by action, for he relied heavily on John Pintard's *Letters* and quoted extensively from them.[45] But as shown above there was often a considerable difference between what Pintard said and what the Bank for Savings actually did. As Confucius might have said: "One good account book is worth a thousand letters."

## Depositor Response to Interest Differentials

This last section investigates the response of depositors to the interest differentials that existed between various banks. It has been suggested that mutual depositors of the prewar era were primarily interested in security and were not particularly responsive to interest rates.[46] The evidence presented below suggests that in fact many depositors were keenly aware of interest rates offered by different banks and transferred their savings in response to interest differentials.

Figures 2 and 3 plot the yearly percentage change in the amount due depositors. As one might expect, the amplitude of the fluctuations in the percentage change in deposits declined as the banks grew in size and the deposit base grew larger. In most cases banks experienced high percentage changes in their early years. This was not due entirely to the relatively small deposit base. Mutuals were almost always founded during periods of economic prosperity when all the banks were enjoying rapid rates of growth. Second, when a new bank opened, it could draw customers from its immediate neighborhood who previously had saved at other mutuals or hoarded their savings. Third, its trustees had a number of friends, family members, and employees who could be induced to help get the bank started by opening an account.

Except for a few cases, the peaks and valleys in the percentage change of deposits occur simultaneously for all banks. This similarity suggests that common exogenous forces dominated the pattern of growth of the industry as a whole. The most notable exception to the common pattern was the Seamen's Bank for Savings in the 1840s. This bank's extremely rapid rate of growth was the result of its attractive interest policy. In January 1840 the Seamen's commenced paying 6 percent on all accounts, and until January 1849 it paid a rate that ranged from one to two percentage points above that paid by any other mutual. For every year from 1841 through 1850, the Seamen's

**Figure 2**  Rate of Change of Deposits for Four Mutuals

The point above any year shows the percentage change in the amount due depositors for that year $[(d_2 - d_1)/d_1]$. Thus in 1860 the deposits of the Bank for Savings increased by about 5.5 per cent. The figures used to derive these percentage changes included interest payments credited to accounts.

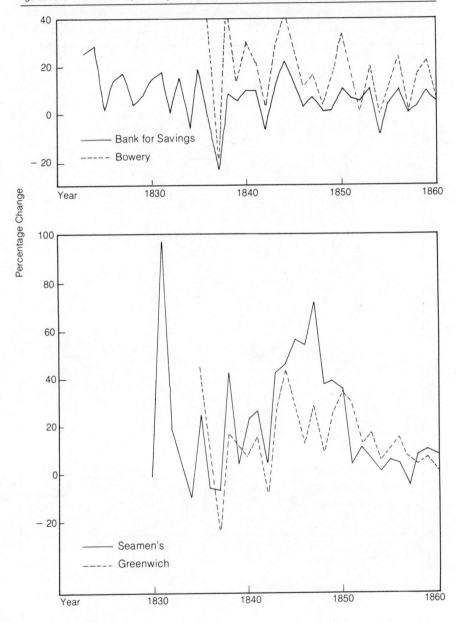

Source: Appendix B.

**Figure 3**   Rate of Change of Deposits for Five Mutuals Founded after 1848

The point above any year shows the percentage change in the amount due depositors for that year [$(d_2 - d_1)/d_1$]. The figures used to derive these percentage changes included interest payments credited to accounts.

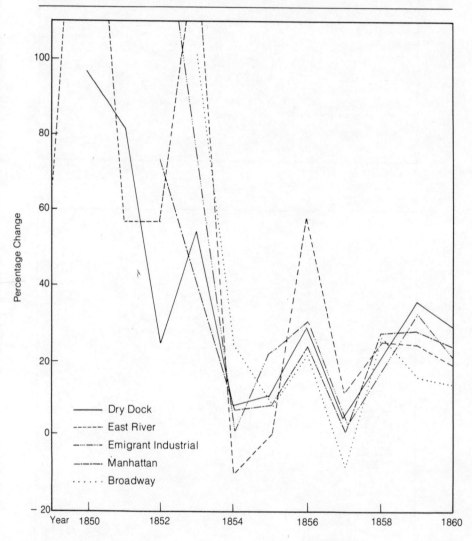

had a higher percentage change in the amount due depositors than any of the other three banks listed in Figure 2. The lag of one year between the time the Seamen's changed its interest rates and the depositors responded is consistent with the findings in Chapter 2 that the other banks did not announce interest increases until after they became due.[47] The relatively small percentage increases for the Seamen's in the 1850s was probably the result of switches by many of its customers to other banks after the Seamen's started paying a lower rate on sums over $500 instead of $1,000.

Several other trends plotted on Figures 2 and 3 suggest that after an appropriate lag at least some depositors were sensitive to interest rate differentials. A comparison of the Dry Dock and East River savings banks illustrates the responsiveness of depositors to interest rates. Both of these banks were founded in 1848. They were originally open six hours a week and were similar in other respects, except that the Dry Dock paid 1 percent higher interest rate for most years until 1856. During this period the Dry Dock grew at a considerably faster rate, and by 1856 its deposits were twice those of the East River's. The trustees of the East River Savings Institution later confirmed this explanation for their bank's sluggish start. "The slow growth of the Institution during its early history may be attributed in a great measure to the over conservative policy of its management, which followed the methods and example of the older banks of the city in the payment of interest. . . ."[48] In July 1856 the East River raised its dividend rate by 1 percent to make it comparable to the Dry Dock's rate. This accounts for the noticeable increase in the rate of growth of East River's deposits in 1856. The East River's directors advertised the proposed increase in dividend rates six months in advance, which suggests that the trustees hoped that the increase would attract new deposits.[49] The bank's trustees were not disappointed. From 1856 to 1861 the average rate of growth of the East River exceeded that of the Dry Dock. It should be noted that the drop in the annual growth rate (from 81 to 25 percent) experienced by the Dry Dock in 1852 came at a time when it temporarily lowered its interest rate by 1 percent. In these instances there was not a year's lag between interest-rate changes and depositor response, as was the case with the Seamen's. The absence of such a lag is evidence of the effectiveness of the newly adopted practices of announcing dividend changes ahead of time and of offering grace periods. It appears that these policies were working to make savers more responsive to interest rate differentials. If so, this segment of the capital market was becoming more efficient.

There is other evidence that many depositors were keenly aware of interest rates and were marginally responsive to them. The records of almost every bank refer to the long lines of customers who insisted on waiting hours in order to get the past six months' interest credited into their passbooks. These customers could have waited a few days and avoided the lines, but for many of the poorer savers it must have been very gratifying to watch their funds grow. The peak-load problem common at these times was not the fault of just these unsophisticated savers; they were joined by numerous persons who were timing their deposits and withdrawals in order to be able to transfer their funds without losing any interest.

In order to earn six months' interest, customers had to make deposits the last day of December and June, and to earn three months' interest, they had to make deposits by the last day of March and September. One would expect net deposits to peak in these four months and to trough in the months of January and July, as customers withdrew their interest and principal for alternative uses. The available quantitative evidence indicates that depositors behaved as predicted.

Monthly data for six New York City mutuals show that there were distinct seasonal fluctuations in total deposits and withdrawals and net deposits.[50] Furthermore, the larger a bank's average balance the greater the regularity and the amplitude of these seasonal variations. This finding supports the observation made by several mutual trustees that wealthier depositors were more likely to adjust their savings to conform to interest payments. One would predict that wealthier savers were more responsive because they probably had more information about other markets as well as enough money to gain entrance into those markets. Furthermore, because transactions costs were independent of account size, it was more profitable for persons with large balances to adjust their assets when interest rates changed.

The Seamen's, which consistently had the highest average balance, also had the most responsive depositors. Monthly data for this bank show that over a thirty-two-year period from May 1830 through September 1861, net deposits seldom deviated from the predicted pattern. This can be seen from Table 12, which lists the number of times net deposits were positive and negative for each month.[51] Many of the exceptions to the general pattern can be explained by panics or changes in the bank's dividend policy. As a rule, the average amount deposited in June and December was over twice the average for the other ten months of the year, and withdrawals in January and July averaged over twice that of the other months. Daily data show that deposits increased sharply during the last few days of March, June, September, and December as savers transferred their funds just before the interest deadline. Similarly, the heavy withdrawals of January and July were bunched at the beginning of the month.

Data for the Bank for Savings, Greenwich, Bowery, Dry Dock,

Table 12    Fluctuations in Net Deposits, Seamen's Bank for Savings,
            1830-1861

| Month | Number of years for which there were data | Number of times that the net change in deposits was: Positive | Negative |
|---|---|---|---|
| January | 31 | 3 | 28 |
| February | 31 | 19 | 12 |
| March | 31 | 30 | 1 |
| April | 31 | 8 | 23 |
| May | 32 | 29 | 3 |
| June | 32 | 31 | 1 |
| July | 31 | 4 | 27 |
| August | 31 | 17 | 14 |
| September | 32 | 27 | 5 |
| October | 31 | 12 | 19 |
| November | 31 | 24 | 7 |
| December | 31 | 31 | 0 |

Source: Deposit and Withdrawal Books, Seamen's Bank for Savings, 1829-1861.

and Broadway yield results similar to, but less pronounced than those described for the Seamen's. The Dry Dock and Broadway did not experience as sharp a drop in net deposits in January and July as the other banks did because these two banks employed grace periods to attract business. As a result the heavy deposits that were normal for the last weeks of June and December continued into the first week or two of July and January. Evidently the grace period had its desired effect on savers.

Mutual passbooks were never the exclusive property of indigents, the poor, industrious toilers, laborers, or even all of these and middle-class artisans and craftsmen. As was the case with the English trustee savings banks, American mutuals were a haven for the savings of many middle- and upper-class individuals whose accounts composed a substantial proportion of all mutual funds. This finding does not mean that savings banks failed to perform a real service to the poor and laboring classes. The majority of mutual customers were domestics, unskilled laborers, or semi-skilled persons of small means for whom the first mutuals were intended. Given their meager incomes, it is surprising that some of these individuals actually managed to accumulate sums in excess of $1,000. The account books of the Bank for Savings contain numerous examples of unskilled persons' accumulating substantial balances by depositing a few dollars a month over several years, but these cases of frugality were the exception rather than the rule.

The examination of mutual policy toward large accounts illustrates the danger of accepting trustee claims (and, for that matter, any commentary) at face value. The only New York City mutual to turn away deposits regularly was the Bank for Savings, which as late as the 1850s closed accounts and refused to accept deposits from many wealthy individuals. In all, this bank turned away several million dollars during the antebellum years. These refusals testify to this bank's philanthropic goals. If its trustees were primarily interested in personal profit, they would have accepted all deposits or lowered the interest rate paid to its customers. The more money deposited, the more that would have been available for trustee projects; the lower the dividend rate paid to savers, the lower the rate the bank would have to charge its favored borrowers. The turning away of deposits indicates that this bank could have lowered its dividend rate and still have attracted as much savings as it did. But this would have affected all depositors indiscriminately—the rich and the poor. Instead the bank's trustees paid a higher rate than required to attract poorer customers and refused to serve less needy persons. The split-dividend policy—paying a higher interest rate on smaller sums than paid on larger balances—was part of the bank's attempt to subsidize the poor at the expense of the rich. A profiteering mutual could be expected to have introduced a set of varying interest rates, but with the higher rates paid on larger accounts, not on smaller balances.[52] The Bowery Savings Bank was the only other New York mutual to consider ferreting out large accounts, but it did not actually do so on a large scale. Though its trustees may have refused some deposits during brief periods, they did not systematically close accounts. Most mutuals had an upper limit on account sizes; however there is no evidence to indicate whether these limits were strictly enforced or whether some banks allowed depositors to open several accounts. The same question can be asked of the split-interest policy adopted voluntarily by most mutuals organized before 1853.

Previous studies have not only been misleading in describing the occupations and social standing of many depositors, but have also inaccurately specified saver motives and behavior. Antebellum depositors behaved much like their twentieth-century counterparts; they responded to bank inducements, timed their deposits and withdrawals to coincide with interest periods, and transferred their savings out of mutuals when alternative interest rates were higher. The larger a mutual's average balance, the more pronounced were the monthly fluctuations in deposits and withdrawals. This suggests that persons with large accounts were more sensitive to interest payments and alternative opportunities than were persons of lesser means.

The reinterpretation of depositor occupations and of the distribution of account sizes indicates that in the absence of mutuals a substantial proportion of the savings they accumulated still would have been generated and invested, albeit in different markets and presumably less efficiently. By offering middle-class depositors a relatively secure and liquid investment for idle balances, mutuals allowed them to better allocate their resources between fixed and liquid assets than would otherwise have been possible. Deposit records as well as trustee statements suggest that standing in the same lines with the provident poor were numerous small businessmen who were shuffling their financial assets in and out of their savings accounts with an eye on alternative business opportunities.

CHAPTER 4

# Investment Constraints and the Financing of Early American Development

The investment opportunities available to the trustees of the Bank for Savings in 1819 were legally limited to New York state and United States government debt, but by the Civil War, New York City mutuals had a much wider choice of investments. They held bonds issued by more than a dozen states ranging from Massachusetts and Wisconsin in the North, to California in the West, and Mississippi, Georgia, and Alabama in the South. These mutuals were the most important supplier of mortgage loans in New York City and some were allowed to make mortgage loans outside the state's borders; they also held a substantial portion of New York City's bonds and were an important source of credit for several other cities in the state. Many mutuals made call loans secured primarily by commercial bank stocks, government bonds, and railroad stocks. Most of the city's mutuals deposited their liquid reserves in banks of discount. These accounts, which generally drew interest and were usually subject to payment on demand, ranged as high as $750,000 in one commercial bank. Table 13 lists the dates when various types of investments were added to mutual charters.

This chapter analyzes the evolution in savings bank portfolios from 1819 to 1861. Its primary aim is to provide a better appreciation of the impact mutual savings banks had on the development of the antebellum economy, but it also sheds light on several aspects of bank behavior and trustee motivation. The efforts of mutuals to invest in the limited number of markets open to them and their responses to changes in constraints show that the trustees of the older mutuals were both far-sighted and aggressive in their portfolio management. This applies especially to the trustees of the Bank for Savings: their actions offer numerous examples of profit-maximizing behavior.[1]

Table 13    The Dates When Various Types of Investments by Mutual
Savings Banks First Became Legal[a]

| Date | Type of Investment |
|---|---|
| 1819 | New York state debt |
| | United States government debt |
| | Deposits in commercial banks[b] |
| 1820 | New York City debt |
| 1827 | Ohio state debt |
| 1829–1830 | Pennsylvania state debt |
| 1830 | Debt of all other states |
| | Mortgage bonds of the New York Public School Society |
| 1834–1836 | Mortgage loans on real estate |
| 1848–1853 | Debt of other cities |
| 1848–1853 | Call loans |

Source: Compiled from the Laws of the State of New York, 1819–1861.

[a] Each bank was governed by its particular charter, and it was common for charters written in the same year to prescribe different investment guidelines.

[b] The Bank for Savings and the Seamen's made such deposits from the date they first opened even though their charters were not revised until 1830 and 1832, respectively.

## The Financing of New York Canals

Until the 1830s the New York state legislature severely restricted the type of investments that mutuals could make in the hope that such a policy would direct mutual funds into the state's debt and thus lower the financial cost of building its canal network. The effort by governments to force financial institutions to support state projects was not limited to this period in history or to mutual savings banks.

The economic histories of the United States and many developing nations offer numerous examples of such government manipulation of financial institutions in order to help finance projects that governments considered important but were unwilling or unable to finance entirely by direct taxation. In the antebellum years many states required commercial banks to help finance social overhead capital expenditures in return for their charters. In other cases, states required banks to purchase stock in canal companies, contribute to state transportation projects, or grant the state long-term loans at favorable interest rates as payment for their charters. States generally stipulated the kinds of investments that banks could make, and these regulations often favored the state's securities.[2]

These and other forms of state intervention in the economy were symptoms of an imperfect capital market. In order to begin to understand and analyze the American economy (or regional economies) in the first few decades of the nineteenth century, one must appreciate the severity of financial constraints. The total amount of savings the economy could generate in any period was constrained by relatively low levels of income and productivity. Furthermore, the nation's ability to invest its savings efficiently was limited by its relatively small and undiversified financial sector. If savings were to be employed economically, they had to be transferred from surplus spending units (savers) to deficit spending units (investors). Particularly, if output was to be maximized, savings had to be transferred to investors who could use them most productively. Traditional economic theory largely ignores or takes for granted the process by which savings are transferred to investors. A key aspect of the early American economy was the lack of financial institutions that could collect and allocate savings, and fundamental to the process of development is the creation and growth of institutions that perform these services. By reducing the costs associated with transport and uncertainty, financial intermediaries can introduce substantial economies into the underdeveloped society.

The absence of a large financial sector was not the only impediment to capital mobility. The primitive transportation and communications networks resulted in a high cost on interregional investments. This was particularly important in a geographically large nation such as the United States. Many states had laws forbidding financial institutions chartered by them to make loans outside their borders, and other states had regulations that interfered with the workings of market mechanisms. Usury laws and internal exchange rates between the various circulating media further complicated and increased the cost of financial transactions. These obstacles prevented savings from flowing where they could earn the highest rate of return and necessarily resulted in a less efficient allocation of financial resources.

Most research investigating the effect of government policy on early American development has concentrated on the direct impact that the state had on the investment process as a saver, intermediary, or promoter. There has been relatively little analysis of the indirect and more subtle consequences of government regulation and interference with market mechanisms. In New York lending restrictions imposed on mutuals enabled the state to mobilize financial capital that many officials thought could not be raised by direct taxation and at a lower rate of interest than the state could have obtained in an unrestricted market. Largely as a result of these constraints directing funds into a limited number of markets, the Bank for Savings in the City of New York became the most important financier for the internal improvement projects of New York state, Ohio, and New York City. Bits and pieces of the story of this bank's impact on early American development have been uncovered by Nathan Miller and Harry Scheiber in their studies of the New York and Ohio canals,[3] but to date the full magnitude of this bank's financial dealings has not been appreciated.

A simple test is used to determine whether legal restrictions actually constrained investment behavior. When a law was changed, did mutuals quickly attempt to adjust their portfolio position? Their doing so implies that the laws had been binding. The test reveals that prior to the Panic of 1837 lending restrictions were in fact binding, but that their importance diminished significantly in the post-Panic era. In the period when constraints were tightest, the history of New York mutuals was dominated by the Bank for Savings, for as late as 1837 this one mutual still held about 90 percent of all New York City mutual assets. Thus a discussion of the impact of lending restrictions necessarily concentrates on the Bank for Savings.

When New York state commenced construction of the Erie Canal in 1817 there was no established capital market it could count on to purchase its debt. Nathan Miller has demonstrated that many New Yorkers were concerned that the financial expenditures on the canal would bankrupt the state and many of its citizens. According to Miller there was a general opposition to increasing taxes to pay for the proposed canal, and there was apprehension even by those favorably inclined, as to whether the canal bonds would find buyers at any price. The canal's detractors had good reason to deprecate the state's ambitious undertaking, especially because the only previous effort to unlock the treasures west of the Catskills had been marked by incompetence, inadequate financing, and eventual failure.[4] The memory of this failure still influenced policymakers responsible for the success of the state's project.

The type of financial problems New York state faced early in the nineteenth century were not unique to that place or period in history, but have confronted almost every developing nation. In general, the amount of financing needed for transport investment can be so large that a government's freedom to allocate funds to other uses may be severely restricted. Traditionally, governments have relied on foreign capital imports and on heavy taxation to force the needed savings from the populace.[5] But as noted above, there was much opposition to raising taxes and, unlike those of more powerful central governments, New York state politicians were unable to disregard the popular will. Additionally, in 1817 there was little prospect of attracting much foreign capital.

CHARTER CONSTRAINTS: AN ALTERNATIVE TO DIRECT TAXATION

In this setting of widespread government manipulation of financial institutions, severe capital scarcity, and state commitment to massive public works expenditures, the Bank for Savings was chartered in 1819. The bank's impact on the state's finances was unprecedented, and it is doubtful that any legislators fully appreciated the effect the bank would have. For more than a decade, this institution was by far the largest holder of the state's Erie Canal debt, at times owning as much as 30 percent of the issue. The main reason that the bank played such an important role in the financing of the Erie Canal was that the state allowed the bank very few other investment opportunities. The state essentially forced the bank's trustees to buy canal bonds or turn away depositors, and the trustees did both.

The source of the trustees' problem lay in the bank's charter, which required its trustees to invest "in Government Securities or stock created and issued under and by virtue of any law of the United States, or of this State, and in no other way . . . ."[6] The rapid growth in the bank's deposits coupled with the fact that the federal government was retiring its small debt forced the trustees to invest almost entirely in canal bonds and prompted them to appeal for a wider range of investment opportunities. On 10 November 1819, just four months after the bank received its first deposit, the trustees petitioned the state legislature to allow the bank to invest in New York City debt and to make mortgage loans.[7] The bank's first annual report reveals that its trustees did not wait for the legislature to act, because by the end of November 1819 the funding committee had already purchased $50,000 of New York City bonds.[8] On 24 March 1820 the legislature amended the bank's charter in order to permit this type of investment, but at the same time the legislature denied the board's request to permit mortgage loans.[9] In 1820 the legislature was still too concerned with financing the Erie Canal to allow the Bank for Savings much freedom in its choice of investments.

By requiring the bank to invest in its debt, the state taxed the bank and indirectly taxed its depositors in order to subsidize its canals. This subsidy resulted in the bank's receiving a lower rate of interest on all its New York state bonds and the state's paying a lower rate of interest on all its new bonds, not just those subscribed to by the Bank for Savings. The size and the form of this subsidy depends upon the assumptions one makes about the bank's investment policy in the absence of constraints and about the elasticity of demand and supply of New York state bonds and the other types of debt the bank would have purchased. The subsidy and its impact on state finances (which are not the same) would also depend on what long-run policy the state might have followed had it been forced to pay a higher interest rate on its debt.

If the bank's investments opportunities has not been constrained, or at least had not been constrained as much as they were, and if the bank had behaved as a profit-maximizing institution, then its trustees would have attempted to invest so as to equate the marginal yield (considering risk) on each type of asset in its portfolio. Pursuant to this policy it would not have invested as much of its total assets in state bonds; presumably it would have made mortgage loans, purchased New York City bonds, and made other types of investments. In other words, in the absence of constraints, the bank would have acquired other assets, which would have resulted in a more efficient allocation of its resources than actually existed under state regulations.

A static, partial-equilibrium supply-and-demand model gives an idea of the form this tax on the bank might have taken and of its effect on state finances. Consider two cases: in Case I the bank is required to invest *all* its assets in New York state debt and in Case II the bank has *no* constraints on its portfolio.[10] The supply curve for bonds is defined as the number of bonds of given par value (e.g., $1,000) which the state will offer at various prices. Assume these bonds are of infinite maturity so that their price ($P$) is equal to the inverse of the effective interest rate ($1/r$), where the effective rate of interest is the dollar amount of interest payments per year divided by the price received by the state when the bonds were initially sold. Thus, the supply of state bonds is inversely related to the effective interest rate and therefore directly related to the price, and for any point in time the supply curve is given (see SS in Figure 5).

Figures 4 and 5 depict both Case I and Case II. In Figure 5, SS and $D_1D_1$ represent the market supply-and-demand curves for a stock of state bonds when the bank is forced to invest all its assets in state bonds. The bank's demand curve ($d_1d_1$), which is shown in Figure 4, is perfectly inelastic. Both the X and Y axes in Figures 4 and 5 have the same scale. Under these assumptions the state sells $Q_1$ number of bonds for a unit price $P_1$ and its total revenue from the sale of $P_1Q_1$. The Bank buys $Q'_B$ bonds at the market price $P_1$.

In Case II without constraints the bank's demand curve for state bonds becomes more elastic. This assumes the bank will buy other assets in addition to state bonds. The bank's new demand curve for state bonds is $d_2d_2$ in Figure 4. As a result of the difference in the bank's demand curve, there is a different market demand curve $D_2D_2$, which is to the left of and more elastic than the market demand curve in Case I. Under the assumptions of Case II, the bank buys fewer state bonds and receives a higher interest rate on its entire holdings of New York state debt. The state sells $Q_2$ bonds for a price $P_2$. Its total receipts are $Q_2 P_2$, which is less than it received in Case I. The difference in the state's receipts between the two cases is shown by the shaded area in Figure 5. The essential point illustrated by this analysis is that *the state has to pay a higher interest rate on its entire debt, not just that portion held by the bank.* The subsidy the bank paid the state in Case I would be equal to its total

**Figure 4** The Supply and Demand for State Bonds: The Bank

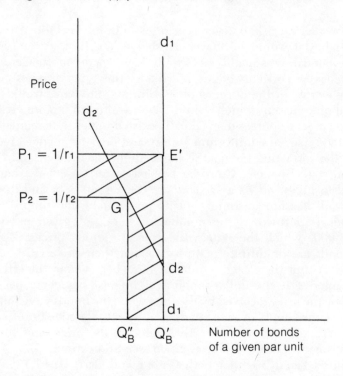

**Figure 5** The Supply and Demand for State Bonds: The Market

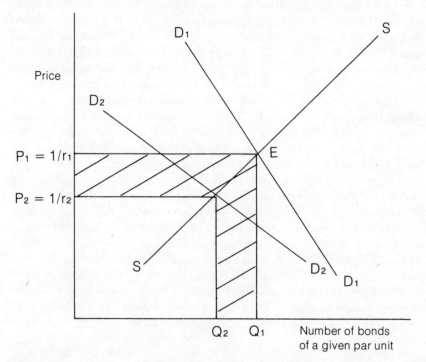

interest earnings in Case II minus its total interest earnings in Case I. (Its total interest earnings in Case II would be $r_2 Q''_B + r_3$ $(Q'_B - Q''_B)$—where $r_3$ is the average rate it earns on its "other" assets. The bank's total interest earnings in Case I are $r_1 Q'_B$.)

By forcing the bank to invest in its debt the state is able to obtain more money at a lower rate of interest from the bank *and* from non-bank purchasers. But this statement does not suggest how to measure the consequences of the subsidy in real terms. The real effects would depend on the state's dynamic response to the changed demand conditions, and this consideration takes us far afield.

Much of the material that follows describes the investments of the Bank for Savings and analyzes its responses to changes in state constraints. To measure the bank's influence in the markets to which it was restricted, we would need the various elasticities of demand and supply, which we do not know. However, descriptive evidence, the bank's share of the market, the size of its holdings relative to other investors, and the timing of its purchases suggest that its impact was substantial. Its impact on the financing of the public works of New York state, New York City, and Ohio was particularly important to the development of the American economy. The Bank for Savings held a substantial proportion of the debt of all three governments. Furthermore, many of its purchases occurred when these governments were trying to establish their credit ratings, when their debts were relatively unknown entities. It was during these critical periods in government financial history that the Bank for Savings often bid for and purchased entire issues. The ability to sell early issues helped create public confidence in a government's ability to finance and complete its undertakings and thus affected the demand for future issues.

The fear of high finance cost had deterred several governments from pursuing projects of their own. The relative ease with which New York state financed the Erie Canal and New York City financed its water works demonstrated that relatively favorable terms could be found and encouraged other governments to proceed with similar undertakings. So in an indirect sense, the Bank for Savings' investments may have influenced decisions made in numerous state capitals with which it had no direct financial dealings.

THE TIMING AND MAGNITUDE OF THE BANK FOR SAVINGS' PURCHASES

From 1819 to 1831 over half of the bank's assets were in New York canal bonds, and as late as 1833, the bank was the largest single holder of the state's debt. This relationship between the bank and the state started on 7 July 1819, when the bank purchased $4,332 of Erie Canal bonds at 98.25 percent of par value ($4,256). As deposits mounted the bank's purchases continued, and by 1 January 1820, as a result of nine separate transactions, it held $97,912 of New York state debt. At that point, less than six months after it had opened, the Bank for Savings held approximately one-eighth of the total debt issued (since 1817) to finance the Erie Canal. Between January and June 1820 the trustees made six more purchases of canal equities ranging in size from $3,247 to $35,700.[11] The bank made these transactions through the larger commercial banks and private banking houses in New York City, which performed the investment banking function before the age of specialization.[12] By summer of 1820, just a year after it opened, the Bank for Savings had become large enough to bypass the commercial banks and negotiate directly with state officials. Largely at the insistence of William Bayard and John Pintard, the board decided to take a bold step and bid for an entire issue of bonds. In July 1820 the trustees sent William Bayard to Albany "to obtain $200,000 of new Canal Stock ['stock' was the common terminology for bonds] on the best terms possible." Though Bayard was successful, the funding committee was still unable to keep up with the rapid growth in deposits. To solve the problem the committee, at the insistence of Pintard and Bayard, suggested that when the next "Canal loan opened the Bank subscribe to an amount which will absorb the anticipated deposits to January, 1821." The trustees agreed to this idea, and in September and October of 1820 they contracted for issues of $151,000 and $100,000 of canal securities. When the time came in December to pay for these subscriptions, the bank had not yet taken in enough deposits, so the trustees borrowed $98,889 from the Mechanics' Bank. The funding committee estimated that it would take four or five months before deposits would grow enough so that the loan could be paid back.[13] Borrowing an amount equal to 20 percent of the bank's total deposits in order to invest in a still unproven canal scheme is hardly the type of action one would expect of an institution dedicated, first and foremost, to the safety and liquidity of its depositors' savings. This extraordinary behavior is neither consistent with the general picture of mutual trustees as unimaginative, habitual risk-minimizers, nor is it consistent with the Bank for Savings' strong emphasis on safety in later years. This episode demonstrates the severity (or perhaps, from the point of view of the state, the effectiveness) of the lending restrictions and how the bank's trustees, trying to work within a narrow legal framework, had to compromise one of their primary objectives—the bank's safety.

As a result of its aggressive buying, by January 1821 the bank had accumulated $475,465 of Erie debt. In June 1821 as a result of mounting deposits, Bayard traveled to Albany again with the intention of purchasing a $200,000 new issue of canal bonds, but he was outbid by an Albany bank, which took the entire issue. After failing in an attempt to purchase part of the issue from the victorious competitor, Bayard returned empty-handed to New York City, where he was able to obtain $50,000 of canal bonds from Nathaniel Prime.[14] By the end of 1821, the bank's holdings of $581,515 represented almost 30 percent of the outstanding canal debt.[15] The Bank for Savings in the City of New York, which was still considered by its founders and the public in general to be a philanthropic organization, almost incidentally was also the Erie Canal's most important source of funds.

The mere statement of the absolute and relative size of the bank's holdings does not begin to convey the magnitude of its contribution to the success of the canal. It was during these early years, from 1817 through 1820, that the canal commissioners experienced their only difficulty in raising money. During this period investing in New York canal bonds was not considered a particularly safe venture. European investors were rarely interested and did not begin purchasing canal bonds on a large scale until the middle of 1822.[16] The bank invested in the canal during what Nathan Miller describes as the era of the "small investor." Through 1820 the canal loans were supported "chiefly by individuals of substantial, but not great savings, whose investments were made in relatively small amounts." In January 1821, when the Bank for Savings held almost $500,000 of canal equities, the next largest domestic holding was less than$40,000.[17]

Miller argues that wealthy Americans did not become convinced that Erie securities were safe and profitable until the end of 1820. He is especially critical of the bank's trustees, accusing them of being too timid to risk their personal fortunes while readily investing their depositors' savings in the canal. Of all the bank's trustees, only William Bayard and Brockholst Livingston risked their own capital in canal stock. Through his firm, LeRoy, Bayard and Company, Bayard purchased $50,000 of the Erie's debt in 1821; Livingston waited until 1822 before investing.[18] At that point Miller maintains that there was little possibility of failure, for more than half the canal was finished and the state had proven itself capable of financing and administering its enterprise.

The hesitancy of many trustees to invest their own funds is particularly interesting in light of the handsome profits many of them could expect to make if the canal was a success. Many were engaged in trade-connected businesses that would later profit from the new markets, and others had speculated heavily in lands along the canal route. These individuals may have expected larger returns from land than bonds. In any case their land holdings certainly would indicate some faith in the canal's success. But the principal reason for the trustees' behavior was probably no more linked to such alternative investments than it was to personal timidity. Rather, it was the product of their serious problems in finding investments for the bank's deposits. Realizing the bank's predicament, many trustees probably abstained from purchasing canal bonds in order not to further depress the expected yield on the bank's investments.

TRUSTEE ENTREPRENEURIAL INPUTS

Many of the bank's trustees were also leaders in promoting the idea of a western canal and actively participated in the struggle to transform this dream into reality. Thomas Eddy, John Murry, and William Bayard all were connected with the Western Inland Lock and Navigation Company, which first attempted to build a canal in the 1790s. Eddy served as the treasurer and as a director of this early enterprise. At an early date, Eddy advocated that the state take over the actual construction of the project, and in 1810 he was instrumental in eliciting DeWitt Clinton's support for the proposed canal. Eddy served as secretary and treasurer of New York state's first canal board. In 1810 this board issued a report that set in motion the campaign for public rather than private construction of the western canal. In 1811 Eddy and Robert Fulton were given the task of finding an engineer to direct the canal project.[19]

In 1815 a mass meeting was called in New York City to organize political support for the proposed canal. Three of the six organizers of this meeting would become trustees of the Bank for Savings. William Bayard was chairman of this meeting, and John Pintard served as its secretary. Clinton later claimed that the memorial drawn up at this meeting was "the basis for the whole canal system."[20] In their other capacities as politicians, civil servants, and merchants the Bank for Savings' trustees were essentially supplying entrepreneurial inputs to the canal that the bank later helped to finance.

THE REDEMPTION OF THE BANK'S ERIE DEBT

After 1821 the bank continued to invest heavily in Erie Canal bonds. Although it was still the largest holder of this type of debt as late as 1833, its relative importance declined as big and small lenders in Europe and New York City entered the market and as the bank diversified its portfolio. In 1826 the commissioners of the canal fund started to use canal revenues to retire the outstanding Erie debt. On several occasions the commissioners attempted to persuade the trustees of the Bank for Savings to sell the bank's Erie and Champlain Canal "stock," but the trustees flatly refused to give up any portion "unless an opportunity was offered them of re-investing the money in other stock."[21]

Finally, after lengthy negotiations, the trustees agreed in 1833 to sell $600,000 of Erie-Champlain bonds, which were due in 1837, for a 9 percent premium.[22] The cash received from this sale was immediately reinvested in 5 percent Pennsylvania bonds payable in 1857.[23] The trustees had contracted for this purchase before consummating the New York transaction in order to guarantee that the bank would not be stuck with a large amount of idle cash. In June 1833 the trustees still held almost $600,000 of the state's debt, $393,347 of which was Erie and Champlain "stock." The commissioners approached the bank's trustees in an effort to purchase their remaining Erie-Champlain debt, but the hard-bargaining trustees refused to sell "at any price on account of the difficulty of reinvesting the money." Negotiations continued and the trustees finally agreed to an exchange for other New York bond issues due at later dates.[24] Reflecting on this transaction, Secretary of State John A. Dix referred to the bank's trustees as " 'a damned pack of sharpers' " and accused them of squeezing an extra "2 or 3 per cent out of the Canal Fund."[25] The record of the bank's bargaining with the state reveals no signs of the irrationality or "provincialism" that supposedly dominated mutual trustee behavior. On the contrary, the bank's trustees exploited the state's desire to retire its debt in order to obtain charter amendments allowing a wider range of investments, and the trustees bargained aggressively to obtain the best possible terms for their depositors.

The trustees' decision to redeem about one-half of their Erie holdings in less than a year caused a short-lived but serious credit restriction for numerous commercial banks located along the canal route and in New York City. Since 1826 the commissioners of the canal fund had been depositing their surplus revenues in commercial banks. In essence, by 1833 almost $1 million of the Bank for Savings' money was deposited in commercial banks throughout the state. To meet the Bank for Savings' terms, the commissioners made large and unexpected withdrawals (their demand deposit balances plunged from over $600,000 at the end of January 1833 to $95,000 by the middle of June), and in May they called in all the tolls that had been deposited that month in banks along the canal.[26] This episode offers yet another example of the Bank for Savings' far-reaching impact on the state's economy.

Given the relative size of the Bank for Savings' holdings and its aggressive bidding for almost every issue of bonds during its first few years of business, it seems that the state's policy of restricting the bank's portfolio paid off in reducing the cost of financing New

York's canals. New York state was just one of several governments which benefited from the constraints on the bank's investments.

## The Financing of New York City Public Works

As pointed out earlier, the original charter of the Bank for Savings restricted it to investing in New York state and federal securities. Only after the bank had made its first purchase of New York City securities did the legislature legalize the holding of the city's debt. From this premature beginning to the end of the antebellum era, New York City debt constituted an important part of the bank's portfolio. Not until 1836 did the bank's holdings of city debt exceed its holding of New York state debt. But the bank's impact on the city's finances was probably greater than it had been on the state's because for a number of years the bank held a larger percentage of the city's total debt than it had held of the state's total issue. In many years the bank's purchases of city securities constituted a considerable proportion of the total demand and thus most likely reduced the rate the city had to pay to its creditors. For example, in 1828 the bank made several large purchases of new city bond issues; by the end of the year it held $349,800, which was about half of the city's total outstanding debt.[27]

THE CROTON WATER WORKS

In 1832 New York City embarked upon one of the largest and most important municipal construction projects of the time: the Croton reservoir and aqueduct. Over several years the city spent more than $11 million on this project. This was an enormous amount for the time, as can be appreciated by the fact that the initial section of the Erie-Champlain canals required an investment of only about $7 million. As was the case with the Erie Canal, the financing of this undertaking was significantly aided by the Bank for Savings' relatively large purchases of bonds during the early stages of construction. The Croton system also resembled the Erie Canal in the sense that both were innovative steps in government ownership, one state and the other municipal, and the success of both encouraged other governments to engage in similar ventures. The first sale of securities to finance this undertaking was a $1 million issue in 1835.[28] The Bank for Savings' funding committee purchased $400,000 of this issue, or two-fifths of the total.[29]

As was the case with the Erie Canal, several of the bank's trustees were directly involved with the planning and management of the Croton water works. John Pintard was especially interested in improving sanitary conditions and was the leading figure on the New York Board of Health. In 1832, when New York City was in the grip of a serious cholera epidemic, Pintard remarked that he expected that Philadelphia would pass through the ordeal better than New York because Philadelphia had "g[rea]t advantages, [a] pure & copious supply of water . . . ." Pintard was especially upset by the fact that New York City had been empowered to raise $2 million to improve its water system, but that the city was dragging its feet for financial reasons. He considered the city's delay inexcusable because "Our Savings B[an]k c[oul]d take the whole [amount] . . . ."[30] At this time Pintard was the president of the Bank for Savings, and the bank was soon to become the major subscriber of the city's water bonds.

Philip Hone was another trustee who led in the effort to improve the city's water supply. As mayor of New York City in the 1820s he had worked for a better water system. In 1845 Hone was elected president of the Bank for Savings and three years later, in 1848, he was appointed to the presidency of the Croton Water Works.[31] Under Hone the water works continued to expand and the Bank for Savings continued to be an important source of funds [32]

THE FIRE LOAN

In 1836 the Bank for Savings became the principal subscriber to another city loan when it purchased $300,000 of New York City 5 percent "fire stock."[33] This transaction occurred in the wake of the Great Fire of 1835, which raged for days and inflicted losses estimated at between $18 million and $20 million. At the request of Philip Hone and New York mayor Cornelius Lawrence (both men were trustees of the Bank for Savings) the state legislature authorized the city to float a fire loan to relieve the business community. About $1 million worth of debt was issued, and the money collected was lent to fire insurance companies on the brink of ruin.[34] As was the case with so many of its previous investments, the Bank for Savings' purchase (about 30 percent of the total issue) represented a considerable proportion of the total demand and probably affected the price the city received on the entire issue.

## Interstate Flow of Mutual Funds

The Bank for Savings would have played an even more important role in financing New York City's public works if the legislature had not extended the bank's investment horizons at about the same time that the city embarked on its projects. The first change was made in 1827, when the bank was authorized to invest in Ohio State bonds. Emerson Keyes commented that there was nothing in the historical record that explained why the "stock" of Ohio was singled out as the exception, but he speculated that "Probably the action was taken upon petition . . . of the trustees of the Bank for Savings, who were incited thereto by negotiations for the sale to them of Ohio stocks on advantageous terms."[35] In fact Keyes's guess was correct, but he did not dig deeply enough.

Ohio started its canal construction in 1825, the same year that the Erie and Champlain canals were completed. The proposed Ohio network was an extension of the Erie in the sense that it would increase the size of the market served by the New York canals. Both New York City merchants and the state legislature were aware of the complementary effects the Ohio works would have on their system, and both merchants and legislators took steps to encourage their construction.

One of the primary concerns of Ohioans was that the state would be unable to attract outside funds. Scheiber has recorded how Micajah T. Williams, the leading advocate and promoter of the Ohio canals, frequently corresponded with canal enthusiasts in New York to gain information and to elicit backing for his state's program. In 1823 Williams traveled to New York City to consult with William Bayard and Cadwallader Colden about the possible sources of finance available in New York City. "On the basis of their experience with Erie Canal finance, they assured him that eastern capital would be forthcoming if the State of Ohio built the projected canal and put the public credit behind bond issues to finance construction."[36] What Scheiber failed to mention is that at this time Colden was a trustee and Bayard was the president of the Bank for Savings.

Realizing that the time was right, in 1826 the trustees applied to be allowed to invest in Ohio State debt, and in March 1827 the legislature acted favorably on the bank's petition.[37] Given the keen interest that some of the trustees had expressed in the proposed Ohio canals, the fact that the bank petitioned for the amendment, and the difficulty it was having investing in the limited number of markets open to it, one would expect the trustees to respond rapidly to the new situation. In June 1827 the funding committee purchased $138,731 of Ohio 6 percent canal bonds, and by the end of the year the bank had increased its holdings to $280,000, which was over 10 percent of the total amount issued.[38] These were timely purchases which antedated the acceptance of Ohio's debt in the London bond market.[39] The trustees continued to purchase Ohio bonds, and in 1832 the bank's holdings amounted to $568,552, almost 14 percent of Ohio's total debt.[40]

This percentage probably does not convey the marginal impact the bank's purchases had on the market for Ohio debt. Scheiber recently found that in 1840 the Bank for Savings was by far the most important holder of Ohio state debt. "Of the 6 per cents sold initially during 1826–1832 . . . , $1,185,161 had remained in the United States. Of this portion, one third ($362,552) was owned by the Bank for Savings . . . . Aside from the Bank for Savings lot, nearly all the 6 per cents were held by small-scale individual investors in America; and of the larger portion, $2,664,158, in foreign hands, nearly all had been widely diffused, similarly among small purchasers."[41] The bank's importance relative to other investors probably has been even greater in earlier years; from 1832 to 1837 it owned $568,552 of Ohio "6 per cents."[42] It seems likely that the bank's holdings of Ohio debt, as was the case for New York state and New York City debts, were large enough relative to the total issue and relative to the size of other investors' shares of the total to have had a considerable impact on the market. In all three cases, when the size of the bank's holdings are considered along with the key timing of its purchases, it is entirely probable that its actions affected the entire market, not just the marginal conditions.[43]

The addition of Ohio debt to the Bank for Savings' portfolio was significant because it represented the first crack in the barrier to the interstate and inter-regional flow of mutual funds. In 1829 this crack widened further when the Seamen's Bank for Savings was granted the right to invest in both Ohio and Pennsylvania state bonds. In March 1830 the legislature passed a bill, significantly titled "An Act For The Relief Of The Bank For Savings In The City Of New York," which authorized the trustees to invest "in any stock or securities, for the redemption or payment of which the faith of any State in the Union shall be pledged . . . ."[44] This same act also authorized the bank to lend "money to the Public School Society of New York, on satisfactory real security; and also to make temporary deposits in any of the incorporated banks in the said city, and to receive interest thereon . . . ."[45]

The legislature started liberalizing the investment sections of mutual charters only after New York completed the Erie Canal, when the commissioners of the canal fund were attempting to persuade bond holders to turn in their certificates. From their negotiations with the trustees of the Bank for Savings, the commissioners were well aware that the primary obstacle to the redemption of the bank's Erie bonds was the limited number of investment alternatives open to the bank's trustees. The commissioners hoped that the trustees would be more willing to sell some of their holdings if the bank were offered a wider range of investment opportunities. In fact, it was only after the bank had contracted for a large issue of Pennsylvania securities in 1833 that it finally agreed to part with most of its Erie bonds.[46]

As they had done previously, the trustees of the Bank for Savings responded to the new situation by investing in new and often distant markets. In 1830 the bank loaned $60,000 to the public school fund, bought $162,500 worth of Pennsylvania state bonds, and contracted for $100,000 of Alabama state bonds. Again, the Bank for Savings took the lead in establishing a market for a state's securities, for Alabama bonds did not appear on the London bond market until 1833.[47]

The bank continued to expand its out-of-state investments by acquiring some Indiana bonds in 1834 and increasing its holdings of Pennsylvania debt to $862,500.[48] In 1835 the bank increased its holdings of Alabama bonds to $400,000.[49] From 1834 to 1837 over half the bank's portfolio consisted of out-of-state securities. The funding committee's willingness to invest so far from home is another indication of its difficulty in keeping up with the growth of deposits. It is also further evidence that the bank's trustees were responding to new opportunities, that they were evidently adjusting their portfolio in order to maximize its real rate of return (given the constraints under which they operated), and thus were relatively efficiently allocating the bank's funds. The Panic of 1837 brought a halt to the geographical spread of the bank's influence, and not until 1850 was another state, New Jersey, added to the list of the bank's debtors.

Although not alone in making out-of-state investments, the Bank for Savings was more active in this area than was any other mutual. During the years preceding the Panic of 1837 the Seamen's Bank for Savings held as much as 44 percent of its assets in Ohio securities, but the amount involved never exceeded $28,000 and declined as that bank's trustees found other investments. The Greenwich Savings Bank, like the Seamen's, held a small amount of Ohio debt, and for two years—1835 and 1836—some Pennsylvania bonds. The Bowery Savings Bank refrained entirely from investing out of state.[50]

The record of the New York banks, especially the Bank for Savings, in sending financial capital over state lines was not matched by mutuals in other states. The Savings Bank of Baltimore did not invest in any state bonds except those of Maryland until 1855, and the Philadelphia Saving Fund Society did not purchase the issues of states other than Pennsylvania until 1870. The Provident Institution for Savings in the Town of Boston did not purchase any out-of-state bonds during the prewar period.[51] As was the case for mutuals in most other states, these mutuals in Baltimore, Philadelphia, and Boston, were allowed to make loans to private citizens secured by real estate, stocks, or in some cases personal notes, and thus could find sufficient local outlets for their deposits. The Philadelphia bank made loans on real estate as early as 1818.[52] The Savings Bank of Baltimore started making call loans secured by stocks and bonds to private individuals in April 1822, and by 1827 about 85 percent of the bank's funds were invested in this manner. The Provident of Boston could make loans "to commercial banks on no security, to business firms on the signature of the officers and two guarantors, and, for a short time, to mercantile and manufacturing concerns on commercial paper." In addition to having more freedom in the investments they could make, mutuals in other states were not responsible for investing nearly as much money as was the Bank for Savings. As late as 1835, this one bank still held over 35 percent of all mutual deposits with almost twice as much on deposit as the second largest savings bank, the Provident of Boston.[53]

Before 1834 the trustees of the Bank for Savings responded rapidly to every change in legislation governing the bank's portfolio. There was also a significant difference between the Bank for Savings' portfolio and the portfolios of banks in other states. Both of these observations attest to the importance of lending restrictions in determining the composition of the Bank for Savings' portfolio. The degree to which New York City mutuals were constrained in their investments declined sharply in the 1830s with the addition of mortgage loans to their portfolios and the drop in the rate of deposit growth following the Panic of 1837.

## Real Estate Loans

Even after mutuals were granted the right to make mortgage loans they were hampered by charter provisions. Mutuals could not lend an amount exceeding one-half the value of the property used for security.[54] In all cases the loans had to be on unencumbered real estate, and until 1848 all charters required the property to be situated in New York City or Brooklyn. The charters of most of the banks chartered after 1848 did not include the geographical limitations. All the banks chartered before 1850 could lend as much to one person as the trustees considered prudent, but at least four of the banks formed after that date had charters that limited the amount they could lend to one person.[55]

The four oldest banks (the Bank for Savings, the Seamen's, the Greenwich, and the Bowery) all sent petitions to the legislature asking for the right to make mortgage loans. As pointed out earlier, the trustees of the Bank for Savings had petitioned for this right in 1819 and probably on other occasions, only to have their request rejected.

The Seamen's Bank for Savings was the first New York City mutual to obtain the right to grant mortgage loans when its petition was granted on 19 April 1834. This bank wasted little time in adjusting its portfolio to the new situation; by August the funding committee was authorized to sell $20,000 of bonds so as to be able to lend the money on bond and mortgage, and on 3 September 1834 the board approved a loan of $20,000 to the firm of Yates and McIntyre.[56] By January 1837 over 71 percent of all the Seamen's assets were invested in mortgage loans.[57]

The Greenwich and the Bowery also responded rapidly by investing a large proportion of their assets in mortgage loans. By January 1836 the Bowery had over 94 percent invested in mortgage loans, and in January 1838 (there are no data for 1837) the Greenwich had over 50 percent of its assets invested in this manner. It should be emphasized that the Seamen's, Greenwich, and Bowery were still new banks with relatively small amounts of assets compared to those of the Bank for Savings. Thus the absolute amount they lent on real estate was not very significant, but as a percentage of their total assets mortgage loans were very important. A comparison with the Bank for Savings shows that the directors of the three newer banks had a much stronger preference for this type of investment.

For the first time in the history of the Bank for Savings, its trustees did not rapidly take advantage of a change in the constraints governing the bank's portfolio. Between 23 April 1836 (when the charter was amended) and January 1837 the funding committee lent only about $100,000 on bond and mortgage, and in 1837 the committee made only one loan, of $2,000.[58]

A lengthy report made in January 1836 by a special committee of the board of the Bank for Savings offered a number of reasons explaining why the newer mutuals were investing so much of their funds in the mortgage market.

> The price of . . . Stocks . . . have [sic] been so exorbitantly high for a few years past that nearly all the earnings of the Bank . . . have been absorbed in paying premiums upon Stocks, bearing a low rate of Interest. It does not require any extraordinary degree of Sagacity to discover that if we confine our investments to those descriptions of Stocks and at such prices, the time cannot be very distant when the Stocks bearing six per cent interest will be paid off and consequently the Bank must reduce the interest paid to all its depositors. It should be borne in mind that at an early period in the business of this Institution, Stocks of the State bearing six per cent interest were purchased at two per cent below par. . . . Without these early advantageous investments it is evident the Bank could not have paid the premiums it has upon late investments and the dividends it has paid to depositors. . . .[59]

About half of the committee's report argued that to prepare for financial crises the trustees should increase the bank's surplus, but the report also noted that this would not be possible with the present portfolio. It was in this context that the committee recommended that the trustees start making mortgage loans, which the committee estimated would yield a 2 percent higher rate of interest than government bonds.

The trustees of the Bank for Savings decided that they would have to make mortgage loans in order to maintain their present dividend rate to their depositors and increase the bank's surplus. The trustees felt that mortgage loans were not as safe, or at least not as liquid an investment as government bonds, but they were willing to give up some safety for a higher rate of interest in the short-run in order to build up a surplus for long-run security. With this attitude, it is not surprising that they moved rather cautiously into the mortgage market.

The Bank for Savings' report indicated that the trustees of the newer banks were not in a situation that would allow them to be as cautious. One would predict that the new banks would move more rapidly into the mortgage market than the Bank for Savings, because their younger portfolios could not have been earning as high a rate of interest as the Bank for Savings' investments. Much of the older bank's portfolio consisted of bonds that were paying 6 percent and could be marketed at a price above what the bank had paid for them. But according to the report quoted above, bonds purchased in the last several years had been relatively poor investments, paying only 5 percent or less. All of the bonds held by the newer mutuals would have been of this type. Furthermore, the Bank for Savings had an interest-earning surplus of about 3 percent in 1836, while the other banks had virtually no surpluses. Thus while the newer banks were compelled to invest immediately in higher-earning assets if they were going to maintain their dividend rates to their depositors, the Bank for Savings was not.

These varying pressures on the different banks were intensified by the movement in deposits and withdrawals during 1836. In 1836 the Bank for Savings experienced a 2 percent decline in deposits, which meant its funding committee was pressed to invest only the proceeds of bonds that matured during the year. The funding committees of both the Greenwich and the Bowery had to find investments for the new deposits received during the year, which in the case of the latter bank amounted to a 38 percent increase, equal to about $100,000.

The mid-1830s marked the end of the period when New York City mutual investments were severely constrained by state limitations.

Given the addition of other states' debts and mortgage loans and the growing supply of these types of debt, mutuals had a wide number of investment choices compared to earlier years. Furthermore, their need for new areas of investment diminished in the late 1830s and the early 1840s because of the relatively slow rate of growth of deposits during those years.

## The Debt of Other Cities and Call Loans

The preceding discussion of the period up to 1837 showed that mutuals adjusted to new investment opportunities fairly rapidly, which implies that they previously had been constrained by their charters. However, in the period after the mid-1830s mutuals were not so severely constrained, as is indicated by their failure to shift rapidly into new markets when they became available options.

Two major changes in the provisions governing New York City mutual portfolios were introduced in the late 1840s and early 1850s. The first was the addition of the bonds of any town, city, or county in New York state authorized by the legislature to create debt. The second change allowed mutuals to make call loans.[60]

The available data indicate that New York City mutuals were an important source of finance for some city projects, but that type of debt never made up a large percentage of mutual assets in the prewar era. The Bank for Savings did not purchase any city bonds except those of New York City and Brooklyn. The Seamen's and Bowery savings banks never invested much more than 1 percent of their total assets in the bonds of other cities. Although some newer banks did purchase other cities' debt, the total amount held probably never exceeded a few percentage points of all New York City mutual assets.

The same conclusion applies to call loans. Most of the newer mutuals made call loans, with a few lending as much as 50 percent of their assets on call. But for safety reasons, the more established institutions were reluctant to undertake this type of loan, and since they held the bulk of all mutual assets, call loans never composed more than 3 percent of all New York City mutual investments. The fact that the addition of call loans and other cities' debt did not lead to a significant change in the overall composition of mutual assets suggests that the legislation preventing these types of loans had not been as binding as the prohibitions of earlier years.

This chapter has traced the evolution of New York City mutual portfolios over four decades as the banks responded to changing legal conditions. The investments made by the Bank for Savings in the City of New York differed substantially from those made by mutuals in other states primarily because of the stricter lending restrictions in New York. These same institutional constraints also help explain why this one mutual played such a prominent role in the financing of key social overhead investments. The record of this bank's trustees' struggle to invest within the confines of the constraints reveals that they energetically pursued their bank's interests.

New York state (and other governments) reaped substantial benefits in the form of lower interest payments on its *entire* debt from both the lending restrictions and the usury law. The early constraints were successful not only in channeling the Bank for Savings' assets into the Erie Canal, but in indirectly attracting savings from other investors who entered the market only after the canal was partially opened and was not nearly as risky a venture. The initial success of New York state in financing its public works encouraged other governments to embark on similar projects. The New York experience not only demonstrated that a market existed for state and municipal government debt, but it actually helped create the market for other governments' bonds by introducing many Americans and Europeans to this type of investment.[61] By its key bond purchases during critical periods of New York state's and later New York City's financial history, the Bank for Savings was instrumental in establishing the state's credit, which in turn directly facilitated its acceptance in wider markets, both domestic and foreign. Less sophisticated investors, who often failed to discriminate adequately between states and who generalized from the success of the Erie Canal, represented a large market for other governments' bonds. It is ironic that a financial innovation, which significantly affected the financing of the Erie Canal, directly and indirectly influenced investment decisions made in numerous state capitals, and stimulated the development of the European demand for American state debt, was not designed as an engine for development but as an eleemosynary institution. The men who organized the Bank for Savings were primarily motivated by their commitment to philanthropy. Their bank's investment activity was considered necessary to achieve their charitable goals. Although the first mutual was not organized specifically to mobilize capital, it was founded when the economy needed large blocks of capital in a relatively new area. One of the pressing problems a developing society must confront is that of transferring financial capital from developed to underdeveloped geographical regions, and from old to new industries or activities. In New York, largely because of legal constraints, the new institutions responded to this need far more effectively than did already existing institutions.

Economists have identified among several nations' financial institutions what have come to be called "development banks" or "investment banks."[62] William Diamond credited two French institutions

founded in 1852, the Crédit Foncier and the Crédit Mobilier, as being
the first modern development banks.[63] These French banks became
the models for similar institutions established throughout western
Europe. The proponents of the Crédit Mobilier hoped that a bank
specializing in railroad and industrial loans would "lower the rate
of the interest in those industries . . . ." This, it was thought, would
encourage the development of key sectors of the national economy
"and lessen the need for state subsidies to the railways." These were
the very services which New York City mutual savings banks had
been performing since 1819. The similarity with American mutuals
did not end with the type of investments made, for the backers of
the Crédit Mobilier hoped to attract the savings of "the smallest
merchants, peasants, and even the day laborers . . . ."[64]

Another characteristic often attributed to investment banks is that
they supplied entrepreneurial inputs for the projects they financed.
In many cases development bankers, acting as promoters as well as
financiers, were instrumental in planning new projects and often
obtained seats on the boards of companies with which they did
business.[65] Again there is a similarity with the early mutuals, for
in many cases mutual trustees were involved in planning projects
that their banks later helped to finance, and in other instances mutual
trustees prodded government planners to proceed with social overhead
investments by assuring that the mutuals' funds would be forthcoming.
Cadwallader Colden, Thomas Eddy, William Bayard, Philip Hone,
and John Pintard were just a few of the Bank for Savings' trustees
who were actively engaged in promoting internal improvements at
the municipal, state, and regional levels.

The subject of development banks does not appear in most
financial histories of the United States dealing with the first half
of the nineteenth century. Perhaps most writers, failing to find an
institution patterned after the European model, concluded that there
were no development banks. Future works in this area should include
a discussion of the role which New York City mutual savings banks
played in financing early American growth.

CHAPTER 5

# The Convergence of Mutual Portfolios:
## Efficiency Considerations and Trustee Objectives

An inconclusive exchange between Lance Davis and Barbara Vatter represents one of the few times that economic historians have even questioned the motives of early mutual trustees. In an article only tangentially concerned with mutuals, Davis argued that mutuals, the primary suppliers of long-term industrial credit in the Boston area, did not charge more than 6 percent interest on their loans because of the state usury law. He then maintained that because the free-market interest rate often exceeded the usury rate, "non-price rationing must have played an important role in finance. This conclusion suggests that industries less well connected than textiles—and new industries in particular—may well have found loan finance almost impossible to obtain through traditional channels in times of credit stringency."[1]

In a comment on this article Professor Vatter suggested that it was in the private interest of mutual trustees to obey the usury law because the trustees were also stockholders and directors of the textile mills that received the loans. In effect they were lending to themselves at an interest rate below the prevailing free-market rate and thus were profiting from their trusteeships.[2] In his reply, Davis does not purport to test her hypothesis, and at times he actually assumes away her basic issue: "Since they [the trustees] had launched the intermediaries [Boston mutuals] for non-profit reasons, it is not strange that they did not use them for further profit."[3] But the question still remains— were the mutuals really launched for non-profit reasons? Even if this were the case, one still must ask if objectives changed as the banks grew in importance.

To answer these questions this chapter examines the evolution of mutual portfolios over time and asks if the observed investments were more consistent with the "philanthropic" hypothesis that the trustees were attempting to maximize their depositors' well-being or with the "profiteering" hypothesis that the trustees were trying to profit from their positions.

## Investment Determinants and Implications of Portfolio Convergence

As the legal constraints discussed in Chapter 4 became less binding and more similar for all banks, mutual trustees could pay more attention to alternative market opportunities in making their investment decisions. This in itself should have led to a more efficient allocation of mutual funds over time. Since the banks were operating in the same market, and assuming that they were trying to maximize the same objective function, one might reasonably expect them to make similar marginal investment decisions. If so, the portfolios of all banks should have converged over time. One would not expect the various portfolios to be similar at first because banks founded at different dates faced different sets of initial constraints. Past constraints and a bank's previous investment decisions were both important determinants of current investment decisions.[4]

Several other factors influenced portfolio decisions. Of those most easily identified, the expected real rate of return on different types of assets was probably the most important. Changes and expected changes in a bank's deposits and the maturation schedule of its portfolio were important since they affected the amount of "new" money a bank had to invest. Other factors such as the recent memory of a panic and individual differences between trustee preferences also were undoubtedly important.

A profit-maximizing mutual, without any constraints and with zero cost of adjustment, would have attempted to equate the expected marginal real rates of return on each type of asset in its portfolio. But there were legal constraints. In addition, because one observes only nominal interest rates, banks may have differed in their subjective evaluations of risk. Expectations did not necessarily correspond with actual, *ex post* observations, and it is not possible to determine with certainty whether or not any mutuals were in fact acting as profit maximizers. Furthermore, one would not expect banks to have continuously adjusted their portfolios to every change in market conditions because the banks incurred real costs in making such adjustments; gathering and analyzing information and exchanging assets entailed administrative costs. Some banks were also constrained in their actions because their marginal adjustments could have been large enough, relative to the market for a particular type of security, to affect the price of the assets they were exchanging. Therefore one would not expect rapid portfolio convergence, but a gradual process of continual adjustments on the margin.

The failure of portfolios to converge could indicate many possibilities, each the consequence of imperfect markets. The market signals of interest rates, prices, and risk may not have been distinct enough for all the banks to identify and to interpret consistently; alternatively, some banks may have been more sluggish in identifying changes in market conditions and responding to them. A failure to converge could also indicate that no optimal mix of assets existed or that banks did not all have the same objective functions or risk aversion.[5]

## The Investments of the Four Oldest Mutuals

In fact, the marginal investments made by the four oldest mutuals (the Bank for Savings, Seamen's, Greenwich, and Bowery) tended to be similar in the 1840s and 1850s, resulting in an noticeable convergence in the composition of their portfolios.[6] Figure 6 exhibits the percentage of each bank's total assets invested in government securities for each year, and Figure 7 exhibits the percentage invested in mortgage loans. By 1860 all four banks had between 42 and 47 percent of their assets in mortgage loans and 52 to 62 percent in government securities. The percentage of assets held in these two forms by the Seamen's, Bowery, and Greenwich (in the years for which data exist) tended to converge in the 1840s and to fluctuate in the same direction over the next twenty years (see Figures 8 and 9 for the amount of government securities and mortgage loans outstanding each January for each bank). The composition of the Bank for Savings' portfolio differed noticeably from that of the other three institutions until the 1850s.

The rather late movement into mortgage loans by the Bank for Savings can be explained by the different set of market conditions it faced. During the brief interlude of prosperity between the Panic of 1837 and the downturn in 1839, all four banks attempted to diversify their portfolios at the margin. Thus, while the three newer institutions holding portfolios heavily laden with mortgage loans invested almost exclusively in government issues, the Bank for Savings, with a much smaller percentage of its portfolio in mortgages, showed a distinct preference for mortgage loans. With the advent of the 1839 depression, all four banks denied almost all applications for mortgage loans and invested primarily in the securities of those governments that had proved to be financially solvent during the recent crises. Almost all new investments consisted of United States government bonds and Treasury notes, New York state and city securities, and Ohio state debt (in 1840 and 1841). The issues of these governments were

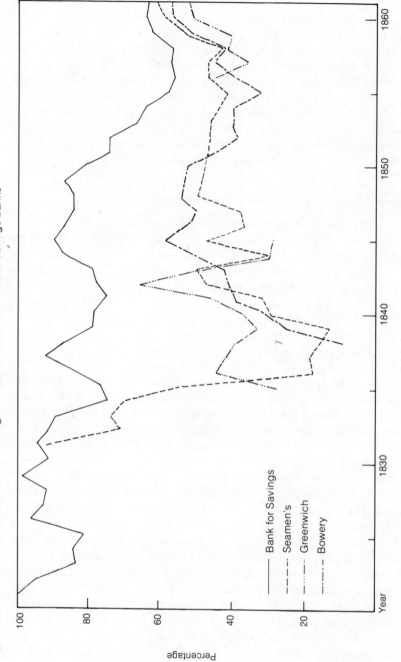

**Figure 6** Government Securities as a Percentage of Total Assets of Four Mutual Savings Banks

Legend:
— Bank for Savings
–·–· Seamen's
······ Greenwich
—·— Bowery

Source: Appendix C.

**Figure 7** Mortgage Loans as a Percentage of Total Assets of Four Mutual Savings Banks

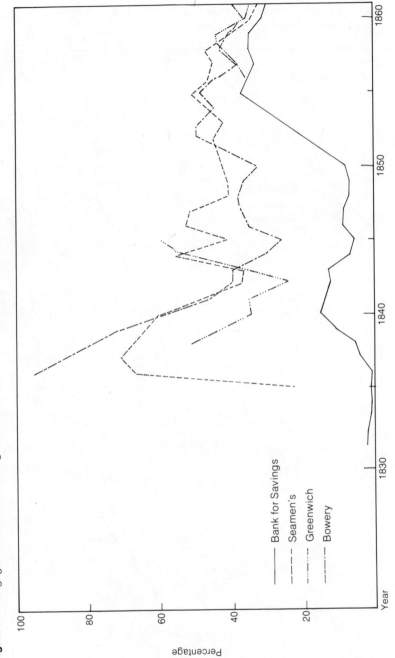

Bank for Savings
Seamen's
Greenwich
Bowery

Percentage

100
80
60
40
20

1830    1840    1850    1860

Year

Source: Appendix C.

**Figure 8**  Total Amount Invested in Government Securities
by Four Mutual Savings Banks

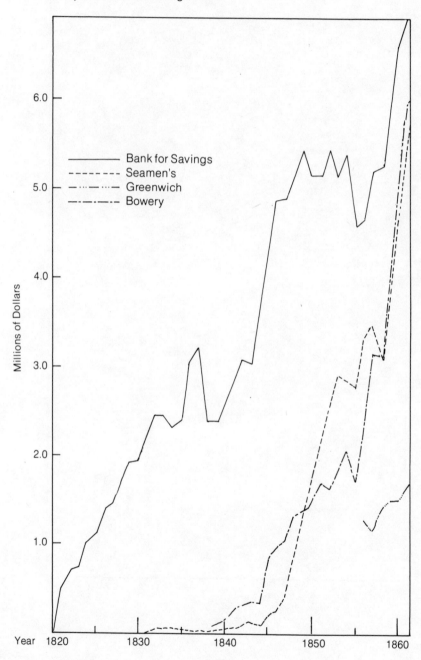

Source: Appendix C.

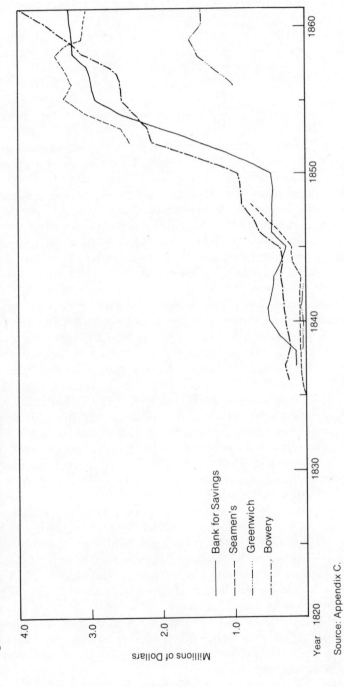

**Figure 9** Amount Loaned on Bond and Mortgage by Four Mutual Savings Banks

Source: Appendix C.

Table 14   Rate of Growth of Deposits for Bank for Savings, Seamen's, and Bowery, 1846-1850 (in percentages)

| Year | Bank for Savings | Seamen's | Bowery |
|------|------------------|----------|--------|
| 1846 | 2.1 | 54.0 | 11.3 |
| 1847 | 6.4 | 71.2 | 15.6 |
| 1848 | 1.0 | 37.7 | 2.6 |
| 1849 | 0.9 | 39.3 | 15.6 |
| 1850 | 9.9 | 36.3 | 33.0 |

Source: Appendix B.

considered more secure and more liquid than mortgage loans, and during the period from 1841 to early 1843 they paid a comparable nominal rate of return.[7]

An examination of Figures 8 and 9 shows that in 1845 all three of the banks for which we have data started making new mortgage loans. In 1846 and 1847 the Bank for Savings did not increase the amount loaned on real estate, though the other two institutions continued to make new loans. During these two years the Bank for Savings had a substantially lower rate of growth in deposits than did the Bowery and the Seamen's, as can be seen from Table 14. As a result, the Bank for Savings made almost no permanent investments of any sort, choosing instead to build up its commercial bank deposits (cash reserves), which had fallen to an unusually low level in 1845.

In 1848 only the Seamen's experienced a significant increase in deposits, and it was also the only bank to increase its mortgage loans. In the early 1850s all three banks invested primarily in mortgage loans. Thus only during 1846 and 1847 did the Bank for Savings' marginal investment pattern differ substantially from the Bowery's, and this occurred when the former had almost no new funds to invest.

Past investment decisions of the Bank for Savings severely limited its ability to transfer its existing funds out of government bonds into mortgage loans. The market value on a considerable portion of the bank's government securities was well below both par and what the bank had originally paid for them, which locked the bank into its portfolio. As late as 1850, up to $900,000 of its bonds could be sold only at a substantial discount. The bank held approximately $270,000 of Pennsylvania bonds, $400,000 of Alabama bonds, and $175,000 of Indiana bonds in the late 1840s, most of which paid only 5 percent during a period when almost all new issues were paying 6 percent and some were paying 7 percent.[8] The relatively slow growth in deposits, during years when other banks were making mortgage loans, combined with the fact that the Bank for Savings was locked into much of its portfolio, explains the bank's relatively low percentage holdings of mortgage loans.

Although the composition of these four older banks' portfolios clearly converged over time, it is difficult to judge whether the variation observed in 1860 was small or large. Donald Hester has pointed out that in 1963 the percentage of mortgage loans in eighteen New York City mutuals' portfolios varied by as much as 20 percent, ranging from 64 to 84 percent of individual bank portfolios.[9] This occurred when mutuals employed full-time investment specialists and had much better access to market information than was available in the nineteenth century. Hester attributed much of this difference in portfolios, and the fact that many present-day mutuals often require as much as three years to recognize and respond to changes in market conditions, to the relatively poor management of some banks. The movement of the four oldest New York City mutuals toward convergence in overall portfolio composition suggests that even by modern standards their trustees responded fairly rapidly to market forces, and is at least an indication that they allocated their resources more efficiently as legal barriers were lowered.[10]

### The Investments of the Newer Mutuals

An examination of the portfolios of the other mutuals founded before 1860 shows that there was less conformity in their yearly movement and that there was more diversity between the portfolios in 1860. Figures 10 and 11 show the percentage of each bank's holdings in government securities and mortgage loans. The banks included in Figure 10 were all founded between 1848 and 1851, and those in Figure 11 were all founded between 1851 and 1860. Figure 10 indicates that by 1860 there was a noticeable convergence in the percentage of mortgage loans among these banks' assets, but that there was still a relatively wide variation in their bond holdings. Figure 11 shows that there was little if any tendency toward convergence by those banks formed after 1851.

These results are difficult to interpret, especially because past portfolio decisions influenced present and future investments and because the smaller size of these banks probably magnifies the amplitude of the observed fluctuations. Newer banks paid their depositors the competitive rate of interest and therefore, lacking the cushion of a surplus, needed to earn a higher average yield on their portfolios. This required the newer mutuals to undertake riskier investments and to behave more aggressively. Furthermore, they may not have been large enough to efficiently pool independent investment risks or to operate efficiently in the capital market if, for example, it was difficult to buy government securities in small blocks. However, this does not explain why banks formed within a few years or months of each other decided on such diverse investments.

**Figure 10**  Mortgage Loans and Government Bonds as a Percentage of Total Assets of Six Mutual Savings Banks

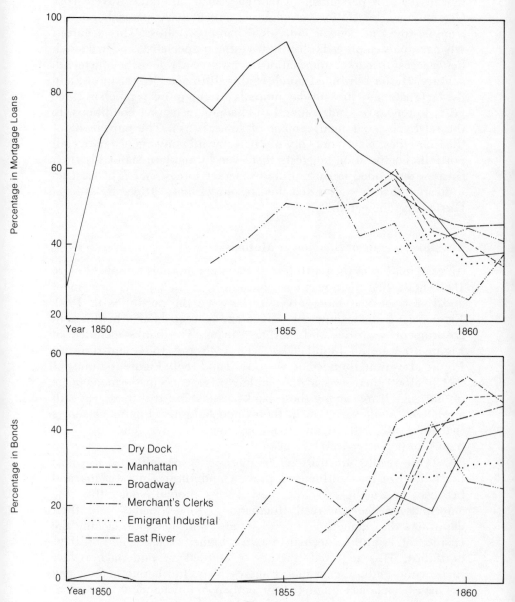

Source: Appendix C.

**Figure 11** Mortgage Loans and Government Bonds as a Percentage of Total Assets of Seven Mutual Savings Banks

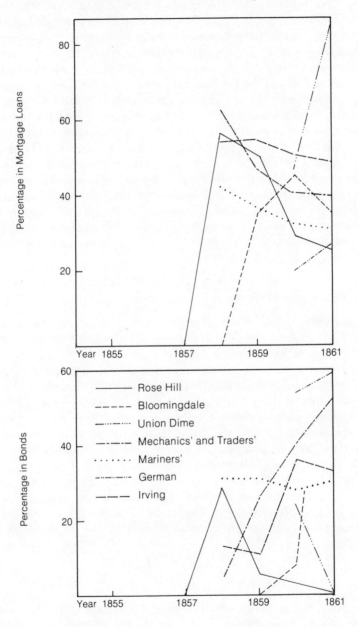

Source: Appendix C.

Another possible explanation for the lack of convergence of newer mutuals' portfolios is that the trustees were not as philanthropic as those of older mutuals and that they had different objective functions. After all, these same institutions were more competitive in their search for deposits, and they more readily turned over management positions to employees. Perhaps the newer mutuals were designed to raise capital for projects in which the trustees had special interest. Such a purpose would explain why these banks made relatively more mortgage and call loans to private citizens. One could also argue that the managers of the newer banks were not as experienced or as competent as those of the older institutions, and that as a result the newer banks did not so readily recognize and react to changing market conditions. It is also possible that the directors of the newer banks did not clearly define their objectives or that they changed their subjective evaluation of risk in the wake of some exogenous event such as a panic. This discussion presents only some of the plausible explanations for the observed differences in investment behavior and does not purport to list or test all possible hypotheses.

## A Test of Trustee Objectives

So far it has been established that there was a significant convergence in the portfolios of the four older banks. The portfolios converged because these banks behaved very much alike in both the allocation of their funds between government securities and mortgage loans and in the timing of their marginal investments in these two markets. This similarity in investment decisions gives reason to suggest that these mutuals endeavored to satisfy the same objective function. The marginal investments of the banks formed later in the period did not conform to any clear pattern, except insofar as these banks tended to allocate more of their resources to mortgage and call loans than did the older mutuals. I shall now attempt to determine the nature of the objective function that the older institutions were attempting to satisfy. Specifically, it is important to ascertain if the trustees attempted to maximize their own interest at the expense of their depositors.

### THE STATE USURY LAW

Throughout the prewar years the New York state usury law set the maximum rate of interest at 7 percent. Loans tainted by usury were subject to forfeiture of principal, and criminal charges could be brought against the lender. Thus, though a trustee had personal incentives to charge low rates when dealing with friends, business associates, or commercial banks with which he was connected, he faced legal disincentives to charging usurious rates. Contemporary statements indicate that by the 1850s most lenders had found ways to circumvent the law, but the mutuals continued to obey it. Evidence of widespread evasion was often presented as a reason for repealing the law. For example, on 17 January 1850 a large group of prominent New Yorkers met at the Merchants' Exchange to petition for the repeal of the state usury law. In a memorial addressed to the state legislature, the group noted: "Yet a higher rate than seven per cent is continually, nay, almost daily taken, and amid the changes in the money market will continue to be required and paid, notwithstanding the restrictions and the penalties of the Law."[11]

A priori reasoning suggests that a philanthropic mutual would obey the law, for one of its most important assets was the goodwill derived from its reputation for honesty. It seems doubtful that its trustees would risk tarnishing this esteemed commodity, especially since personal risks were involved. The records of eight New York City mutuals give no indication that these institutions ever charged rates higher than 7 percent, but this in itself is not conclusive, because records of illegal transactions might have been kept apart from the "official books" and destroyed when no longer needed.[12] In his study of the industrial borrowing in the Boston region, Lance Davis concluded that Boston mutuals obeyed a much more stringent 6 percent Massachusetts usury law.[13]

Compelling evidence that some New York City mutuals were in fact constrained by the usury law is found in an address delivered by James De Peyster Ogden at the Merchants' Exchange meeting referred to above. Ogden, one of the Bank for Savings' most active trustees, was also an organizer of the meeting and its principal speaker.[14] He observed that a reason cited for not repealing the law "was an apprehension lest any interference with this subject would interfere with the security of the vast sums invested on bond and mortgage [i.e. loans on real estate]." Ogden argued strongly for "repeal of [the] law because it kept lenders from the markets. . . ."[15]

Several inferences can be drawn from this statement. First and most significantly, Ogden was not devoting several hours a week to the Bank for Savings in order to lend money below the free-market interest rate to some firm in which he owned stock, which is Vatter's explanation for the Boston mutuals' compliance with the Massachusetts usury law. If this had been his intention, he would have demanded the usury law be retained instead of lobbying for its repeal.[16] Second, he recognized that the real estate market would suffer if the law were changed. He suggested that "vast sums" were lent on real estate and would move into other markets if lenders could obtain a nominal rate of interest high enough to compensate for the added risk. At that time mutual savings banks were the most important suppliers of mortgage loans in New York City. Third, Ogden observed that the law "kept lenders from the markets. . . ." This offers another indication that the usury law was not uniformly disregarded, but that it did constrain some lenders; it discriminated against those who were most risk averse and most aware of their public image, or who viewed this matter on strictly moral grounds.

The usury law in New York state effectively lowered interest rates in some markets largely because of the particular nature and size of mutuals. This was probably also true for Boston, Baltimore, and other areas where mutuals were influential. The direct effect of the law was to channel mutual funds into low-risk investments, such as real estate loans and government debt. This action tended to depress the interest rates in these markets and possibly caused an "over-investment" in low-risk debt and a social misallocation of finance. Other investors, already on the margin, transferred their funds into other markets because the interest rate in the mortgage market was abnormally depressed. Thus the effect of the usury law was diffused in varying degrees to all markets, not just those dominated by mutuals. In general, the usury law had the following distributional effects: issuers of relatively low-risk debt benefited and issuers of higher-risk debt paid higher interest rates. Furthermore, the holders of low-risk debt, such as mutual savings banks, received a lower rate of return than they would have earned in the absence of the law. Not surprisingly, the primary beneficiary of this law was the state, which was a net debtor throughout the period.[17]

The imperfect market that prevailed in this situation is analyzed with the help of Figure 12. SS is a supply curve showing the quantity of money lenders are willing to lend on mortgages at various interest rates; $D_1 D_1$ and $D_2 D_2$ are demand curves representing the quantities of mortgage loans that will be demanded at various interest rates under two sets of assumptions. If the rate of interest in the mortgage market was $r_1$, mutuals would make $q_1$ in loans (Case I). If the demand curve for mortgage loans happened to be farther to the right (or the supply curve farther to the left) reflecting a tight money market, the resulting equilibrium market rate of interest ($r_3$) would exceed the usury rate ($r_2$), the maximum rate savings banks could charge (Case II). In this latter situation, mutuals would ration their loans by lending an amount less than $q_3$ (the amount lent if there were no usury law). As long as the interest rate in any market (e.g., the discount or call-loan markets) exceeded 7 percent, an individual who owned real estate could potentially profit by financial arbitrage.[18] One could obtain a loan at 7 percent from a mutual and reinvest it at a higher rate of interest.

We know that the interest rate charged private borrowers and the rate charged the government moved in the same direction over the business cycle, and that the rate at which most governments borrowed was below the private rate. Thus, when the equilibrium private rate in the mortgage market went above 7 percent, the spread between the rates in the two markets would narrow. This spread

**Figure 12**   Real Estate Mortgage Market with a Usury Law

$r_1$ = actual rate in Case I
$r_2$ = usury rate
$r_3$ = equilibrium rate in Case II

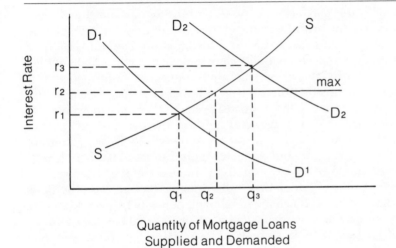

Quantity of Mortgage Loans
Supplied and Demanded

under equilibrium conditions would represent the expected difference in risk and liquidity between the two markets. If the trustees were maximizing their depositors' well-being, one would expect mutuals to shift into government securities as the rate differential between government and private debt narrowed. On the other hand, during tight money situations, when the equilibrium rate of interest was above 7 percent, the personal incentives and pressures to lend to friends and associates would be greater. Therefore, an examination of mutual lending policy during periods of high interest rates should illuminate trustee motivation.

INVESTMENTS DURING A PERIOD OF HIGH INTEREST RATES

The available annual investment data conceal rather wide transitory monthly movements, so it is necessary to find a fairly prolonged period of high interest rates in which to apply this model. Such a period existed during the entire year of 1848 when commercial bank discount rates reached a plateau "that has rarely, if ever, been duplicated in the decades for which we have any sort of data. Rates did not fall below 13-1/2 per cent for any month throughout the whole calendar year 1848, and they averaged nearly 15-1/2 per cent in those twelve months."[19] During this same period, the decline in bond prices increased the yield the banks could have expected on this type of investment.[20] With a spread of at least 7 percent between the maximum rate that mutuals could legally charge and the short-term rate then current, there was substantial room for personal gain if trustees had wanted to take advantage of the situation.

A look at the portfolios of the Bank for Savings and the Bowery shows that both institutions reduced the amount they had outstanding on mortgages during the year. As illustrated in Table 14, both of these banks experienced relatively slow deposit growth in 1848, which helps explain why their bond holdings increased only moderately. But the fact remains that they both purchased new government issues at the expense of their loans on real estate. If they had wanted to profit from their position at the expense of their depositors' overall interest, they could have transferred some of their assets out of government securities in order to have more funds available to loan.[21] Trustees could also have profited by increasing their deposits in commercial banks of which they were stockholders. In 1848 the Bank for Savings decreased its commercial bank deposits by over $100,000. The Bowery increased its deposits by about $75,000 between January 1848 and January 1849, but a look at the monthly data for this mutual indicates that in January 1848 its commercial bank deposits as a percentage of assets had fallen to 6.2 percent, the lowest level since 1840. Furthermore, its average monthly balance during 1848 was lower than it had been since 1843.

The evidence strongly suggests that the trustees of the Bank for Savings and the Bowery were basing their investment decisions on market conditions (given legal constraints) in order to maximize the rate of return on their portfolios—this was consistent with their depositors' interests. Evidence also suggests that in doing so they were foregoing possible personal gain. The data for the Seamen's, although not so clear-cut, lead to the same conclusion.

The Seamen's was the only mutual with a substantial amount of new money to invest during 1848 (over $700,000). Its funding committee invested approximately $345,000 in stocks and lent about $315,000 on mortgages. The bank also increased its commercial bank deposits by about $62,000. Because of the bank's rapid growth, this increase in its commercial bank deposits (which constituted less than 1 percent of its total assets) may have represented a temporary build-up, authorized while the funding committee searched for permanent investments.

To review, if mutuals were trying to maximize their depositors' welfare, one would expect them to invest in government securities during this period since the nominal rate they could earn on this type of investment approached or surpassed the rate they could earn on mortgage loans, which were constrained by the usury law. The nominal rate they expected to earn on government securities would not have had to reach 7 percent to make this type of investment more attractive than mortgage loans because the banks associated higher risk with loaning to individuals.

But as a result of recent bond purchases, the Seamen's trustees were not particularly worried about the overall liquidity of their portfolio. An examination of the changes in the bank's assets during the late 1840s shows that the funding committee took steps to improve the bank's liquidity posture by investing heavily in United States government securities, the safest and most liquid investment available. From 1845 the bank's holdings of United States government debt increased from about $36,000, or less than 8 percent of its total assets, to almost $700,000, or over 25 percent of all assets. During 1848 alone, the bank purchased over $260,000 of United States debt.

A look at the specific mortgage loans made during 1848 indicates that the bank rationed its funds by lending to borrowers with excellent credit ratings. Approximately one-fifth of the amount lent went to churches and over one-fourth went to persons listed by Moses Beach among the "most wealthy men in New York City."[22] Almost all of the money lent during 1848 was kept for over one year and about two-thirds of it was still outstanding in 1855, which indicates that it was not borrowed to take advantage of short-run market conditions.[23] The evidence on the Seamen's is thus not as convincing as that for the other banks. The fact that its trustees made mortgage loans to churches and to the exceptionally wealthy could be consistent with the philanthropic hypothesis insofar as these loans entailed lower risks and thus higher real returns. On the other hand, these loans could be consistent with selfish behavior insofar as they went to friends or to trustees' churches. Nevertheless, if the Seamen's trustees were behaving strictly in accordance with Vatter's hypothesis, it is doubtful that approximately one-half of their new investments would have gone into government debt.

The evidence presented for the Bank for Savings, the Bowery, and, to a lesser extent, the Seamen's supports the hypothesis that these banks' trustees were pursuing their depositors' interest even during a unique period when the opportunity for personal gain was exceptionally large. This conclusion can probably be extended to most of the prewar era for two reasons. First, there were no basic changes in the composition of the boards of trustees, which might suggest that their motives could have changed. Second, all three banks tended to make similar marginal investment decisions through most of the 1850s, which implies similarity of objectives. So, unless all three boards changed their objective functions at the same time, which is highly unlikely, they all probably continued to work in their depositors' behalf. This does not mean that financial advantages were not associated with being a trustee of one of these banks. This caveat notwithstanding, when there existed a potentially profitable conflict of interest, the trustees resolved it in favor of their depositors' long-run interests. A prospering mutual increased the trustees' esteem in the financial community—a return in lieu of a pecuniary reward.

## A Comparison with Mutuals in Boston and Baltimore

It is interesting to compare the New York mutuals with the two large mutuals in Boston and Baltimore that Payne and Davis studied. Since both of these banks were constrained by 6 percent usury laws, there must have been many periods in which the free-market rate exceeded the legal limit.[24] If they were maximizing the real rate of return on their portfolios, they should have invested relatively more of their assets in government securities than did the New York mutuals, but on the contrary, they both held a markedly lower percentage of their assets in public debt.[25] This difference in holdings might indicate that the Boston and Baltimore banks were less risk averse and more willing to help finance "friendly" projects—especially since the interest rate they received on private loans often was no greater than what New York mutuals received on more secure government issues. If trustees were using state usury laws for their personal advantage they would have increased their loans to private borrowers during high-interest periods. There is some evidence that the Provident of Boston followed this policy. The percentage of the Provident's portfolio that was invested in government issue fell from 25 to 15 percent in 1848 while loans to private parties increased from 54 to 64 percent. Interestingly enough, almost all those new loans appear to have been made where the free-market interest rate was highest—in 1848 discounts increased from 4 to 14 percent of the bank's portfolio.[26] On the other hand, the Savings Bank of Baltimore did make substantial purchases of United States government debt in 1848.[27] But its directors were not above lending to themselves. Professor Davis dismissed this observation by pointing out that the directors "were charged the going [interest] rate. . . ."[28] But did the bank demand as much collateral of its directors? Would the bank have called in a director's loan as rapidly as the loans of other businessmen? Payne and Davis concluded their analysis of mutual investment policy by noting the importance of market imperfections and trustee irrationality:

> The investment policy of both banks was marked by a considerable degree of provincialism. It is almost as if the managers refused to invest in any asset that they could not touch. The bank shares that they held were the shares of local banks; their loans were almost entirely loans to local residents; and, until the mid-'fifties, the state and local bonds that they held were limited to the issues of their own states. Because of their provincialism the banks failed to take advantage of a great range of investment opportunities. For example, during the 'twenties the Provident was making the bulk of its loans at a rate of interest well below the 6 per cent received by the Savings Bank. The provincialism in investment policy strongly suggests that in this early period long-term capital was relatively immobile, and that the geographic concentration of industry may well have been one manifestation of this immobility.[29]

The apparent capital immobility may only indicate that local businessmen who had connections with the mutuals were pre-empting the mutuals' funds. Furthermore, the reason they were able to do this was because they were serving as directors, in part, for this very purpose. If this is "provincialism," it certainly need not be condemned. Instead, this is a noteworthy example of mature, shrewd business practice—and nothing more.

This chapter has examined the response of mutual portfolios to changes in market forces in order to identify trustee objectives. Four tentative conclusions can be drawn from this examination. First, the trustees of the four oldest mutuals (the Bank for Savings, Seamen's, Greenwich, and Bowery savings banks) attempted to maximize the real rate of return on their portfolios given legal constraints. Second, the *primary* objective of these trustees was to pursue their depositors' interests; there is little support for the profiteering hypothesis. Conflicts of interest, when they occurred, had a minimal aggregate impact on the operating characteristics of these mutuals. Third, the findings presented here, when coupled with the evidence of aggressive bargaining on the part of mutual trustees presented in Chapter 4, suggest that the trustees of the four mutuals were relatively efficient in the pursuit of their objective. The aggregate data do not allow us to conclude that these banks *never* played favorites. The important conclusion is that even if the older mutuals did occasionally play favorites, the aggregate allocative and efficiency impact was nil. Finally, a cursory comparison with the leading mutuals in Boston and Baltimore does not warrant extending these conclusions to those two institutions.

CHAPTER 6

# The Determinants of
# Mutual Behavior:
## Commercial Bank Deposits
## and Call Loans

Were the interlocking directorates connecting mutuals and commercial banks abused to the detriment of the mutual? For example, did mutuals make deposits in "friendly" commercial banks at a lower rate of interest than they could have obtained elsewhere? If so, how large were the resulting transfers? Were many loans made to trustees' friends, business associates, or relatives, and did they pay lower interest rates than other borrowers? Such questions have seldom been raised and have never been subjected to a detailed investigation. Yet their answers are crucial to our understanding not only of mutuals but of the broader business community as well.

These answers will obviously help specify the nature of trustee objectives, because if the trustees were profiting from their positions, their philanthropic pretenses would be doubtful. This inquiry will shed light on the efficiency with which mutuals allocated their financial resources. To achieve efficient allocation, mutuals should have bargained with borrowers and lent to whoever offered the highest real rate of interest.[1] The answers to these questions also bear on the issue of bank safety. Assuming uniform managerial skill, for a group of trustees to pay the same dividend rate paid by other mutuals and still profit required them to make riskier investments or accumulate less surplus. Either would lower a mutual's resistance to financial crises. The answers to these questions have a wider application: other things being equal, if one segment of the business community had preferential access to credit, it would have a lower cost of production than its competitors. As long as the economy or even a relevant sub-sector was in a sufficient state of disequilibrium, businessmen who were not "well-connected" would have higher average (interest) costs of production and thus lower profit margins. In periods of intensified competition with falling profit margins, businessmen without this favorable financial leverage would be exposed to a greater risk of failure. These individuals would have a great incentive to protect themselves by gaining access to a source of credit. Thus the existence of a few financial institutions that discriminated in favor of "insiders" could create an unstable situation as "outsiders" attempted to improve their competitive position by associating with financial intermediaries.

Neither the existence of interlocking directorates nor the discovery that trustees made loans to friends, associates, and relatives necessarily implies that funds were misused. To expect mutual trustees not to lend to persons close to them would be naïve for a number of reasons. It was common practice in the nineteenth century, as it is today, for individuals and institutions to prefer lending to someone with whom they had had previous business dealings, rather than to strangers. Such loans could reduce administrative cost and lower risk. Similarly, when seeking a loan one generally inquires first at banks where one has references. In the less developed financial markets of the nineteenth century, economic activity was often conducted on a personal basis; one would expect fo find many loans going to entrepreneurs known to the trustees through other dealings, for these were the very people whom they trusted most. Thus the practice of lending to friends, relatives, and associates could be perfectly consistent with a trustee's effort to maximize his depositors' welfare. To show otherwise we would need to establish that the mutual lowered its collateral requirements for these individuals or that it demanded a lower rate of interest than it could have obtained elsewhere (at the same write-up cost).

## Some Determinants of Reserve Policy

All mutuals confronted two issues. First, *how much* cash should it keep on reserve? Second, *where* would it keep its cash reserves? This section analyzes the diversity in the behavior of several mutuals on these issues. It is not always possible to reconcile the behavior of every single mutual with our paradigm, especially the latecomers, but a discussion of the "maverick" mutuals is included for the sake of complete analysis.

How much cash a mutual had on reserve at any time depended on a number of factors, some transitory and others more basic to long-run objectives. A large, unexpected influx of deposits relative to withdrawals could lead to a temporary increase in unwanted reserves. If a bank's investment committee expected bond prices to fall or interest rates in the mortgage market to rise, it might prefer to hold cash and to refrain from making permanent investments. More indica-

tive of long-run objectives would be a board's evaluation of what
constituted sufficient liquidity to meet unexpected withdrawals. This
evaluation would itself be a function of numerous variables. If interest
rates increased over the business cycle, the marginal cost of liquidity
would increase. Assuming no corresponding upward re-evaluation of
risks that would increase the marginal desirability of liquidity, a
rational intermediary should substitute on the margin out of cash
and into interest-earning assets. A bank's overall liquidity posture
depended upon the composition of its entire portfolio, not only on
its cash reserves. Mutuals could make marginal adjustments between
cash and highly liquid Treasury notes. The more successful mutuals
relied heavily on secondary reserves of liquidity. In order to maintain
the same overall degree of liquidity, a large percentage of its portfolio
in relatively illiquid mortgage loans should hold a larger cash reserve
than another bank that had substituted state and federal bonds for
mortgages. Changes in legal constraints could affect a board's evaluation of what constituted a proper reserve ratio. As constraints were
lowered mutuals could diversify their portfolios and to some extent
lessen their need for cash reserves. In the short-run, tight constraints
could drive a bank to reduce its reserves. For example, as noted in
Chapter 4, the trustees of the Bank for Savings went heavily into
debt in 1820 to the Mechanics' Bank in order to purchase a new
issue of Erie Canal bonds. This bank's trustees were so constrained
that they considered the advantages gained from relieving investment
pressures greater than the short-run risk incurred. As a final point,
discussions found in the minute books of several banks indicate that
their trustees placed more emphasis on maintaining high reserve ratios
if they had recently experienced a run by depositors associated with
a financial panic.

## Mutual Deposits in Commercial Banks: A Key to Mutual Objective Functions

During the antebellum years, New York City mutuals deposited most
of their cash reserves in commercial banks. The Bank for Savings
initiated this policy in 1819, although the bank was not explicitly
granted the right to make such deposits until 1830.[2] The commercial
bank deposits of individual mutuals often exceeded $100,000 and
reached as high as $750,000. On occasion these substantial sums
exceeded the entire capital stock of the commercial bank. The benefits
from these deposits could accrue to either institution, depending upon
which of three competing models is chosen to explain these transactions. The first is the perfectly competitive model, in which case
a mutual would bargain with several commercial banks and adjust

its account to maximize the real rate of interest it received. The second possibility is that some mutual trustees connected with a commercial bank were using their influence to the benefit of the latter's stockholders. If this situation prevailed, one would expect the mutual to carry relatively large, stable balances in the commercial bank at a rate of interest below the equilibrium rate under perfect competition. The effect of the interlocking directorate would be to transfer profits from the savings bank to the commercial bank. The third possibility is that the commercial bank subsidized the mutual by paying a rate of interest higher than the equilibrium rate under perfect competition.

Equilibrium interest rates for a perfectly competitive market are not available, but if mutuals negotiated with commercial banks, shifted deposits to obtain higher interest rates, and received interest rates as high as other depositors, it would appear that interlocking directorates were not misused. If on the other hand a mutual favored one commercial bank, maintained a large stable account in it, and received a lower rate of interest than did other mutuals, it is possible that some trustees discriminated in favor of the commercial bank. It is also possible that managers of such mutuals were less competent managers or that the commercial bank was in turn treating the mutual preferentially. For example, the commercial bank may have lent to the mutual at preferential rates, promised an "open line of credit" when other borrowers were turned away, performed valuable consulting services, given favorable repayment terms, allowed early payment without penalties, allowed the mutual use of its vault, and given the mutual office space. These and other services have a positive market value, but they seldom if ever are quantified and never appear in *ex post* data available to most researchers. This type of information is almost always regarded as privileged and is known only to corporate executives. This almost insurmountable problem plagues researchers today who try to show that banks "discriminate" against small borrowers. The confidential records of several mutuals considered below offer abundant evidence both on the motivation of mutual trustees and on the relative importance of market and non-market forces in explaining bank behavior.

The data on mutual deposits in specific commercial banks are presented in Appendix F in Tables F-1 through F-7. These tables exhibit the amount deposited, the name of the commercial bank in which the deposits were made, and, when available, the terms of the accounts.

From these tables and other evidence to be presented below, it appears that most of these mutuals demanded and received a competitive rate of interest on their deposits. In most cases mutuals preferred to deposit their reserves in commercial banks that had some of the mutuals' trustees as directors, but this generally did not conflict with the optimization of the mutuals' behavior. The two exceptions discussed below are the Bowery Savings Bank and the Broadway Savings Institution, which at times were not as aggressive in their negotiations as other banks. This conclusion undoubtedly applies to many of the institutions for which we do not have detailed data. Many of the above conclusions can be documented by turning to case studies of individual mutuals.

THE BANK FOR SAVINGS

The Bank for Savings kept all its cash reserves on deposit in the Mechanics' Bank from 1819 to 1833. These deposits were interest-bearing and subject to immediate withdrawal. The Bank for Savings probably received 5 percent from the Mechanics' Bank for the entire period from 1819 to 1835. The records of the Bank for Savings never explicitly listed the rate it received, so this conjecture must be based on information obtained elsewhere. First, the trustees of the Seamen's Bank for Savings (many of whom were also trustees of the Bank for Savings) noted in June 1829 that the Mechanics' Bank was paying the Bank for Savings 5 percent per year. Second, the Mechanics' Bank paid 5 percent in 1838 to the Seamen's Bank for Savings. Third, semi-annual statements exist which show the amount of interest the Bank for Savings received from the Mechanics' Bank, and the amount on deposit at various times. From these data it is possible to make a rough calculation of the rate received.[3]

The comparative evidence available strongly indicates that the Bank for Savings did better than other commercial bank depositors, many of whom received no interest on their balances during many of these years. Paying interest on deposits in the early 1820s was a relatively new practice not employed by all of New York's commercial banks. An investigation of New York City banks in 1820 revealed that, although a few city banks were paying interest on country banks' deposits, this was an uncommon practice.[4] In the mid-1820s the New York City branch of the "Second Bank of the United States was hard pressed by its large customers, e.g. Nathaniel Prime of New York, to pay interest on their deposits," but the bank turned down their request.[5] Furthermore, the Mechanics' Bank, in which the Bank for Savings kept its account, was noted for being one of the first New York City banks to pay interest on deposits.[6] By the end of the 1820s, the payment of interest on demand deposits by commercial banks had become more common, but it was by no means universal. There is interest rate information on some better known deposits with which we can compare the rates received by the Bank for Savings.

Table 15   Interest Rates on New York Canal Fund Deposits in Commercial
Banks (in percentages)

| Year | Demand Deposits | Time Deposits (required 60-day notice) |
|------|-----------------|-----------------------------------------|
| 1826 | 5.0 | |
| 1827 | 3.5 | |
| 1828 | 3.5 | |
| 1829 | 3.5 | |
| 1830 | 3.5 | |
| 1831 | 3.5 | |
| 1832 | 4.5[a] | 4.0-4.5 |
| 1833 | 4.5[a] | 4.5-5.0 |
| 1834 | 4.5[a] | 4.5-5.0 |
| 1835 | 4.5[a] | 4.5-5.0 |
| 1836 | 4.5[a] | 4.5-5.0 |
| 1837 | 4.5[a] | 4.5-5.0 |

Source: Compiled from Nathan Miller, *The Enterprise of a Free People*, pp. 116-25.

[a] The rate on these deposits was in essence less than 4.5% because "the banks had 'free use' of the deposits for fifteen days beyond the end of the month during which they were made." Miller, *Enterprise*, pp. 118-19.

Nathan Miller in his study of the Erie Canal quoted rates the canal fund received on its deposits in commercial banks over several years. This information is given in Table 15.

Another account for which there is information belonged to the state of Ohio. The Manhattan Company Bank held the state's balance and acted as its agent in New York City: "The bank paid interest to the stockholders, issued and registered the certificates and transfers, and transacted other business of an agency. Proceeds of loans were placed in this bank and transferred as wanted, in small installments, to Ohio banks, which were selected by the fund commissioners. The Manhattan Bank allowed the state 5 per cent interest on all undrawn deposits (this was soon reduced to 4 per cent), with the exception that so long as the deposits should continue, $20,000 of them should be exempt from the charge of interest as a compensation to the bank for its work."[7] The Manhattan Company Bank performed many services for the state of Ohio, and it is difficult to say with certainty exactly what rate the state would have received on its deposits in absence of these services. If we take Bogart literally and consider the deposit of $20,000 interest free as payment for other services, it follows that the state received 5 (and later 4) percent on its balance.

It thus seems that the rates received by the Bank for Savings and by the Seamen's from 1829 to 1837 were as high or higher than those received by the state of Ohio and the Erie Canal fund. In 1829 the canal fund received only 3.5 percent on its deposits and the state of Ohio received 4 or 5 percent. At this time both mutuals extracted 5 percent from the commercial banks with which they did business.

In 1833 the Bank for Savings made two time deposits of $100,000 and $300,000 in the Bank of America and the Bank of New York, respectively.[8] The Bank for Savings continued to make demand deposits at the Mechanics' Bank until 1835, when it transferred this account to the Union Bank. Unfortunately the Bank for Savings' records do not mention the interest rates it received on its two time deposits, but secondary sources indicate that its trustees drove a hard bargain and attempted to maximize the mutual's interests.

Throughout much of 1836 the Bank of New York, along with most of the city's financial institutions, experienced a liquidity crisis.[9] As a relief measure the commissioners of the canal fund increased their loans to New York City banks, and the state legislature authorized commercial banks to treat borrowed funds as capital stock for the purpose of expanding their own loans and discounts.[10] With this inducement the Bank of New York took the unusual step of borrowing £112,500 from London bankers for thirteen months at 5 percent. Henry Domett, the historian of the Bank of New York, noted that this institution's troubles were soon intensified by the Bank for Savings' decision to close its account. "The difficulties which had already proved so embarassing were increased by the fact that the Bank of New York was called upon in May, 1836, to return to the Bank for Savings $300,000 which it had held on special deposit. . . . Fortunately, on the 4th of May, the commissioners of the canal fund offered to the bank $100,000 at five per cent., to be repaid on the 1st of July, 1837; and on the 23rd of August the receivers of the Washington Insurance Company also made to the bank a loan of $194,000 at five per cent., to be repaid on twenty days' notice."[11] If the Bank for Savings' trustees' primary concern was the prosperity of the commercial bank's stockholders, it is unlikely that the trustees would have withdrawn their entire deposit at such an inopportune moment. Had the Bank for Savings been confronted with a run by its own customers, and was thus desperately in need of converting its deposits into cash, one might argue that it had no choice but to close its account. But there were no such compelling reasons behind the mutual's decision. Instead, the bank's balance sheets reveal that its funding committee decided to convert these bank deposits into New York City bonds.[12]

In 1835, the Bank for Savings transferred its demand deposits from the Mechanics' Bank to the Union Bank. This action was particularly noteworthy because none of the mutuals' trustees were directors or officers of that commercial bank.[13] That was the first time that a New York City mutual entrusted its deposits to a commercial bank with which it did not have an interlocking directorate, and not until the 1850s would another mutual do likewise.[14] Although the Bank for Savings had an interlocking directorate with all three of the commercial banks in which it made deposits before 1835 (the Mechanics' Bank, Bank of America, and Bank of New York), there is no indication that this interfered with the savings bank's negotiations with these commercial banks.[15] The record of this mutual's relations with commercial banks and its negotiations with various government agencies noted in earlier chapters suggest that its trustees consistently acted as profit maximizers, i.e., they attempted to maximize the rate of return on the mutual's portfolio.

THE SEAMEN'S BANK FOR SAVINGS

In 1829 the Seamen's trustees opened an account with the Fulton Bank, which paid the mutual 5 percent per year on the average monthly balance. This arrangement continued until September 1838, when the Fulton Bank notified the Seamen's that it would no longer pay 5 percent. The Seamen's trustees discussed the situation at their board meeting of 5 September 1838 and resolved to inquire about terms other banks might offer. The board also voted that it would be willing to accept 4 percent. At the next regular meeting Seamen's funding committee announced that the bank's deposits had been transferred to the Mechanics' Bank, which paid 5 percent.[16] This was particularly significant since the Seamen's board had expressed a willingness to accept 4 percent and because several commercial banks potentially had access to this information via their interlocking directorates. The fact that the funding committee obtained 5 percent on the Seamen's balance strongly suggests that its trustees were attempting to maximize the mutual's interest and not that of any particular commercial bank.

In July 1839, less than a year after it had last transferred its account, the Seamen's moved its entire deposit to another commercial bank: the Leather Manufacturers' Bank.[17] The Seamen's kept all its cash reserves in this one bank for over ten years. The Seamen's records do not indicate why it switched its deposits from the Mechanics' to the Leather Manufacturers' Bank, nor do the records mention if there was a change in interest rates. The next and the last mention of interest rates on commercial bank deposits found in the Seamen's records was dated 4 December 1844. At that time the Leather Manufacturers' Bank informed the Seamen's that beginning in January 1845 it would only pay 3 percent on the mutual's average monthly balance.[18] This reduction occurred when interest rates in general were falling, and the Seamen's evidently was unable to obtain more favorable terms elsewhere.[19] Because of a concern that its account had become too large to be kept safely in one bank, the Seamen's opened a second account in the Bank of Commerce in 1850. It maintained both accounts throughout the 1850s.[20]

The records of both the Bank for Savings and Seamen's over the period for which interest rate data are available indicate that neither institution was being manipulated to the benefit of a particular commercial bank. Both boards of trustees bargained effectively with the commercial banks and both seem to have been managing their deposits as if they were rational, unconstrained investors. This conclusion is consistent with that reached in Chapter 5.

The Bank for Savings and the Seamen's had another common characteristic in their relations with commercial banks. The trustees of both mutuals were particularly careful to differentiate their product by establishing a separate identity in the public's mind from any particular commercial bank or from commercial banks in general. Neither the Seamen's nor the Bank for Savings ever operated out of a commercial bank office, and both commented in advertisements that they had no ties with banks of discount. Both mutuals were also careful to have directors of several commercial banks on their boards and at the same time not to allow the number of trustees associated with any particular commercial bank to gain anything approaching a majority of board seats. In this regard the Seamen's and the Bank for Savings stood apart from the next two mutuals organized in New York City.

THE GREENWICH SAVINGS BANK

Both the Greenwich Savings Bank (1833) and the Bowery Savings Bank (1834) were organized and for several years controlled by the directors and stockholders of the Greenwich Bank and the Butchers' and Drovers' Bank, respectively. Half of the founding trustees of the Greenwich Savings Bank held stock in the commercial bank of the same name, and in 1835 about one-third of the mutual's trustees were either officers or directors of the commercial bank. The Greenwich Bank listed thirteen officers and directors in 1835, eleven of whom were also trustees of the savings bank.[21] These two institutions remained closely tied by interlocking directorates well into the latter half of the nineteenth century.[22]

The information available on the Greenwich Savings Bank is summarized in Appendix F, Table F-3. These data show that the Greenwich Bank paid the savings bank 5 percent for several years, which was the same rate the Bank for Savings and the Seamen's were getting on their deposits. The data show that the savings bank drew on its two commercial bank accounts during the Panic of 1837, which must have aggravated the drain faced by its two depository banks. There is no specific evidence to suggest that in later years the savings bank kept its deposits in the Greenwich Bank when it could have received more favorable terms elsewhere, but given its strong ties with the commercial bank the chances that this might happen were probably greater than for mutuals whose trustees had more diverse outside economic interests. It is also doubtful that the savings bank would have made large enough withdrawals to force the commercial bank to borrow elsewhere, as was the case when the Bank for Savings closed its account with the Bank of New York in 1836. The above speculation about the effect of closely interlocking directorates is applicable to at least the Bowery Savings Bank, an institution with which the Greenwich had much in common.

THE BOWERY SAVINGS BANK

The records of the Bowery Savings Bank indicate that for several years its trustees kept relatively large deposits in the Butchers' and Drovers' Bank on less favorable terms than it probably could have obtained elsewhere or from the bank itself. The Bowery failed to obtain better terms primarily because a large number of its most influential trustees had financial ties with the Butchers' and Drovers' Bank, which interfered with the trustees' ability to bargain with the commercial bank.

On 2 June 1834 the Bowery Savings Bank opened for business in the Butchers' and Drovers' Bank. One-fourth of the Bowery's trustees were also officers or directors of the Butchers' and Drovers' Bank, and one-third were listed among the holders of the commercial bank's stock in 1832.[23] The Bowery kept all its cash reserves on deposit in this one commercial bank until 1851. During its first year of business, the mutual received 5 percent on its deposits, but in July 1835 the Butchers' and Drovers' Bank announced that it would no longer pay interest on the Bowery's account.[24] Apparently without any debate or instructions the Bowery's board referred the matter to its funding committee with power to transfer its account to another commercial bank.[25] There is no record in the Bowery's minutes concerning what arrangement was reached, and it appears that the board did not discuss the decision of its funding committee. The bank's ledgers show that it continued to use the Butchers' and Drovers' Bank as its sole depository. The same individuals who controlled the Butchers' and Drovers' Bank and initiated its policy to suspend interest payments were also charged with determining the Bowery's response; thus it seems most likely that the mutual accepted the announced cut. At that time the president of the Bowery Savings Bank and all three of the members of the Bowery's funding committee had been listed as holders of the commercial bank's stock since 1832.

There were evidently no further changes in the terms of the Bowery's account until February 1844, when the Butchers' and Drovers' Bank offered to pay 4 percent compounded semi-annually on all sums up to $40,000; any balance in excess of that amount would not draw interest.[26] Under this arrangement, which continued until May 1846, the rate of interest the Bowery received on its entire balance averaged slightly over 1 percent per year.[27]

In May 1846 the Butchers' and Drovers' Bank offered to pay 3 percent on all sums up to $100,000. This concession came in the wake of a minor revolt among some of the Bowery's trustees. In February 1846, Joseph B. Collins presented a resolution calling for the transfer of $50,000 to a demand deposit in the New York Life and Trust Company, which was willing to pay at least 3 percent. This resolution was tabled in order to allow the funding committee to study the subject. At the next regular meeting the funding committee reported: "Since the organization of the Bowery Savings Bank, their weekly deposits have been made in the Butchers' and Drovers' Bank. . . . For a part of that period the Bank has paid four per cent upon a balance of $40,000 and the Balances have ranged from $50,000 to between $100,000 and $200,000. The Funding Committee are of the opinion, that the Balance remaining in the Bank should not at any time be reduced below $100,000 and that for such sum a small interest should be paid." The board accepted this report and resolved to ask that the Butchers' and Drovers' Bank pay "not less than three per cent per annum" and that the deposit be subject to withdrawals without notice.[28] These conditions, which were readily accepted by the Butchers' and Drovers' Bank, remained in effect for five years. During this period, when the interest rate was calculated at 3 percent on the first $100,000, the Bowery received less than 2 percent on its entire average monthly balance.[29]

The decision to ask for more favorable terms marked the beginning of a prolonged effort by several of the Bowery's trustees to assert their independence of the Butchers' and Drovers' Bank. In November 1847 several disgruntled trustees suggested that the deposit in the Butchers' and Drovers' Bank be reduced to $50,000 and that a $50,000 deposit be made in another bank at 4 percent. This resolution was rejected at the next meeting by a vote of 20 to 8.[30]

Not until 1851 did the board finally agree to make deposits in other commercial banks. During the previous year the Bowery's monthly balance had averaged over $280,000 and in December it had climbed to $604,533—an amount that exceeded the Butchers' and Drovers' capital stock by over $100,000. By entrusting so large

a deposit to one commercial bank, the board was obviously compro-
mising the safety of the Bowery's assets. By 1 February 1851 the
Bowery's funding committee had opened accounts totaling $300,000
in four other banks. The board agreed to give these banks ten days'
notice on all withdrawals over $10,000. In July 1851 the Butchers'
and Drovers' Bank offered to increase its interest rate on the Bowery's
deposit to 4 percent on the first $100,000 and 3 percent on any sums
above that amount, and declined the notice requirement on future
withdrawals. This offer came too late to persuade the Bowery's trustees
to return to their former policy of depositing solely in the Butchers'
and Drovers' Bank; the board responded by directing its funding
committee to keep deposits "in not less than three banks to our best
advantage."[31]

By 1851 a majority of the Bowery's trustees were insisting that
it receive better terms on its deposits, and for the next six years the
Bowery did not give preferential treatment to the Butchers' and Drovers'
Bank. By January 1857 the board had dispersed its deposits, totaling
about $900,000, among eleven different commercial banks and held
a $130,000 cash reserve in its own vault. In February 1857 the board
debated a proposal requiring all the banks holding its deposits to
increase the rate of interest to 5 percent per year compounded
semi-annually. At the next meeting the board voted 17 to 14 to accept
this resolution. An analysis of this vote suggests that those trustees
who were also directors of commercial banks were not prone to approve
of the increase, while those trustees who did not have this conflict
of interest were so inclined. At least ten of the fourteen trustees voting
to maintain the lower rate of interest were also directors of the banks
in which the Bowery had deposits, whereas only six of the remaining
twenty-nine trustees, who either voted to increase the rate or were
absent, held directorships in these commercial banks.[32] This vote
illustrates how interlocking directorates might influence a mutual's
behavior and its allocation of resources. Requesting a higher rate
of interest on its deposits could only benefit the savings bank, yet
fourteen trustees opposed asking; these trustees were willing to
subjugate the mutual's interests to those of commercial banks. The
majority's decision to require 5 percent on the bank's deposits was
an affirmation of the bank's independence and a continuation of the
1851 policy of bargaining more strenuously with commercial banks.
The board's more competitive behavior in dealing with commercial
banks was likely to have carried over to its negotiations with private
borrowers. If so, the bank became more efficient over time in its
allocation of financial capital. It is also significant that the more
aggressive investment behavior occurred when the entry of new
mutuals was causing the savings banking industry to become more

competitive. In January 1849 the Bowery raised its dividend rate to its depositors.

*An Increased Reliance on Secondary Reserves*

The Bowery's experience during the Panic of 1857 led to a reversal of its newly avowed policy of spreading its deposits among numerous banks. In February 1858 the board "resolved that the moneys now deposited in the several Banks . . . be withdrawn therefrom excepting from the Butchers' and Drovers' Bank in which there be a sum allowed to remain, without interest, but subject to call at any time." The board elaborated by recommending that the unemployed balances in the Butchers' and Drovers' Bank and in the Bowery's own vault not exceed $300,000. One reason given by the board for its extremely cautious policy was that "the experience of the last two seasons of pressure has demonstrated that the deposits in the Commercial Banks interfered with the safety of those Banks."[33] The board recognized the dangers to both mutuals and commercial banks of compounding reserves. This recognition came just a few years before the National Banking Act encouraged the compounding of reserves among commercial banks, which stimulated the movement of bankers' balances to New York City. Half a century passed before the foresight of the Bowery's trustees was validated by legislation eradicating this flaw in the banking system.

Although the policy of not requiring interest on its deposits was a relatively short-lived phenomenon engendered by the recent panic, the board re-evaluated the bank's overall liquidity posture.[34] The board's new policy was to keep a lower percentage of its assets on reserve and to increase the liquidity and safety of its reserves by keeping most of them in its own vault. The percentage of the Bowery's assets in commercial banks dropped from about 10 percent to about 1 percent, and the bank's total reserves dropped from about 13 percent to about 5 percent. The board compensated for this overall drop in primary reserves by increasing the bank's holding of semi-liquid securities, principally United States government bonds and Treasury notes. The percentage of this type of asset increased from a pre-Panic average of about 10 percent to over 20 percent by 1860. This new policy represented the increased awareness of the board that during the current financial stress, should the bank need cash desperately, commercial banks would be hard pressed to meet the Bowery's drafts. Because of past experiences the board was well aware of the liquidity that United States bonds and Treasury notes offered. A subsequent section of this chapter analyzes some of the broader implications of mutual savings bank reliance on secondary reserves.

*An Estimate of the Transfer*

This discussion has demonstrated that from 1835 to 1851 the Bowery's trustees did not negotiate terms as favorable as they could have on their deposits in the Butchers' and Drovers' Bank because several of the Bowery's trustees were also directors and stockholders in the commercial bank. As suggested by the vote taken in 1857, these individuals were not as demanding of the commercial banks in which the Bowery kept its accounts. What remains to be answered is how large was the subsidy—i.e., if the Bowery had received rates comparable to those received by other banks, how much more would it have earned? The following product gives an estimate of the dollar amount of the Bowery's subsidy to the Butchers' and Drovers' Bank or of the tax on the depositors of the mutual: let,

$r_1$ = the rate paid to the Bowery Savings Bank on its deposits,

$r_2$ = the rate paid to other savings banks which we assume the Bowery could have obtained,

B = the Bowery's average balance in the Butchers' and Drovers' Bank; then $(r_1 - r_2)B$ = the subsidy.

Table 16 exhibits the relevant data, the estimate of the subsidy, and this estimate expressed as a percentage of the Butchers' and Drovers' capital stock. Note that this estimate does not include several intangible, but potentially important, aspects of the Bowery's deposits. For example, it could have been that the Bowery's account was more stable than that of other mutuals or that deposits might have been made to tide over the Butchers' and Drovers' when it was temporarily in need of funds. It also should be emphasized that these figures do not estimate the amount of profit the Butchers' and Drovers' made on the Bowery's account, for presumably banks paying higher rates to other mutuals made a normal profit on those accounts. The results in Table 16 are an estimate of the amount in excess of the normal profits that accrued to the Butchers' and Drovers'.

The estimated amount of the subsidy for each year certainly appears to be insignificant, especially in the first few years.[35] However as a percentage of the Butchers' and Drovers' capital stock the subsidy does not appear to be so small; in several years it would have allowed the commercial bank to pay an extra dividend of one-half of 1 percent.[36] In 1842 when the commercial bank paid only a 2.5 percent dividend, the subsidy accounted for 20 percent of the entire payment, but in most years its importance as a percentage of the bank's dividends was considerably less, ranging between 1 and 5 percent.[37] The transfer appears no more significant if viewed as a tax on the mutual's depositors. If the Bowery had received an interest rate comparable to what other mutuals obtained, its total interest earnings would have

**Table 16**    Estimate of the Bowery's Subsidy to the Butchers' and Drovers'
Bank

| Year | $r_1$ | $r_2$ | $r_2-r_1$ | Bowery's Average Monthly Balance | Subsidy | Subsidy as a Percentage of Butchers' and Drovers' Capital Stock[e] |
|------|-------|-------|-----------|--------------------|---------|-------------------|
| 1835 | 5.0 | 5[a,b] | 0.0 | | | |
| 1836 | 0.0 | 5[a,b] | 5.0 | $ 11,599 | $ 580 | 0.12 |
| 1837 | 0.0 | 5[a] | 5.0 | 8,075 | 404 | 0.08 |
| 1838 | 0.0 | 5[a] | 5.0 | 9,185 | 459 | 0.09 |
| 1839 | 0.0 | 5[a] | 5.0 | 27,541 | 1,377 | 0.28 |
| 1840 | 0.0 | 5[b] | 5.0 | 37,999 | 1,899 | 0.38 |
| 1841 | 0.0 | 5[b] | 5.0 | 52,979 | 2,649 | 0.53 |
| 1842 | 0.0 | 4[c] | 4.0 | 88,529 | 3,541 | 0.71 |
| 1843 | 0.0 | 4[c] | 4.0 | 87,635 | 3,505 | 0.70 |
| 1844 | 1.0 | 4[c] | 3.0 | 140,503 | 4,215 | 0.84 |
| 1845 | 1.4 | 3[a] | 1.7 | 117,080 | 1,990 | 0.40 |
| 1846 | 1.7 | 3 | 1.3 | 139,122 | 1,809 | 0.36 |
| 1847 | 2.0 | 4 | 2.0 | 147,895 | 2,958 | 0.59 |
| 1848 | 1.9 | 4[d] | 2.1 | 107,892 | 2,266 | 0.45 |
| 1849 | 1.7 | 4[d] | 2.3 | 174,292 | 4,009 | 0.80 |
| 1850 | 1.1 | 4[d] | 2.9 | 283,708 | 8,228 | 1.65 |

Source: Compiled from Secretary's Minutes, Bowery Savings Bank, 1835-1850.

[a] Seamen's.

[b] Greenwich.

[c] No data, but we know the Seamen's rate was "reduced" to 3% in January 1845.

[d] Dry Dock (received 6% for part of 1848).

[e] The Butchers' and Drovers' Capital Stock was $500,000 during these years.

been only 4 percent greater than what it did receive over the period
1846-1851.

Since it is most unlikely that many individuals held more than
$10,000 of the Butchers' and Drovers' capital stock, the amount that
any one trustee could hope to make from the subsidy would hardly
have compensated him for attending the mutual's board meetings,
let alone for performing the other more burdensome duties required
of a trustee.[38] For example, in 1850 a trustee who held $10,000 of
Butchers' and Drovers' stock could have made a maximum of $16.45
if the entire subsidy were passed on to the stockholders. It is evident
that the subsidy, as defined and measured here, could not have
represented an important source of income to any of the mutual's
trustees. It appears that commercial bank ties influenced some trustees
to vote against proposals that could benefit only the savings bank,
yet a trustee could expect to gain only a few dollars from maintaining
the lower rates. There are several possible explanations for this apparent

contradition. First, in the long run the trustees stood to gain much more than a few dollars if the mutual's deposits kept the commercial bank solvent during a panic. Furthermore, the derived estimates are *ex post;* the trustees might have thought that their personal gain was going to be greater. It is also possible that the amount of the subsidy was underestimated or that externalities existed which have been overlooked. For example, some trustees may have feared that if the commercial bank paid a higher rate on the mutual's deposit, it would have to pay a higher rate on other deposits.

The available evidence indicates that commercial banks did not pay all their depositors a uniform rate and relied on market imperfections (e.g., information barriers, the cost of changing accounts to another bank, and, in the case of savings banks, interlocking directorates) to hold accounts that could earn a higher rate in other banks. Margaret Myers found that "the payment of interest on deposits [of other commercial banks] was not general among all bankers at any time; it was used by them rather as a competitive device than as a routine measure. Some bankers refused to pay interest at all, even before there was any general opposition to it. Even bankers who paid interest did not pay it on all deposits, offering it as an inducement to obtain new accounts, or to draw an account from a rival bank, and paying it more frequently to an out-of-town depositor than to one at home."[39] Myers's description of bank policy implies that commercial bankers were extremely cost-conscious at the margin and that they employed discriminatory pricing policies whenever possible. The record of the Bowery's relations with the Butchers' and Drovers' Bank appears to confirm Myers's observation. The directors of the Butchers' and Drovers' Bank paid the Bowery Savings Bank as low a rate on its deposits as the mutual would tolerate. On the three occasions when some of the mutual's trustees proposed to open accounts with other commercial banks or asked for a higher interest rate, the Butchers' and Drovers' responded with offers its directors knew to be just enough to maintain the Bowery's account and to pacify most of the dissidents on the Bowery's board. The mutual's trustees did not seem to go out of their way to subsidize the commercial bank. During the period of high discount rates in 1848, when the Butchers' and Drovers' Bank could have most profitably employed the mutual's deposits, the latter's trustees drew heavily on their account. The average monthly balance of $129,471 in 1848 was almost $50,000 less than that of 1847 and almost $80,000 less than that of 1849.[40] This indicates that the Bowery Savings Bank was not being flagrantly mismanaged to the advantage of the commercial bank. On the contrary, the analysis in Chapter 5 showed that this mutual's marginal portfolio adjustments closely paralleled those of the Seamen's and Bank for

Savings, suggesting that all three boards had similar objectives. Furthermore, the Bowery's trustees accumulated a surplus, which they proceeded to distribute to depositors in the form of unannounced extra dividends. What this analysis does show is that competitive forces were not as keen in relations between the Bowery Savings Bank and the Butchers' and Drovers' Bank because of the interlocking directorate.

OTHER MUTUAL SAVINGS BANK DEPOSITS

The records of the Dry Dock, the Manhattan, and the Broadway savings banks can be compared with the four banks already examined. As was the case with the past discussion, what follows is based on only sparse interest data. Summarized in Appendix F in Tables F-5 through F-7, these data indicate that the trustees of both the Dry Dock and Manhattan savings banks negotiated regularly with the commercial banks in which they deposited and changed banks to obtain higher interest rates on their accounts. For example, in January of 1856 the Manhattan's board directed its finance committee to ask for 5 percent on its deposits, computed monthly, instead of the 4 percent rate it had been receiving. In February the finance committee reported that only one bank in the city would pay 5 percent and recommended that the bank not change its accounts. The board overruled its committee and moved to transfer its deposits to that bank.[41] In so doing the mutual closed accounts in two banks, of which at least nine of its trustees were directors.[42] In December 1856 the Manhattan made a time deposit of $50,000 in the Bank of North America, which paid 5.5 percent. When the Bank of North America informed the Manhattan that it would no longer pay interest on this account in January of 1858 the board authorized its finance committee to open an account in the bank that would pay the highest rate if the committee considered it secure. The only constraint the board placed on these deposits was that the deposit in any one bank could not exceed 10 percent of the bank's capital stock, in accordance with the General Act of 1853. In January the mutual opened an account in the St. Nicholas Bank, and in March it opened an account with the Shoe and Leathers' Bank—both at 5 percent.[43]

There is not as much information on commercial bank deposits in the Dry Dock's minutes as in the Manhattan's, but what does exist confirms that Dry Dock's trustees behaved much like the Manhattan's. When the Dry Dock opened in June 1848 it deposited almost all of its receipts in the Bowery Bank (not to be confused with the Bowery Savings Bank), which agreed to pay 4 percent. In December 1848, after some prodding, the Bowery Bank agreed to pay 6 percent on the Dry Dock's account.[44] As mentioned in Chapter 5 the entire year of 1848 was remarkable for its high interest rates, with discount rates averaging about 15 percent. Aware of this situation, the Dry Dock's trustees were able to negotiate a temporary increase on the rate they received on their deposit. It is significant that the Dry Dock could obtain 6 percent, because according to Margaret Myers 6 percent is the highest rate ever quoted on such deposits.[45] The rate on the Dry Dock's account was evidently reduced again within a few months, because in April 1850 the board instructed its funding committee to obtain a higher rate from the Bowery Bank.[46] The records do not mention the outcome of these negotiations. Beginning in 1853 the Dry Dock opened deposits in several banks and adjusted its accounts in order to obtain the most favorable terms possible.

The records of the Broadway Savings Institution show that its trustees kept all of its commercial bank deposits in the Broadway Bank throughout the 1850s. Unfortunately, this mutual's records do not mention the interest rates received on these deposits, but from other evidence we can speculate as to the nature of the relationship that existed between these two institutions. This evidence deals primarily with this mutual's call loans and will be presented later in this chapter.

This analysis of mutual deposits in commercial banks is directed at deducing mutuals' motives and the determinants of bank behavior. It has been suggested that most mutuals for which we have data did bargain and adjust their deposits in order to obtain higher rates. The exception was the Bowery, which throughout much of the 1830s and 1840s received a lower rate than it probably could have obtained elsewhere. In the 1850s there was a change in the Bowery's policy, and its board demanded and received rates comparable to those obtained by other mutuals. Several savings banks founded in the 1850s also had particularly close ties with one or two commercial banks. The analysis of call loans presented later in this chapter examines some of the reasons for these ties.

## Secondary Reserves in Times of Crises: An Alternative to Commercial Bank Deposits

Mutuals were engulfed by hysteria during the financial panics of 1825, 1834, 1837, 1854, 1857, and 1861. These panics were harrowing experiences, in the course of which even some of the larger institutions were driven precariously close to the brink of failure by a crush of frenzied depositors. In each of the panics the Bank for Savings' trustees relied mainly on their ability to sell government securities, not on fixed specie reserves or cash deposits in commercial banks. During the Panic of 1837 the bank suffered a decline in its deposits of over 18 percent. The darkest hours came on 9 May 1837, when over $81,000 was withdrawn. Philip Hone described that hectic day:

> The press was awful. The hour for closing the bank is six o'clock, but they did not get through the paying of those who were in at that time till nine. I was there with the other trustees and witnessed the madness of the people. Women were nearly pressed to death, and the stoutest men could scarcely sustain themselves, but they held on, as with a death's grip, upon the evidences of their claims, and exhausted as they were with pressure, they had strength to cry, "Pay! Pay!"[47]

To meet these unprecedented withdrawals the bank's officers sold state and city bonds. The bank's minutes show that it received over $860,000 from these forced sales, including approximately $512,000 for Pennsylvania state bonds, about $206,000 for Ohio canal bonds, and between $40,000 and $50,000 each for Indiana state, New York state, and New York City bonds. The most interesting aspect of this episode is that though this bank sold most of these bonds at the height of the Panic, the weighted average of their price *exceeded* the par price by almost 2 percent and was only about 6 percent below the weighted average of the pre-Panic price (1 January 1837).[48] These bonds were remarkedly liquid given the prevailing financial chaos; at the same time that the bank was selling government bonds, the Bowery, Greenwich, and Seamen's were unable to liquidate many of their outstanding mortgage loans,[49] and Philip Hone claimed that lots in New York City were selling at one-tenth their pre-Panic prices.[50] The records of eight New York mutuals show that in subsequent panics government bonds generally could be sold without exorbitant losses, but that mortgage loans and even call loans were almost totally illiquid. When banks tried to call in loans they received promises, excuses, and additional collateral, but very little cash.

In the 1850s the three largest New York mutuals began to rely heavily—and in some cases exclusively—on United States government bonds and Treasury notes for secondary reserves. For example, during the panics of 1854 and 1857 the emergency authorizations issued by the board of trustees of the Bowery Savings Bank specifically directed the bank's president to sell *only* United States debt.[51] Federal debt remained liquid and held its value in part because the United States Treasury assumed some central banking responsibilities and acted as a lender of last resort. In 1854 the Secretary of the Treasury moved a large quantity of gold from Boston to New York and retired approximately $3.8 million of the Treasury's debt during the crisis;[52]

the Bank for Savings and the Bowery sold the Treasury over $1.5 million of its debt, receiving an average price in excess of par. By 1857 the trustees of the Bank for Savings had become so accustomed to dealing directly with the Treasury that they treated it almost as a reserve bank; during the crisis of that year the board directed its funding committee members to "draw funds from the Sub-Treasury from time to time as they think the interests of this Institution require."[53] The combined sales to the Treasury of the three largest mutuals exceeded $2.1 million, most of which was sold during a single week at the height of the run.

This dependence on secondary reserves is particularly interesting in light of Margaret Myers's assertions concerning commercial bank policy: "Liquidity of assets is of course almost as valuable as a specie reserve for the protection of notes and deposits, but American bankers had never learned to manage their investments from that point of view as did European and Canadian bankers. The specie reserve was therefore of primary importance."[54] Given that savings bankers consciously had relied on semi-liquid assets since the 1820s and that many mutual trustees were also prominent commercial bank directors and managers, it hardly seems plausible that commercial bankers never learned to use secondary reserves. The analysis of mutual savings bank portfolio management also gives reason to question Hinderliter and Rockoff's specification of liquid reserves in their recent paper dealing with commercial bank reserve management in the 1850s. "Any asset which could be converted into specie quickly and at low cost could have potentially satisfied a bank's demand for liquidity. However, since secondary markets of this period did not possess the depth and resiliency of *today's* securities markets, only specie and those assets representing demand claims on specie were considered liquid assets in the econometric analysis."[55] A comparison of the depth of the antebellum bond market with the 1970s is hardly relevant. A more interesting question is whether or not the secondary reserve market in the 1850s was sufficiently "deep" and "resilient" to have provided liquidity during a crisis to one or more commercial banks if they had adjusted their portfolios on the margin to hold more government bonds. The experience of mutuals suggests that the market was indeed sufficiently developed to serve this purpose.

## Call Loans and the Issue of Mutual Objectives

The development of the mutual savings banking industry was closely related to events taking place in the commercial banking sector. As institutional and market conditions changed, there sprang up a new impetus to exploit the close ties between commercial banks and mutuals.

Government attempts to regulate commercial banks as well as changes in mutual portfolio constraints increased the profitability of such ties. One of the most important changes was the addition of call loans to mutual portfolios. We shall see that there were marked differences in mutuals' acceptance of this type of asset; many newcomers invested heavily in the call-loan market while the older mutuals made almost no loans of this type. Part of this difference in response might be explained by the fact that newer firms needed to make more risky, higher-yield investments to compensate for diseconomies of scale and the absence of an interest-earning surplus. Part of the difference might be due to variations in the subjective evaluation of risk. But much of the observed difference is attributed to a fundamental difference in trustee objectives.

In 1838 the New York state legislature passed the Free Banking Act, which greatly eased entry into the banking industry. The number of banks in New York City increased and competition between banks increased. This in itself could be expected to force bankers to become more cost-conscious and to stimulate some individuals to gain access to the credit of a mutual savings bank. Particular aspects of the new legislation increased this incentive. The Free Banking Act and subsequent amendments increased the costs of note issues to banks. Legislation required banks to deposit with the state banking department prime government bonds to back note issues; a list specified acceptable collateral and this list changed over time. For every dollar of notes a commercial bank issued, it had to hold a dollar of government debt.[56] This greatly stimulated the movement to deposit banking and increased the competition for deposits. What better source of deposits than a mutual savings bank?

An added incentive for uniting a commercial bank with a mutual was provided by legislation prohibiting commercial banks from suspending payments. Any bank that did not meet the demands of its note holders or depositors would be put into receivership. But savings bank charters allowed them to require notice of withdrawals. Commercial bankers could thus acquire an added measure of safety by conducting some of their deposit business through a savings bank. Another stimulus for commercial bankers to form a mutual savings bank stemmed from the state requirement that commercial banks pay in and maintain their capital stocks. The following discussion shows that the entrance of some mutuals into the call-loan market was linked to the effort of commercial bank managers to circumvent this state regulation.

THE LEGALIZATION OF CALL LOANS

A wide variety of regulations governed the ability of mutuals to make call loans. The first New York City mutual to be granted the right to invest in this manner was the Emigrant Industrial Savings Bank. Its charter of 1850 stipulated that the bank could create a semi-liquid "available fund" of $100,000 or one-third of deposits, whichever was larger.[57] The available fund could be put out at interest as the trustees deemed best; thus no restrictions were placed on how a large amount of money was to be invested. With slight variations every one of the eleven banks chartered after 1850 was given similar authority.[58] In addition to being able to create an available fund, several banks could evidently make any investment whatsoever as long as none, or in some cases no more than one or two, of the trustees present at a regular board meeting objected.[59] These two sections of mutual charters effectively negated most of the other provisions regulating investments if a board was willing to take full advantage of them.

The General Banking Act of 1853 extended to all New York City mutuals the right to make call loans, but on a much more limited basis than was given in the charters of most banks formed in the 1850s. This act allowed any New York City mutual to make loans secured by bonds issued or guaranteed by the United States government, any state, and any city or county in New York state provided "the cash value of such stocks or securities shall . . . be at or above its par value."[60] The banks could lend amounts up to 90 percent of the par value of the securities deposited as collateral. This act essentially stipulated which securities were acceptable collateral, while the charters written after 1850 left this up to trustee discretion.

The difference in response to the legalization of call loans can be seen in Table 17. The Bank for Savings, the Seamen's, and Greenwich did not make any call loans (there are no data for the latter bank for 1854 through 1857). Furthermore, on several occasions the trustees of the Bank for Savings and the Seamen's expressed strong opposition to making such loans for reasons of risk. The Bowery Savings Bank's yearly balance sheets show that it had call loans outstanding only in January of 1854, 1855, and 1857, and that the amount lent never exceeded 3 percent of its total assets. The Bowery's minutes indicate that these loans were all secured by government securities as required by the Act of 1853.[61] Most of the new mutuals lent relatively more of their funds on call than did the older institutions, often 20 percent or more of total assets.

There was nothing inherently risky about call loans if a mutual applied the same standards in making call loans that it applied in making other investments. But in fact the same standards were not

**Table 17** Percentage of Assets Loaned on Call, Nineteen New York Mutual Savings Banks, 1851–1867

| Year | Bank for Savings | Seamen's | Greenwich | Bowery | East River | Dry Dock | Merchants' Clerks | Emigrant Industrial | Manhattan | Broadway |
|---|---|---|---|---|---|---|---|---|---|---|
| 1851 | | 0 | | | | | | | | |
| 1852 | | 0 | | | | | | | 37.0 | ... |
| 1853 | | 0 | | | | | | | ... | 46.3 |
| 1854 | | 0 | | 0.0 | | 1.7 | | | ... | 25.5 |
| 1855 | | 0 | | 2.6 | | 0.0 | | | ... | 3.9 |
| 1856 | | 0 | | 0.0 | | 0.0 | | | 11.4 | 15.2 |
| 1857 | | 0 | | 0.0 | | 11.3 | | | 14.0 | ... |
| 1858 | | 0 | 0.0 | 3.1 | 0.0 | 13.1 | 0.0 | 12.3 | 9.7 | 5.8 |
| 1859 | | 0 | 0.0 | 0.0 | 3.6 | 3.4 | 0.1 | 3.6 | 3.1 | 6.0 |
| 1860 | | 0 | 0.0 | 0.0 | 8.7 | 8.9 | 1.5 | 11.5 | 1.2 | 13.1 |
| 1861 | | 0 | 0.0 | 0.0 | 1.7 | 5.9 | 1.2 | 10.2 | 4.6 | 10.4 |
| 1867 | | 0 | 6.0 | 0.2 | 9.4 | 0.8 | 0.1 | 0 | 7.3 | 3.1 |

| Year | Knickerbocker | Irving | Mechanics' and Traders' | Mariners' | Sixpenny | Rose Hill | Bloomingdale | Union Dime | German |
|---|---|---|---|---|---|---|---|---|---|
| 1854 | 7.0 | ... | | | | | | | |
| 1855 | [a] | ... | | | | | | | |
| 1856 | | ... | | | | | | | |
| 1857 | | ... | ... | | | | | | |
| 1858 | | 15.8 | 16.8 | 16.5 | 0.0 | 0.0 | 0.0 | | |
| 1859 | | 17.0 | 7.0 | 17.6 | 0.0 | 37.1 | 29.0 | | |
| 1860 | | 0.0 | 1.4 | 24.3 | 0.0 | 52.5 | 36.1 | 0.0 | 0.0 |
| 1861 | | 0.0 | 0.0 | 25.1 | 0.0 | 26.9 | 28.6 | 0.0 | 1.3 |
| 1867 | | 0.8 | 0.3 | 17.0 | 0.5 | 15.9 | 36.1 | 1.7 | 2.1 |

Source: Compiled from Appendix C.

[a] Bank failed.

applied. Furthermore, since call loans were supposed to be liquid they were used as secondary reserves, which proved to be risky. In granting real estate loans most mutuals were allowed to lend an amount equal to only 50 percent of the value of the property.[62] The largest margin mutuals required on call loans was 20 percent, and most banks required only 10 percent. More important to the issue of safety was the type of call-loan collateral accepted. Many mutuals accepted a wide range of relatively risky bonds, stocks, and notes which the banks could not directly invest in themselves. Particularly significant was the practice of securing call loans by commercial bank stock. A brief examination of changes that occurred within the commercial banking sector will show that government attempts to regulate commercial banks had a profound and unintended impact on the savings banking industry.

It was a common practice prior to the passage of the Safety Fund Act of 1829 for commercial banks to operate with only a small portion of their authorized capital stock actually paid in. Stockholders in commercial banks used several procedures that permitted them to retain the use of a large percentage of those funds supposedly backing the bank's operations. Subscriptions were often made in installments extending from less than one year to four years. It was common for subscribers, after paying the first installment, to pledge only their partially-paid-for stock back to the bank as security for a loan. This loan could be used to make subsequent payments if required, but in many cases subsequent payments were not compulsory. For example, the charter of the Mechanics' Bank (1810) allowed its directors "to call for payments from its stockholders in such proportions as they saw fit." This practice not only offered the opportunity for larger profits to stockholders and facilitated the expansion of bank credit, but was also a major cause of instability among financial institutions. The dividends a stockholder received often exceeded the interest rate on the loan he took out to finance his purchase. This difference was a clear gain to individual shareholders who invested little if any of their own money. Commercial banks proceeded to incur liabilities that were secured by their capital stock, much of which existed in name only. "In 1818 a committee of the New York legislature reported that the major portion of the circulation of the State had been issued by banks whose nominal capitals were small and composed largely of notes of stockholders, called stock notes."[63] In 1829 the state took the first of a series of steps that would eventually require all of a bank's capital stock to be paid in and prohibit banks from lending on their own stocks, or in some cases the stocks of other banks. The Safety Fund Act of 1829 required a bank's entire capital stock to be paid in but contained no provisions preventing stockholders from purchasing stock with borrowed funds. By the mid-1830s legislation was passed that prohibited banks from taking their own stock in hypothecation, and in 1837 a legislative committee proposed that no bank be allowed to take any bank's stock in hypothecation.[64]

In the 1850s commercial banks could not legally grant loans secured by their own stock, but many mutuals were allowed to make call loans backed by almost any type of stock. Thus by forming a mutual savings bank commercial bankers could circumvent the law; as mutual trustees they could extend credit to stockholders, taking their bank's stock as collateral. All of the commercial bank's stockholders could benefit from this arrangement, for the mutual created a secondary market for the bank's stock, which would enhance its market value. The mutual's credit also made it easier for the directors of the commercial bank to retain control over a majority of the bank's stock, for any stockholder who had a temporary need for cash was less likely to have to sell his shares. But the person who received the loan stood to gain the most, for under normal circumstances there was an opportunity for financial leverage. This was true no matter what type of stock or bond was used as security for the loan.

Data from several mutuals show that call-loan rates ranged between 6 and 7 percent. The stocks and bonds offered as securities almost always paid a higher rate than that charged by the mutuals for the loan. A survey of three New York City newspapers showed that in the 1850s the annual dividends declared on commercial bank capital stock ranged from 7 to 20 percent; the most frequently quoted rates were 7, 8, and 10 percent, which appeared with about the same regularity. Dividends paid on fire insurance companies' stocks were generally higher than those quoted on bank stocks and probably averaged well over 10 percent a year.[65] As an example of the type of leverage that was possible, assume an individual held $1,000 of stock on which he expected to receive a 10 percent dividend. If he had access to a mutual's credit, using his stock as collateral he could borrow up to $900 at perhaps 7 percent. With this sum he could purchase $900 more stock, which he could use for a second loan of up to $810, using it to purchase yet more stock. He could, at least theoretically, continue this process of pyramiding both stock and debt, and with each step his net interest income would increase. Suppose the process was terminated after his $810 loan; if his stocks paid 10 percent, the return on his initial investment would be 14 percent. This practice obviously parallels bank margin lending on stocks before the Crash of 1929.

This type of manipulation offered prospects of large profits to borrowers, but did so at substantial risk to both borrowers and lenders. During financial panics, the entire pyramid of credit could collapse.

Faced with a run a mutual would attempt to call in those loans upon which it relied for secondary reserves. This was often a painfully slow process. The records of four mutuals show that call-ins were often met by tactics of delay and refusals from overextended debtors, and in some cases mutuals were left holding collateral the market value of which was only a small fraction of the loan it was supposed to back. The following discussion will illustrate that some mutuals lent a large percentage of their assets to directors of adjoining commercial banks and insurance companies and that these loans were often backed by the commercial bank's stock.

## THE KNICKERBOCKER SAVINGS BANK

During the Panic of 1854, the Knickerbocker Savings Bank failed when the commercial bank of the same name collapsed. Both banks did business in the same banking rooms and at least four of the mutual trustees were also directors of the commercial bank.[66] The Knickerbocker had the ignominious distinction of being both the first New York state savings bank to fail and the only one to do so during the entire pre-Civil War era. As a result, the circumstances surrounding its downfall were thoroughly investigated by Emerson Keyes.[67] A noteworthy finding of his study is that the savings bank's depositors did not lose all of their savings, for after its assets were liquidated at public sales its depositors eventually received 86.5 percent on the dollar.[68] Table 18 shows the mutual's assets at the time it went into receivership, the amount for which these assets were sold, and the percentage realized from their sale.[69]

Table 18   Financial Structure of Knickerbocker Savings Bank at Time of
Failure in 1854

| Types of Assets | Amount Invested | Amount Realized | Percentage Realized |
|---|---|---|---|
| Bonds and Mortgages | $324,091 | $275,748 | 85 |
| Deposits in Knickerbocker Bank | 114,582 | 113,939 | 99 |
| Notes (mostly secured by Knickerbocker Bank Stock) | 33,000 | 1,000 | 3 |
| Total | $471,673 | $390,687 | 83 |

Source: Emerson W. Keyes, *Special Report on Savings Banks*, pp. 110-11.

Note: All of the figures given above for the amount realized and the amount invested are from Keyes, but the percentages and totals differ. Keyes's sum for column one was $473,673, and the percentages he gave were 75%, 94%, 3% and 86.3%, which were not consistent with his data. It is, of course, entirely possible that his percentages were correct and that there were printing errors in the other figures. The difference between the percentage realized from the sale of securities (82.8) and the percentage realized by depositors (86.5) may be due to interest received on the bank's assets.

Keyes's data offer an indication of the relative liquidity of the various types of assets immediately following the panic. Most significant was the utter worthlessness of the Knickerbocker commercial bank stock as collateral for call loans; it realized only 3 percent of its previous value. Although this is an *ex post* observation, there was ample precedent from earlier commercial bank failures to have forewarned risk-averse trustees. It is also interesting that the mutual's bonds and mortgages realized only 85 percent of the amount lent. The property securing these loans was supposed to have been worth at least twice the amount lent, which implies that the property's market value plummeted by well over 100 percent, or that the mutual's appraisers had been (perhaps intentionally) careless.

From the information Keyes gathered, he concluded that "The Savings bank was in fact little more than a *side issue* of the bank of discount, which, as we see, held nearly twenty-five per cent of its deposits, and whose friends, as owners of its stock had considerable more in the form of loans secured by pledge of the stock as collateral."[70] If this is a valid conclusion for the Knickerbocker, then there were several other mutuals which were also little more than side issues of commercial banks.

THE BROADWAY SAVINGS INSTITUTION

A look at the Broadway Savings Institution will show that it resembled the ill-fated Knickerbocker in many ways. The Broadway Savings Institution was founded in 1851 by a group of twenty-three men, which included seven of the Broadway commercial bank's sixteen directors.[71] Francis A. Palmer, president of the commercial bank, was a vice-president of the savings bank and in 1853 would be elected its president.[72] Francis P. Schoals, who succeeded Palmer as president of the Broadway Savings Institution in 1858, was also a director of the commercial bank.[73] Throughout the pre-Civil War era both banks shared the same building and for the first few years shared some of the same employees. The savings bank kept all its cash reserves on deposit with this one commercial bank and made a substantial proportion of its loans to stockholders of the commercial bank.

In July of 1852 the savings bank's board of trustees authorized one-third of the mutual's deposits to be lent on call. Between January 1853 and April 1855 the Broadway Savings Institution made call loans to thirty-five different individuals and firms, many of whom received more than one loan.[74] Twenty-two of these individuals secured all or part of their loans with Broadway Bank stock and at least seven of them served as directors or officers of the commercial bank in the 1850s.[75] Table 19 exhibits the various types of securities used

Table 19   Securities Used as Collateral for Call Loans, Broadway Savings
Institution, January 1853 to April 1855

| Bank Stocks | Number of Times Used |
|---|---|
| Broadway Bank Stock | 29 |
| Citizen's Bank Stock | 6 |
| Napan Bank Stock | 4 |
| Peoples's Bank Stock | 1 |
| Bank of Commerce Stock | 1 |
| Bank of Panama Stock | 1 |
| Knickerbocker Bank Stock | 1 |
| Langatrick Bank Stock | 1 |
| Lansingburgh Bank Stock | 1 |
| *Railroad Company Stocks* | |
| Panama Railroad Stock | 2 |
| Syracuse and Rochester Railroad Stock | 1 |
| New York & Harlem Railroad Stock | 1 |
| Junction Railroad Company Stock | 1 |
| New York & Erie Railroad Stock | 1 |
| Michigan Central Railroad Stock | 1 |
| Hudson Railroad Company Stock | 1 |
| Cleveland & Toledo Railroad Stock | 1 |
| Vermont Railroad Stock | 1 |
| *City Bonds and State Bonds* | |
| Troy City Bonds | 1 |
| Boston Bonds | 1 |
| Hartford City Bonds | 1 |
| North Carolina Bonds | 1 |
| Pennsylvania Bonds | 1 |
| Wisconsin State Bonds | 1 |
| Kentucky State Bonds | 1 |
| *Other* | |
| Fox River, Wisconsin Improvement Company | 1 |
| Pacific Mails | 1 |
| Park Fire Insurance Company Stock | 1 |

Source: Compiled from Loans on Stock Ledger, 1853–1855, Broadway Savings Institution.

for collateral and the number of times each was used.[76] Although
the Broadway Bank stock was used as collateral for a majority of
the loans made, it probably did not back more than half the amount
lent during most periods; many of the larger loans were secured by
other types of securities. In 1854 about one-tenth of the Broadway
Bank's entire capital stock was being used as collateral to secure
loans from the Broadway Savings Institution.

The size of individual loans ranged from a low of $450 to a
high of $50,000, and as a result of several transactions some balances
temporarily reached $60,000.[77] The duration of these loans ranged

from a few days to several years, but most were paid off within a year. Interest rate information, although fragmentary, suggests the rate of interest varied between 6 and 7 percent.

It is not difficult to see the various advantages that the directors and stockholders of the commercial bank received from organizing a mutual savings bank. The mutual essentially increased the total amount of funds that the commercial bankers could allocate. Under normal conditions the savings bank would keep a relatively large and stable deposit in the commercial bank. The commercial bank could offer a broader spectrum of services by referring its customers to the mutual for mortage and call loans and thus could hope to attract more business and allocate a higher percentage of its own funds into higher-yielding assets. Much of the mutual's funds were lent directly to friends and business associates of its trustees. We have here an excellent example of what was probably a very common practice for mutuals chartered late in the period under study, that of the directors' pre-empting the credit facilities of the bank they controlled.

The close ties noted above between some savings banks and commercial banks were not peculiar to New York. For example, in 1861 the Massachusetts bank commissioners reported that twenty-seven of the eighty-nine savings banks in Massachusetts were "located in the same rooms with banks of discount, and managed by the same officers."[78] The commissioners were quite frank in their opposition to such arrangements: "The evils resulting from this practice are manifold. There is danger of relations growing between the two institutions more intimate than the law allows, and it is almost certain that the interest of one or the other will be ... neglected.... In our examinations we have often found the books of a Saving Bank sadly in arrear, because the treasurer had been too much occupied with his duties as cashier [of the commercial bank] to keep them written up."[79] The evidence presented in this chapter indicates that the commissioners had good cause for concern. Mutuals that were closely tied to commercial banks were likely to behave differently from those without such connections.

Unlike contemporary studies treating the portfolio behavior of financial institutions, the present inquiry has attempted to go beyond the standard *ex post* explanations of the firm's adjustments to market signals. It is not possible to explain all the observed behavior of financial firms without a hopelessly complex model; many observed inter-firm differences remain an unexplained variation often attributed to the implicit and undefined "risk constraint" that applies uniquely to individual financial firms. This is more precisely a measure of our ignorance. The present study is based in part on access to confidential minutes of mutual trustees' meetings, which provide important insights into the *ex ante* decision-making process of individual firms. Variations in mutual behavior can thus be traced not so much to differences in the maximizing behavior or risk constraints between firms, but to imperfections in the market due to the close ties between the mutual and other debt-issuing institutions. Where this was prevalent, in the cases enumerated above, institutional analysis provided a valuable supplement to the standard theoretical treatment—namely, the competitive hypothesis. This is not to say that the subjective evaluation of the mutual's deposit volatility was not an important factor in the risk function of the trustees; it undoubtedly was, but when choices were made to reallocate portfolios, the main factors influencing the trustees (and recorded by them) in their decisions were either rate differentials or non-market returns culled from their close alliances with particular commercial banks. This methodology is absent in studies of current financial institutions, precisely because the information that was accessible for this study is generally unavailable.

CHAPTER 7

# The End of an Era and a
# Look into the Future

When woven together, the different threads of evidence presented in the previous chapters form a fairly consistent pattern. The first mutuals formed in New York City were indeed philanthropic institutions and they tended to maintain this distinction throughout the antebellum years. These mutuals generally had a large amount of trustee input; they refrained from competing for deposits, and some were relatively strict in prohibiting large accounts. They also tended to emphasize portfolio liquidity and safety more than did many of the mutuals organized later in the prewar era. The newer entrants into the savings bank industry differed distinctly in their operating procedures. These banks' trustees readily hired full-time managers, advertised on a daily basis in the financial pages of leading newspapers, raised interest rates on deposits to encourage savers to switch their accounts, and openly welcomed deposits from businessmen. Their portfolios show that they made relatively more risky investments, which offered considerable opportunity for trustee profiteering. In the cases of the few banks for which detailed investment information is available, it is evident that trustees indeed took advantage of this opportunity to further their own financial interests.

By 1861 one phase of the history of mutual savings banks had come to a close. The pressures of almost half a century had transformed what began as a part-time basement operation into a competitive industry of more than twenty firms. The Bank for Savings and the Seamen's still adhered to many of their traditions, but the stress generated by the Civil War accelerated their movement from trustee to professional management. The trustees of the Bank for Savings, more than those of any other mutual, had been faithful to their original motive. The standard objective functions of profit maximization or growth maximization do not adequately summarize this bank's behavior. The bank's trustees had a wider vision, and they were satisfying a deeper need than these objectives convey. The trustees were of an era when success measured a man's worth, but success involved more than amassing personal fortunes. Political activity, patronage of the arts, and philanthropic ventures all increased a man's stature. A trusteeship of the Bank for Savings was the epitome of success; for many New Yorkers there was no higher honor. To John Pintard the bank was the "apex of my little molehill"; to Philip Hone it was the "greatest associated institution in the United States"; to George Templeton Strong it was "the most important of our [philanthropic] institutions." A trusteeship offered another highly desirable commodity—power. What better outlet for the energies of "development enthusiasts" who pioneered canal and railroad networks? Where else could one help finance a transport system and also help the poor? How pleasing it must have been to John Pintard to be able to tell a hesitant New York City Council to go ahead with the Croton Water Works, that as president of the Bank for Savings he would help to see that it was financed. It was in this role as development bankers that the bank's trustees made one of their most lasting contributions. As shown in Chapter 4, their decisions were enormously important to the success of several internal improvement projects and more fundamentally were instrumental in establishing the market for state and municipal debt. But there was an important distinction between the trustees of the Bank for Savings and most other development bankers. Most development bankers view the social overhead project as an end in itself and consider a bank's depositors and subscribers as a means to achieving that end. The Bank for Savings' trustees' public and private statements testify that the trustees considered their investment activity as a means for serving their depositors.

Although early mutual trustees were not motivated by the prospect of personal monetary reward, this did not prevent them from behaving *as if* they were profit maximizers whenever it was consistent with their broader objectives. For a decade the Bank for Savings was the only savings bank in New York City and for another two decades its deposits exceeded the combined deposits of all other mutuals in the city. Thus for several decades the Bank for Savings had considerable monopsony power. At the same time it was the most important institutional lender in a number of markets and had some degree of monopoly power in these markets. By increasing output it drove down the interest rates received on its loans.

The bank's trustees recognized these facts and to a certain extent behaved as profit-maximizing monopolists. The trustees limited inputs and restricted output. Furthermore the trustees, that "damned pack of sharpers," bargained strenuously with borrowers, whether they were state or municipal governments, commercial banks, or individuals. The method the trustees chose to limit deposits was not consistent with profit-maximizing behavior. They favored small acounts and discriminated against large accounts. Because a portion of the cost of servicing accounts was independent of account size and because persons with smaller balances had few alternative investment opportunities, a rational profit maximizer could have captured some of the consumer surplus of poorer savers by paying lower rates on smaller balances. The policy actually followed clearly provided a subsidy to the poorer savers. In another area the trustees did not utilize their monopoly power; they not only allowed but actually encouraged new firms to enter the industry. The evidence indicates that the trustees were following a rational set of policies to accomplish their original goals.

Because of the multiplicity of constraints, the scarcity of comparative data from other types of institutions, and the absence of a well-specified counterfactual world, it is difficult to judge what net impact mutuals had on the efficiency of resource allocation. But as noted above, the bargaining of the larger banks as well as their adjustments to changes in market conditions suggest that there was not a serious misallocation. Furthermore, given the argument that financial intermediaries introduce economies of scale and economies of information that allow them to reduce risks and the average cost of portfolio management, one would expect that mutuals performed a more efficient allocation than private individuals would have in the absence of an intermediary. It is possible to explain most aspects of the investment behavior of nineteenth-century mutuals with the conventional tools of economic analysis. This is an important conclusion, because it means that economists need not resort to cries of irrationality and provincialism in order to explain investment decisions. It is true that most New York mutual loans were made to local residents, but legal constraints along with the greater safety and the lower administrative costs associated with local property loans explain much of their preference for holding local paper. The New York mutuals certainly were not provincial in their purchases of state bonds or in their acceptance of certain securities as collateral for call loans. Their greater willingness to purchase the debt of "foreign" states may have been because New York City was a larger financial center, with more inter-regional and international ties than Boston or Baltimore; hence dealing in the issues of other states was more common. Alternatively, it is possible that one of the reasons why New York City developed as a more prominent source of inter-regional finance was because its mutuals were willing to accept the debt of other states. In addition, long-term credit supplied to local businessmen by New York City mutuals reinforced the other urban agglomeration economies that attracted businesses to the city.

The analysis of mutuals during their formative years provides insights into a wide spectrum of issues. Most obviously it offers a better picture of the banks themselves, of their depositors, and of their trustees. The picture contains more detail than had been supposed—early mutuals were far more than quaint charitable organizations that served the city's downtrodden classes. The banks' part-time nature and humble origins belie the financial power that the larger institutions wielded. More generally, the analysis of New York mutuals provides a standard for evaluating mutuals in other cities and for assessing aspects of commercial bank behavior. It also offers fresh insights into the rationale of state development policies.

These insights are primarily of historical interest; for the most part the issues I have analyzed have their origins in the existing historical literature and only have a tangential bearing on the present and future. At this juncture it would be useful to let contemporary problems guide one last look into the past.

The 1970s have been turbulent years for mutual savings banks. Locked into long-term mortgages, mutuals have been hit by rising interest rates. Given the low average yield on their portfolios, mutuals and savings and loans were unable to raise passbook interest rates high enough to prevent massive disintermediation. (Legally established maximum interest rates on savings accounts obviously played a part, and it is questionable whether in their absence savings institutions could have survived.) In addition to the unfavorable secular rise in interest rates, thrift institutions have been victims of adverse, but quite understandable, fluctuations in net deposits and market interest rates. The banks generally have little new money to invest during periods when interest rates in mortgage and bond markets are high, because many of their more astute customers buy attractively priced securities. Furthermore, because mortgage loans lack the homogeneity of many other types of assets (e.g., government bonds), secondary markets are relatively underdeveloped. These factors mean that once a bank grants a mortgage loan, the bank has undertaken a long-run commitment on which it may be subject to a serious loss or illiquidity. These problems have been so serious that some analysts fear that many thrift institutions will be unable to survive without significant institutional changes. One change that has been widely advocated is that the banks grant variable interest mortgages instead of long-run fixed interest loans. Given this contemporary concern it is worth asking how early mutuals overcame similar difficulties.

As shown in Chapter 3, many nineteenth-century depositors behaved much like present-day customers; the fundamental laws of economic rationality have not changed. The trustees of both the Bank for Savings and the Bowery Savings Bank were incensed by depositors who transferred funds in and out of their accounts to take advantage of alternative investments, and it was in part to rid the Bank for Savings of its more volatile accounts that its trustees took such stern measures to limit the size of accounts. Most antebellum mutuals were unwilling to take such extreme measures, and accordingly their deposits were subject to greater cyclical fluctuations.

An important distinction between the antebellum era and the 1970s is the duration of mortgage loan contracts. In the recent discussions of variable interest rate loans it has generally been ignored that early mutuals granted mortgages similar to those currently being proposed. As a result, when interest rates increased antebellum mutuals were not stuck with a portfolio of low-interest mortgages as their present-day counterparts are. Very few references to the duration of loan contracts appear in bank records. This omission is puzzling, because many records are otherwise very detailed. Out of several thousand entries on mortgage loans only seventeen mention the contract's length. The Bond and Mortgage Books of the Seamen's Bank for Savings show that the bank granted approximately one thousand loans in the prewar era, but only fourteen entries mention the length of the loan contracts; seven were for one year, two were for two years, and five were for three years. All of these loans were made between 1835 and 1845. In addition, the bank's minutes make reference to the duration of two other loan agreements. On 16 June 1845 the board approved a seven-year, $15,000 loan to the American Seamen's Friend Society at an interest rate of 6 percent for the first three years and with the provision that the rate would be renegotiated at the end of three years. On 6 November 1850 the board agreed to extend a ten-year, $6,500 loan on a private house at 7 percent with the provision that the borrower could "pay back at his discretion in sums not less than $1,000 on giving 30 days notice. . . ."[1] These contracts probably were discussed at trustee meetings in part because of their unusual length. The only other reference to the length of a specific agreement appears in the records of the Broadway Savings Bank, which granted a four and one-half year, $1,800 mortgage in 1852.[2]

Although there is no other explicit mention of the contract length, other fragments of evidence indicate that loans were generally of a short duration (probably for one to three years) and in most cases renewed subject to renegotiation of the interest rate. Most banks' records contain numerous references to the trustees' declararing their intentions to change interest rates on loans outstanding. For example, on 12 December 1854 the trustees of the Bank for Savings declared they would increase the interest rate on mortgage loans from 6 to 7 percent as of 1 January 1855 "in all cases where no pre-existing agreement to the contrary intervenes. . . ."[3] In October 1848 the trustees of the Bowery Savings Bank decided to increase the interest rate on all past loans from 6 to 7 percent starting 1 February 1849. In December 1849 the bank's funding committee reported that it had received many applications for reduction of interest on mortgage loans and that competitive pressures compelled the bank to respond favorably. The board decided that as of 1 February 1850 it would reduce until further notice the interest rate from 7 to 6 percent on all old and new loans. These changes in mortgage rates indicate that most loans may have been subject to annual renegotiation. (As of 1841 all interest payable to the bank on mortgage loans was due on the first of February and the first of August, and it is possible that the bank scheduled loans to expire on those dates.) Statements found in 1861 suggest that loans were then made for two years. In May 1861 the board resolved to raise the interest rate to 7 percent starting 1 August 1861 on all mortgages due, "and that interest on the remaining Mortgages be increased to the same per centage [sic] upon the expiration of two years from their respective dates."[4] Similar examples of trustees' changing interest rates on outstanding loans appear in the records of the Dry Dock, Manhattan, and Seamen's savings banks.

Although interest rates on loans were subject to periodic renegotiation, it remains unclear what bounds were placed on these negotiations. As noted in previous chapters, banks were constrained by a 7 percent usury law. One can only speculate as to the importance of this constraint because it appears that the free market rate never exceeded 7 percent for an extended period of years. But if it had exceeded 7 percent for a considerable period of time the banks might have had difficulty calling in loans very fast even though it was legally permissible to do so. Nonetheless, the banks could have adjusted on the margin by calling in some loans and demanding more security to back others. Whatever the formal duration of the loan agreements, as a matter of practice many loans remained outstanding for a decade, and it was not at all unusual to find loans outstanding without any payment having been made on the principal for two or more decades. With a few exceptions the only cases of trustees' threatening to foreclose on loans occurred when the debtor was in arrears. The exceptions came during the worst days of financial panics when a bank's very survival was in question. In such trying moments trustees appealed to borrowers to pay up all or part of their loans. For example, during the Panic of 1837 the Seamen's trustees demanded that four of its borrowers pay 10 percent of the amount loaned them within thirty days.[5] Such appeals usually met with little or no success. Incomplete as it is, the evidence indicates that antebellum mutuals had considerably more flexibility in adjusting the yield on their mortgage portfolios to meet changing market conditions than do today's savings institutions. This extra flexibility was of course a mixed blessing, because it worked to the early banks' disadvantage when interest rates declined.

Further investigation of mortgage loan contracts in the post-Civil War era could yield valuable insights for present-day policymakers. In particular it would be interesting to know what agreements or customs, if any, constrained negotiations when it came time to renew a loan. More generally, a cursory investigation of post-Civil War mutuals suggests that further research would prove valuable. In terms of total assets, mutuals continued to be the most important type of non-bank financial intermediary until the second decade of the twentieth century, yet there has been almost no investigation into their activities. Particular attention might be paid to the events surrounding the Civil War, when there was rapid inflation, and the Panic of 1873, when there were many failures.

The rationale of government policy and the impact of policy on institutions and on resource allocation are topics that deserve further investigation. Most inquiries into the effect of government on early American development have concentrated on the state's direct impact on the investment process as a saver, intermediary, or promoter. There has been much less analysis of the indirect and more subtle effects of government regulation and interference with market mechanisms. This book attempts such an analysis of a limited number of policies that related to the development of savings banks. The constraints written into mutual charters were extremely important, not only in influencing firm behavior and the growth of the industry, but also in allocating resources in a way beneficial to New York state. Commercial bank regulations designed to favor state debt and to stabilize the money supply also influenced the development of other types of intermediaries. State usury laws effectively manipulated the price system—again channeling resources to benefit the state. All of these policies tended to reduce the cost of financing state projects, made it easier for the state to assume new responsibilities, and perhaps led to overinvestment in the public sector.

Finally, the pure theory of the firm in perfect competition is notably lacking in its treatment of the organizational and behavioral characteristics as well as objective functions of cooperative firms. The implicit assumption may be that the traditional principles of cost minimization and profit maximization apply in spite of the claim made by cooperatives that many of the services they produce do not appear on balance sheets or in the market place. There has been a recent increase in the literature on cooperatives dealing with such subjects as Russian collective farms, hospitals, and clubs, all of which attempt to provide some theoretical explanation for cooperative behavior. Misconceptions about the past can distort one's perception of current issues. I hope that elucidating some of the institutional and historical aspects of mutuals hitherto neglected will contribute to our more general knowledge of the cooperative firm.

# Occupations of Mutual Depositors

The banks did not classify their customers in the convenient categories of unskilled laborers, skilled laborers and tradesmen, and professionals, merchants, and property owners. The banks' reports listed the specific occupations of new customers, such as "artists, bakers, lamp lighters, lunatic keepers, and land agents." In all, several hundred different occupations were represented among mutual depositors. In organizing these different occupations into meaningful headings I relied on relative wage rates found in Stanley Lebergott, *Manpower and Economic Growth*, and in the United States Census. The amount of capital and training associated with various occupations influenced the categorization, as did the possibility that a person listing a particular occupation might own his own shop and even be an employer.

For most occupations the grouping was obvious, especially for those most frequently listed, but a number of occupations were difficult to classify. There were also a number of cases where persons listed under the same occupations probably had considerable differences in skill, income, and wealth. For example, some coachmakers, cabinetmakers, bakers, and others similarly occupied, all listed in category two, probably owned their own shops and could have been quite prosperous, while others who were employees were much less wealthy. But in either case people with these occupations most likely had a larger income than those listed among the unskilled laborer classification. There is little doubt that some errors were made in the process of organizing the various occupations into meaningful headings, but probably these errors in judgment offset each other in part.

### Category One: Unskilled Laborers

Included under the heading of domestics were all persons who listed their occupations as butlers, chambermaids, coachmen, cooks, domestics, governesses, housecleaners, housekeepers, ladies' maids, midwives, nurses, servants, stewards, washerwomen, and wet nurses.

Included under the heading of unskilled laborers are all the occupations found in the domestic category as well as boatmen, book folders, boot cleaners, cartmen, chimney sweepers, laborers, lamplighters, market women, night scavengers, paupers, porters, quill dressers, sailors, seamstresses, shoeblacks, soldiers, stevedores, street sweepers, tailoresses, waiters, and watchmen.

### Category Two: Skilled Laborers, Craftsmen, and Tradesmen

Bakers, barbers, bath manufacturers, bedstead makers, blind makers, bit and stirrup filers, blacksmiths, block and pump makers, boilermakers, bookbinders, bookmakers, bootleg crimpers, brass finishers, brewers, butchers, cabinetmakers, calico printers, cap makers, card makers, carpenters, carriage makers, carvers, caulkers, chair makers, chocolate makers, clerks, clothiers, coachmakers, combmakers, coopers, coppersmiths, curriers, cutlers, distillers, dyers, engravers, figure makers, file smiths, fishermen, founders, furriers, gardeners, gas workers, gate makers, glassblowers, glass cutters, gilders, glovers, gold-beaters, gunsmiths, hatters, harness makers, ironmongers, japanners, joiners, lamp makers, lapidaries, last makers, leather dressers, locksmiths, looking-glass frame makers, looking-glass makers, machinists, masons, meter makers, milk-men, millers, millwrights, molders, ostlers, oystermen, paint makers, painters, papermakers, peddlers, pilots, plumbers, potters, printers, riggers, rope makers, saddlers, sailmakers, sash makers, sausage makers, saw makers, sawyers, segar makers, ship carpenters, ship joiners, shipwrights, shoemakers, skinners, stereotype finishers, stockmakers, stonecutters, stove makers, sugar bakers, surgical instrument makers, tailors, tallow candlers, tanners, teachers, tin plate makers, tobacconists, trunkmakers, turners, typefounders, umbrella makers, upholsterers, varnish makers, weavers, wheelwrights.

**Category Three: Professionals, Merchants, and Property Owners**

Included in this category are all savers who listed their occupations as accountants, agents, apothecaries, architects, army officers, artists, attorneys, authors, bankers, botanists, brokers, builders, chemists, clergymen, clock dealers, clockmakers, customs house officers, dentists, doctors, druggists, editors, engine makers, engineers, fancy store keepers, farmers, furniture dealers, gentlemen, goldsmiths, grocers, importers, innkeepers, inspectors, jewelers, judges, lumber merchants, musical instrument makers, musicians, oil dealers, organ builders, perfumers, philosophical instrument makers, physicians, piano-fork makers, reporters, ship captains, shipmasters, shop-keepers, silversmiths, speculators, stage proprietors, storekeepers, students, superintendents, surveyors, tavernkeepers, and watchmakers.

APPENDIX **B**

# Total Amount on Deposit and Number of Accounts in Each Mutual, 1 January 1820-1861

Table B-1   Bank for Savings

| Year | Number of Accounts | Amount on Deposit | Year | Number of Accounts | Amount on Deposit |
|------|------|------|------|------|------|
| 1820 | 1,481 | $ 148,194 | 1841 | 27,543 | $ 3,427,653 |
| 1821 | 2,684 | 413,433 | 1842 | 28,553 | 3,758,913 |
| 1822 | 4,116 | 659,846 | 1843 | 27,970 | 3,505,163 |
| 1823 | 5,383 | 863,465 | 1844 | 29,308 | 3,860,915 |
| 1824 | 7,002 | 1,085,069 | 1845 | 32,515 | 4,635,133 |
| 1825 | 9,043 | 1,388,716 | 1846 | 34,874 | 5,252,187 |
| 1826 | 9,564 | 1,409,592 | 1847 | 35,519 | 5,361,433 |
| 1827 | 10,501 | 1,600,392 | 1848 | 36,921 | 5,705,385 |
| 1828 | 12,249 | 1,867,073 | 1849 | 37,850 | 5,759,345 |
| 1829 | 13,420 | 1,923,054 | 1850 | 38,432 | 5,810,686 |
| 1830 | 14,707 | 2,061,091 | 1851 | 41,000 | 6,386,263 |
| 1831 | 16,506 | 2,346,664 | 1852 | 42,455 | 6,790,082 |
| 1832 | 18,492 | 2,733,351 | 1853 | 43,737 | 7,174,666 |
| 1833 | 19,421 | 2,748,511 | 1854 | 46,997 | 7,901,808 |
| 1834 | 21,914 | 3,105,778 | 1855 | 44,138 | 7,236,003 |
| 1835 | 22,594 | 3,085,738 | 1856 | 44,606 | 7,548,001 |
| 1836 | 25,295 | 3,628,783 | 1857 | 47,945 | 8,317,820 |
| 1837 | 26,427 | 3,533,717 | 1858 | 47,915 | 8,350,546 |
| 1838 | 23,938 | 2,710,358 | 1859 | 48,613 | 8,701,923 |
| 1839 | 25,220 | 2,961,887 | 1860 | 51,041 | 9,544,580 |
| 1840 | 26,457 | 3,125,546 | 1861 | 52,480 | 10,062,617 |

Sources: Compiled from the *Annual Reports of the Trustees of the Bank for Savings in the City of New York, 1820-1862*; Secretary's Minutes, Seamen's Bank for Savings, vols. 1-2, 1829-1862; Report Books, nos. 1 and 2, Seamen's Bank for Savings; Deposit and Withdrawal Books, Seamen's Bank for Savings; *Annual Reports of the Trustees of the Seamen's Bank for Savings* in New York State Senate Documents, 1831, 1833-1834, and *New York State Assembly Documents*, 1835-1837, 1839-1840, 1842-1845, and 1847-1848; *Annual Reports of the Trustees of the Greenwich Savings Bank* in New York State Senate Documents, 1834-1836, 1838-1842, 1844-1845; Secretary's Minutes, Bowery Savings Bank, vols. 1-2, 1834-1862; Andrew Mills, *That's My Bank*, pp. 114, 116; Deposit and Withdrawal Books, Broadway Savings Institution; *Banking Department Reports on Savings Banks* in New York State Senate Documents, 1856-1857, and *New York State Assembly Documents*, 1858-1861; Emerson W. Keyes, *A History of Savings Banks in the United States*, 2:176-260.

**Table B-1**    (Continued)

| Year | Number of Accounts | Seamen's Amount on Deposit | Year | Number of Accounts | Amount on Deposit |
|------|------|------|------|------|------|
| 1830 | 67 | $   14,460 | 1846 | ..... | $   736,432 |
| 1831 | ..... | 36,656 | 1847 | ..... | 1,134,250 |
| 1832 | ..... | 72,144 | 1848 | ..... | 1,941,628 |
| 1833 | ..... | 86,707 | 1849 | 9,326 | 2,673,549 |
| 1834 | ..... | 93,721 | 1850 | 11,762 | 3,723,042 |
| 1835 | 458 | 83,906 | 1851 | 15,130 | 5,075,017 |
| 1836 | ..... | 104,981 | 1852 | 16,566 | 5,326,242 |
| 1837 | ..... | 98,700 | 1853 | 18,410 | 5,942,200 |
| 1838 | ..... | 92,293 | 1854 | 20,053 | 6,334,564 |
| 1839 | 761 | 131,554 | 1855 | 20,567 | 6,433,176 |
| 1840 | 690 | 137,707 | 1856 | 22,102 | 6,825,407 |
| 1841 | 768 | 168,970 | 1857 | 22,727 | 7,179,355 |
| 1842 | 922 | 214,877 | 1858 | 22,458 | 6,930,820 |
| 1843 | 1,027 | 225,004 | 1859 | 23,844 | 7,527,541 |
| 1844 | 1,249 | 321,406 | 1860 | 25,825 | 8,384,715 |
| 1845 | 1,724 | 471,217 | 1861 | 27,292 | 9,144,402 |

| Year | Number of Accounts | Greenwich Amount on Deposit | Year | Number of Accounts | Amount on Deposit |
|------|------|------|------|------|------|
| 1834 | 466 | $   70,988 | 1848 | 2,777 | $   716,556 |
| 1835 | 716 | 120,754 | 1849 | 3,136 | 785,880 |
| 1836 | 1,018 | 177,857 | 1850 | 3,716 | 995,468 |
| 1837 | 1,156 | 198,856 | 1851 | 4,855 | 1,338,010 |
| 1838 | 884 | 139,729 | 1852 | 6,036 | 1,736,274 |
| 1839 | 947 | 164,178 | 1853 | 6,778 | 1,971,277 |
| 1840 | 966 | 181,278 | 1854 | 8,123 | 2,323,344 |
| 1841 | 934 | 198,241 | 1855 | 8,665 | 2,430,220 |
| 1842 | 983 | 230,511 | 1856 | 11,968 | 2,710,253 |
| 1843 | 941 | 209,720 | 1857 | 13,587 | 3,127,898 |
| 1844 | 1,065 | 268,006 | 1858 | 14,475 | 3,356,111 |
| 1845 | 1,495 | 386,196 | 1859 | 15,611 | 3,528,851 |
| 1846 | 1,912 | 493,846 | 1860 | 16,850 | 3,786,125 |
| 1847 | 2,220 | 556,670 | 1861 | 18,076 | 3,898,339 |

**Table B-1** (Continued)

| | Bowery | | | | |
|---|---|---|---|---|---|
| Year | Number of Accounts | Amount on Deposit | Year | Number of Accounts | Amount on Deposit |
| 1835 | 531 | $ 65,111 | 1848 | 11,050 | $ 2,288,258 |
| 1836 | 1,836 | 257,140 | 1849 | 11,863 | 2,347,101 |
| 1837 | 2,166 | 354,816 | 1850 | 13,207 | 2,714,142 |
| 1838 | 1,846 | 294,011 | 1851 | 16,783 | 3,610,542 |
| 1839 | 2,339 | 424,828 | 1852 | 18,617 | 4,041,520 |
| 1840 | 2,731 | 481,200 | 1853 | 18,967 | 4,070,613 |
| 1841 | 3,215 | 623,985 | 1854 | 23,484 | 4,899,817 |
| 1842 | 3,855 | 756,595 | 1855 | 22,937 | 4,865,837 |
| 1843 | 4,095 | 777,151 | 1856 | 25,285 | 5,358,577 |
| 1844 | 4,998 | 989,515 | 1857 | 30,905 | 6,645,566 |
| 1845 | 6,818 | 1,399,988 | 1858 | 30,520 | 6,697,393 |
| 1846 | 8,478 | 1,777,756 | 1859 | 35,393 | 7,818,143 |
| 1847 | 9,610 | 1,978,711 | 1860 | 41,692 | 9,573,400 |
| | | | 1861 | 44,003 | 10,294,995 |

| | East River | | | Dry Dock | |
|---|---|---|---|---|---|
| Year | Number of Accounts | Amount on Deposit | Year | Number of Accounts | Amount on Deposit |
| 1849 | 138 | $ 15,573 | 1849 | 197 | $ 18,887 |
| 1850 | 207 | 25,498 | 1850 | 535 | 86,157 |
| 1851 | 384 | 69,620 | 1851 | 908 | 169,958 |
| 1852 | 606 | 109,052 | 1852 | 1,429 | 306,997 |
| 1853 | 902 | 170,696 | 1853 | 1,787 | 384,804 |
| 1854 | 1,972 | 392,535 | 1854 | 2,506 | 597,709 |
| 1855 | 2,024 | 351,560 | 1855 | 2,655 | 646,600 |
| 1856 | 2,138 | 351,008 | 1856 | 2,944 | 716,968 |
| 1857 | 3,140 | 559,140 | 1857 | 3,560 | 918,890 |
| 1858 | 3,592 | 626,368 | 1858 | 3,653 | 959,119 |
| 1859 | 4,086 | 785,782 | 1859 | 4,235 | 1,147,225 |
| 1860 | 4,652 | 979,451 | 1860 | 5,904 | 1,565,572 |
| 1861 | 5,235 | 1,161,234 | 1861 | 7,121 | 2,026,908 |

| | Merchants' Clerks | | | Emigrant Industrial | |
|---|---|---|---|---|---|
| Year | Number of Accounts | Amount on Deposit | Year | Number of Accounts | Amount on Deposit |
| 1849 | ..... | $ 21,370 | 1849 | ...... | ........ |
| 1850 | ..... | 129,968 | 1850 | ...... | ........ |
| 1851 | ..... | 346,950 | 1851 | 265 | $ 34,899 |
| 1852 | ..... | 596,477 | 1852 | 1,098 | 186,313 |
| 1853 | ..... | 731,585 | 1853 | 2,183 | 455,310 |
| 1854 | 3,150 | 830,811 | 1854 | 3,661 | 813,996 |
| 1855 | 3,859 | 844,355 | 1855 | 3,691 | 822,453 |
| 1856 | 4,072 | 965,830 | 1856 | 4,291 | 1,001,233 |
| 1857 | 4,861 | 1,145,924 | 1857 | 5,461 | 1,302,791 |
| 1858 | 5,240 | 1,191,150 | 1858 | 5,698 | 1,348,730 |
| 1859 | 6,148 | 1,509,889 | 1859 | 6,686 | 1,628,755 |
| 1860 | 7,203 | 1,826,776 | 1860 | 8,487 | 2,172,873 |
| 1861 | 8,079 | 2,103,286 | 1861 | 10,096 | 2,627,542 |

Table B-1   (Continued)

| | Manhattan | | | Broadway | |
| Year | Number of Accounts | Amount on Deposit | Year | Number of Accounts | Amount on Deposit |
|---|---|---|---|---|---|
| 1852 | 1,764 | $   397,221 | 1852 | 263 | $    46,081 |
| 1853 | 2,853 | 688,239 | 1853 | 1,190 | 213,959 |
| 1854 | 3,967 | 969,887 | 1854 | 1,689 | 438,509 |
| 1855 | 4,372 | 1,040,707 | 1855 | 2,196 | 543,542 |
| 1856 | 4,684 | 1,126,836 | 1856 | 2,464 | 587,340 |
| 1857 | 5,783 | 1,394,739 | 1857 | 2,921 | 722,831 |
| 1858 | 6,173 | 1,408,044 | 1858 | 2,951 | 662,446 |
| 1859 | 7,710 | 1,782,067 | 1859 | 3,421 | 841,347 |
| 1860 | 9,554 | 2,278,609 | 1860 | 3,757 | 973,479 |
| 1861 | 11,346 | 2,794,934 | 1861 | 4,063 | 1,102,794 |

| | Irving | | | Mechanics' and Traders' | |
| Year | Number of Accounts | Amount on Deposit | Year | Number of Accounts | Amount on Deposit |
|---|---|---|---|---|---|
| 1852 | 59 | $   35,819 | 1852 | ..... | ....... |
| 1853 | 822 | 198,107 | 1853 | 502 | $   104,340 |
| 1854 | 1,277 | 328,691 | 1854 | 1,260 | 251,974 |
| 1855 | 1,826 | 440,680 | 1855 | 1,613 | 285,525 |
| 1856 | 2,052 | 496,509 | 1856 | 1,641 | 288,758 |
| 1857 | 2,577 | 586,825 | 1857 | 1,736 | 310,646 |
| 1858 | 2,725 | 588,627 | 1858 | 1,834 | 311,687 |
| 1859 | 3,204 | 719,498 | 1859 | 1,956 | 361,612 |
| 1860 | 3,829 | 894,898 | 1860 | 2,106 | 437,474 |
| 1861 | 4,470 | 1,086,548 | 1861 | 2,738 | 532,934 |

| | Mariners' | | | Sixpenny | |
| Year | Number of Accounts | Amount on Deposit | Year | Number of Accounts | Amount on Deposit |
|---|---|---|---|---|---|
| 1854 | 223 | $   37,946 | 1854 | ..... | $   39,080 |
| 1855 | 669 | 119,975 | 1855 | 3,120 | 85,076 |
| 1856 | 580 | 137,070 | 1856 | 3,948 | 82,442 |
| 1857 | 1,369 | 250,694 | 1857 | 4,762 | 81,157 |
| 1858 | 1,539 | 295,967 | 1858 | 5,606 | 85,922 |
| 1859 | 2,032 | 430,054 | 1859 | 6,946 | 112,361 |
| 1860 | 2,635 | 613,746 | 1860 | 8,369 | 146,295 |
| 1861 | 3,244 | 789,025 | 1861 | 8,764 | 176,322 |

| | Rose Hill | | | Bloomingdale | |
| Year | Number of Accounts | Amount on Deposit | Year | Number of Accounts | Amount on Deposit |
|---|---|---|---|---|---|
| 1855 | 93 | $   8,076 | 1855 | 28 | $    1,533 |
| 1856 | 118 | 23,118 | 1856 | 24 | 1,222 |
| 1857 | 143 | 20,836 | 1857 | 33 | 2,274 |
| 1858 | 162 | 35,306 | 1858 | 28 | 668 |
| 1859 | 275 | 71,854 | 1859 | 273 | 56,300 |
| 1860 | 454 | 105,527 | 1860 | 770 | 125,062 |
| 1861 | 555 | 119,020 | 1861 | 1,508 | 302,073 |

**Table B-1**   (Continued)

| Year | Union Dime Number of Accounts | Amount on Deposit | Year | German Number of Accounts | Amount on Deposit |
|------|------|------|------|------|------|
| 1860 | 1,078 | $ 62,013 | 1860 | 1,873 | $ 239,912 |
| 1861 | 3,016 | 254,244 | 1861 | 4,669 | 759,368 |

# Assets of New York City Mutuals on the First of Each Year

**Table C-1** Bank for Savings, 1820–1861

| Year | Total Assets | Mortgage Loans | Total Bonds | Commercial Bank Deposits | Cash | Call Loans | Building | Other |
|---|---|---|---|---|---|---|---|---|
| 1820 | $ 147,912 | $ 0 | $ 147,912 | $ 0 | $0 | $0 | $ 0 | $ 0 |
| 1821 | 535,683 | 0 | 535,683 | 0 | 0 | 0 | 0 | 0 |
| 1822 | 744,480 | 0 | 701,745 | 42,735 | 0 | 0 | 0 | 0 |
| 1823 | 865,238 | 0 | 722,435 | 142,803 | 0 | 0 | 0 | 0 |
| 1824 | 1,098,477 | 0 | 1,005,582 | 92,895 | 0 | 0 | 0 | 0 |
| 1825 | 1,381,637 | 0 | 1,122,847 | 242,944 | 0 | 0 | 15,846 | 0 |
| 1826 | 1,420,327 | 0 | 1,367,690 | 30,350 | 0 | 0 | 22,287 | 0 |
| 1827 | 1,611,044 | 0 | 1,483,863 | 104,888 | 0 | 0 | 22,293 | 0 |
| 1828 | 1,878,397 | 0 | 1,721,807 | 134,297 | 0 | 0 | 22,293 | 0 |
| 1829 | 1,948,325 | 0 | 1,920,307 | 5,724 | 0 | 0 | 22,293 | 0 |
| 1830 | 2,098,394 | 0 | 1,920,307 | 155,794 | 0 | 0 | 22,293 | 0 |
| 1831 | 2,389,982 | 0 | 2,260,912 | 46,777 | 0 | 0 | 22,293 | 0 |
| 1832 | 2,691,684 | 60,000 | 2,448,759 | 160,632 | 0 | 0 | 22,293 | 0 |
| 1833 | 2,751,131 | 60,000 | 2,448,759 | 230,079 | 0 | 0 | 22,293 | 0 |
| 1834 | 3,074,503 | 50,000 | 2,301,599 | 710,661 | 0 | 0 | 22,243 | 0 |
| 1835 | 3,077,498 | 40,000 | 2,345,599 | 679,657 | 0 | 0 | 22,243 | 0 |
| 1836 | 3,564,629 | 30,000 | 3,045,598 | 466,787 | 0 | 0 | 22,243 | 0 |
| 1837 | 3,503,693 | 30,000 | 3,229,599 | 121,851 | 0 | 0 | 22,243 | 0 |
| | | 130,000 | | | | | | |

**Table C-1**  (Continued)

| Year | Total Assets | Mortgage Loans | Total Bonds | Commercial Bank Deposits | Cash | Call Loans | Building | Other |
|---|---|---|---|---|---|---|---|---|
| 1838 | $ 2,749,804 | $ 159,000 | $2,383,192 | $165,985 | $0 | $0 | $ 22,506 | $ 19,122 |
| 1839 | 3,026,609 | 346,000 | 2,383,192 | 254,336 | 0 | 0 | 23,061 | 20,020 |
| 1840 | 3,228,303 | 502,000 | 2,558,192 | 113,723 | 0 | 0 | 23,376 | 31,013 |
| 1841 | 3,565,418 | 502,000 | 2,658,192 | 351,119 | 0 | 0 | 23,376 | 30,731 |
| 1842 | 3,960,735 | 488,000 | 3,054,392 | 364,174 | 0 | 0 | 23,376 | 30,792 |
| 1843 | 3,750,869 | 469,000 | 2,988,843 | 242,027 | 0 | 0 | 23,376 | 27,624 |
| 1844 | 4,138,018 | 319,660 | 3,596,827 | 151,483 | 0 | 0 | 23,376 | 46,672 |
| 1845 | 4,930,744 | 293,400 | 4,427,052 | 84,101 | 0 | 0 | 57,776 | 68,414 |
| 1846 | 5,548,152 | 485,218 | 4,798,472 | 178,753 | 0 | 0 | 31,260 | 54,449 |
| 1847 | 5,736,950 | 489,718 | 4,834,483 | 301,176 | 0 | 0 | 51,993 | 59,580 |
| 1848 | 6,141,875 | 483,718 | 5,181,183 | 360,022 | 0 | 0 | 51,993 | 64,959 |
| 1849 | 6,268,099 | 451,218 | 5,456,669 | 257,400 | 0 | 0 | 30,000 | 72,812 |
| 1850 | 6,314,680 | 499,718 | 5,151,087 | 560,663 | 0 | 0 | 30,000 | 73,211 |
| 1851 | 6,926,513 | 926,918 | 5,150,387 | 745,324 | 0 | 0 | 30,000 | 73,884 |
| 1852 | 7,376,167 | 1,481,518 | 5,459,576 | 347,030 | 0 | 0 | 30,000 | 58,044 |
| 1853 | 7,635,996 | 1,999,268 | 5,116,806 | 420,733 | 0 | 0 | 30,000 | 69,190 |
| 1854 | 8,363,862 | 2,553,433 | 5,400,006 | 380,422 | 0 | 0 | 30,000 | 0 |
| 1855 | 7,846,786 | 2,882,433 | 4,576,806 | 287,847 | 0 | 0 | 99,700 | 0 |
| 1856 | 8,267,888 | 2,950,433 | 4,644,145 | 309,143 | 0 | 0 | 174,323 | 189,844 |
| 1857 | 9,038,581 | 3,062,933 | 5,216,120 | 424,588 | 0 | 0 | 133,925 | 201,015 |
| 1858 | 9,192,534 | 3,229,618 | 5,258,659 | 366,638 | 0 | 0 | 135,925 | 201,694 |
| 1859 | 9,259,997 | 3,231,618 | 5,767,085 | 125,369 | 0 | 0 | 135,925 | 0 |
| 1860 | 10,240,342 | 3,263,868 | 6,555,999 | 49,858 | 0 | 0 | 135,925 | 234,692 |
| 1861 | 10,898,884 | 3,319,450 | 6,953,035 | 264,053 | 0 | 0 | 135,925 | 226,422 |

Sources: Compiled from Trustees' Minutes, Bank for Savings, Vol. 1–7, 1819–1862; Annual Reports of the Trustees of the Bank for Savings in the City of New York, 1820–1862.

Table C-2   Geographical Itemization of Bonds, Bank for Savings

| Year | New York State | New York City | United States | Other States | Other Cities |
|------|---------|---------|---------|---------|---------|
| 1820 | $    97,912 | $    50,000 | $      0 | $      0 | $0 |
| 1821 | 475,465 | 60,218 | 0 | 0 | 0 |
| 1822 | 581,515 | 120,230 | 0 | 0 | 0 |
| 1823 | 581,515 | 140,920 | 0 | 0 | 0 |
| 1824 | 783,087 | 151,713 | 70,782 | 0 | 0 |
| 1825 | 940,507 | 151,300 | 31,039 | 0 | 0 |
| 1826 | 940,507 | 151,300 | 275,882 | 0 | 0 |
| 1827 | 1,090,507 | 151,300 | 242,055 | 0 | 0 |
| 1828 | 1,090,507 | 151,300 | 200,000 | 280,000 | 0 |
| 1829 | 1,090,507 | 349,800 | 200,000 | 280,000 | 0 |
| 1830 | 1,090,507 | 349,800 | 200,000 | 280,000 | 0 |
| 1831 | 1,138,507 | 349,800 | 200,000 | 572,605 | 0 |
| 1832 | 1,138,507 | 313,200 | 66,000 | 931,052 | 0 |
| 1833 | 1,138,507 | 313,200 | 66,000 | 931,052 | 0 |
| 1834 | 591,347 | 113,200 | 66,000 | 1,531,052 | 0 |
| 1835 | 591,347 | 113,200 | 66,000 | 1,575,052 | 0 |
| 1836 | 591,347 | 413,200 | 66,000 | 1,975,052 | 0 |
| 1837 | 591,347 | 713,200 | 0 | 1,925,052 | 0 |
| 1838 | 546,884 | 673,200 | 0 | 1,163,108 | 0 |
| 1839 | 546,884 | 673,200 | 0 | 1,163,108 | 0 |
| 1840 | 546,884 | 673,200 | 100,000 | 1,238,108 | 0 |
| 1841 | 546,884 | 673,200 | 200,000 | 1,238,108 | 0 |
| 1842 | 546,884 | 563,200 | 706,200 | 1,238,108 | 0 |
| 1843 | 546,884 | 563,200 | 634,700 | 1,244,059 | 0 |
| 1844 | 718,698 | 997,070 | 637,000 | 1,244,059 | 0 |
| 1845 | 902,698 | 1,463,395 | 879,400 | 1,181,559 | 0 |
| 1846 | 1,174,448 | 1,906,167 | 511,400 | 1,206,458 | 0 |
| 1847 | 1,127,878 | 1,877,747 | 622,400 | 1,206,458 | 0 |
| 1848 | . . . . . . . . | . . . . . . . . | . . . . . . . . | 1,206,458 | 0 |
| 1849 | 876,878 | 1,910,033 | 1,463,300 | 1,206,458 | 0 |
| 1850 | 704,696 | 1,957,633 | 1,547,300 | 941,458 | 0 |
| 1851 | 576,896 | 1,972,133 | 1,659,900 | 941,458 | 0 |
| 1852 | 629,161 | 1,797,833 | 1,798,500 | 1,234,082 | 0 |
| 1853 | 584,161 | 1,801,013 | 1,277,550 | 1,454,082 | 0 |
| 1854 | 535,161 | 1,751,013 | 1,572,350 | 1,541,482 | 0 |
| 1855 | 504,961 | 1,751,013 | 684,350 | 1,636,482 | 0 |
| 1856 | 640,650 | 2,251,013 | 86,000 | 1,666,482 | 0 |
| 1857 | 815,025 | 2,127,013 | 532,600 | 1,741,482 | 0 |
| 1858 | 1,409,464 | 1,806,713 | 56,000 | 1,986,482 | 0 |
| 1859 | 1,221,464 | 1,172,439 | 1,198,700 | 2,174,482 | 0 |
| 1860 | 1,709,464 | 1,411,353 | 1,466,700 | 1,968,482 | 0 |
| 1861 | 1,572,100 | 1,698,353 | 1,714,100 | 1,968,482 | 0 |

Sources: See Table C-1.

**Table C-3** Seamen's Bank for Savings

| Year | Total Assets | Mortgage Loans | Total Bonds | Commercial Bank Deposits | Cash | Call Loans | Building | Other |
|---|---|---|---|---|---|---|---|---|
| 1831 | $ 36,612 | $ 0 | $ 33,287 | $ 3,325 | $ 0 | $0 | $ 0 | $ 0 |
| 1832 | 72,317 | 0 | 51,374 | 20,942 | 0 | 0 | 0 | 0 |
| 1833 | 87,186 | 0 | 64,769 | 22,417 | 0 | 0 | 0 | 0 |
| 1834 | 94,016 | 0 | 66,166 | 27,851 | 0 | 0 | 0 | 0 |
| 1835 | 84,105 | 20,000 | 47,095 | 17,011 | 0 | 0 | 0 | 0 |
| 1836 | 105,783 | 71,000 | 19,360 | 15,423 | 0 | 0 | 0 | 0 |
| 1837 | 99,769 | 71,000 | 19,209 | 9,560 | 0 | 0 | 0 | 0 |
| 1838 | ...... | ...... | ...... | ...... | 0 | 0 | 0 | 0 |
| 1839 | 134,101 | 84,957 | 17,453 | 31,691 | 0 | 0 | 0 | 0 |
| 1840 | 142,792 | 84,957 | 41,394 | 16,441 | 0 | 0 | 0 | 0 |
| 1841 | 167,620 | 84,957 | 55,602 | 27,061 | 0 | 0 | 0 | 0 |
| 1842 | 225,297 | 84,957 | 107,394 | 32,945 | 0 | 0 | 0 | 0 |
| 1843 | 236,855 | 86,957 | 117,394 | 32,503 | 0 | 0 | 0 | 0 |
| 1844 | 330,934 | 183,755 | 97,394 | 45,769 | 0 | 0 | 0 | 4,016 |
| 1845 | 480,403 | 199,700 | 228,675 | 44,248 | 0 | 0 | 0 | 7,780 |
| 1846 | 735,803 | 391,150 | 272,109 | 63,499 | 0 | 0 | 9,045 | 0 |

**Table C-3** (Continued)

| Year | Total Assets | Mortgage Loans | Total Bonds | Commercial Bank Deposits | Cash | Call Loans | Building | Other |
|---|---|---|---|---|---|---|---|---|
| 1847 | $1,152,856 | $ 597,696 | $ 438,473 | $ 78,438 | $3,336 | $0 | $ 16,795 | $18,118 |
| 1848 | 1,970,399 | 803,550 | 985,647 | 107,175 | 0 | 0 | 36,385 | 37,642 |
| 1849 | 2,731,357 | 1,119,697 | 1,330,497 | 170,591 | 0 | 0 | 58,276 | 52,295 |
| 1850 | ...... | 1,657,000 | ...... | ...... | 0 | 0 | ...... | ..... |
| 1851 | ...... | 1,866,000 | ...... | ...... | 0 | 0 | ...... | ..... |
| 1852 | 5,443,815 | 2,455,969 | 2,603,269 | 182,262 | 0 | 0 | 126,406 | 75,909 |
| 1853 | 6,055,056 | 2,581,225 | 2,899,152 | 376,618 | 0 | 0 | 132,888 | 65,173 |
| 1854 | 6,482,444 | 3,067,050 | 2,867,267 | 352,826 | 0 | 0 | 131,157 | 64,144 |
| 1855 | 6,632,315 | 3,377,350 | 2,783,453 | 275,018 | 0 | 0 | 131,157 | 65,325 |
| 1856 | 7,076,288 | 3,276,650 | 3,337,918 | 254,111 | 0 | 0 | 131,157 | 76,452 |
| 1857 | 7,478,730 | 3,353,400 | 3,484,467 | 435,825 | 0 | 0 | 126,565 | 78,473 |
| 1858 | 7,347,312 | 3,481,017 | 3,156,223 | 517,819 | 0 | 0 | 125,116 | 67,138 |
| 1859 | 7,792,747 | 3,166,617 | 4,097,095 | 370,846 | 0 | 0 | 158,190 | 0 |
| 1860 | 8,634,172 | 3,093,200 | 5,054,945 | 330,090 | 0 | 0 | 155,937 | 0 |
| 1861 | 9,366,383 | 3,121,500 | 5,779,223 | 332,643 | 0 | 0 | 133,017 | 0 |

Sources: Compiled from Secretary's Minutes, Seamen's Bank for Savings, vols. 1–2, 1829–1862; Report Books, nos. 2–3, Seamen's Bank for Savings, 1829–1862; Mortgage Loans of the Seamen's Bank for Savings, 1834–1877 in Ledger A; *Annual Reports of the Trustees of the Seamen's Bank for Savings*, in *New York State Senate Documents*, 1831, 1833–1834 and *New York State Assembly Documents*, 1835–1837, 1839–1840, 1842–1845, and 1847–1848.

**Table C-4**  Geographical Itemization of Bonds, Seamen's Bank for Savings

| Year | New York State | New York City | United States | Other States | Other Cities |
|------|------|------|------|------|------|
| 1831 | $ 11,579 | $  5,514 | $     0 | $  16,194 | $    0 |
| 1832 | 11,579 | 6,718 | 6,100 | 26,977 | 0 |
| 1833 | 27,917 | 6,718 | 13,846 | 16,288 | 0 |
| 1834 | 27,917 | 6,718 | 15,243 | 16,288 | 0 |
| 1835 | 27,917 | 6,718 | 2,247 | 10,213 | 0 |
| 1836 | 19,360 | 0 | 0 | 0 | 0 |
| 1837 | 19,209 | 0 | 0 | 0 | 0 |
| 1838 | . . . . . . . | 0 | 0 | 0 | 0 |
| 1839 | 17,453 | 0 | 0 | 0 | 0 |
| 1840 | 27,394 | 0 | 14,000 | 0 | 0 |
| 1841 | 36,153 | 0 | 0 | 19,449 | 0 |
| 1842 | 67,394 | 0 | 10,000 | 30,000 | 0 |
| 1843 | 87,394 | 0 | 0 | 30,000 | 0 |
| 1844 | 77,394 | 0 | 0 | 20,000 | 0 |
| 1845 | 93,105 | 80,190 | 35,931 | 19,449 | 0 |
| 1846 | 108,129 | 88,980 | 55,000 | 20,000 | 0 |
| 1847 | 143,129 | 126,980 | 148,364 | 20,000 | 0 |
| 1848 | 179,803 | 144,580 | 435,364 | 225,900 | 0 |
| 1849 | 174,653 | 204,580 | 696,364 | 254,900 | 0 |
| 1850 | . . . . . . . | . . . . . . . . | . . . . . . . . | . . . . . . . . | 0 |
| 1851 | . . . . . . | . . . . . . . . | . . . . . . . . | . . . . . . . . | 0 |
| 1852 | 156,753 | 551,384 | 996,000 | 899,132 | 0 |
| 1853 | 106,701 | 993,074 | 569,800 | 1,229,577 | 0 |
| 1854 | 14,523 | 1,132,374 | 210,800 | 1,509,570 | 0 |
| 1855 | 114,523 | 1,061,474 | 96,800 | 1,460,656 | 50,000 |
| 1856 | 264,523 | 1,211,374 | 263,350 | 1,548,671 | 50,000 |
| 1857 | 189,523 | 1,019,236 | 413,850 | 1,811,858 | 50,000 |
| 1858 | 409,308 | 1,019,236 | 0 | 1,677,679 | 50,000 |
| 1859 | 630,394 | 787,322 | 1,228,700 | 1,400,679 | 50,000 |
| 1860 | 856,394 | 734,322 | 2,013,550 | 1,400,679 | 50,000 |
| 1861 | 896,394 | 809,150 | 2,683,000 | 1,325,679 | 65,000 |

Sources: See Table C-3.

**Table C-5**   Greenwich Savings Bank

| Year | Total Assets | Mortgage Loans | Total Bonds | Commercial Bank Deposits | Cash | Call Loans | Building | Other |
|------|------|------|------|------|------|------|------|------|
| 1834 | $ 71,790 | $       0 | $       0 | $ 71,790 | $     0 | $0 | $       0 | $   0 |
| 1835 | 120,158 | 0 | 35,000 | 82,489 | 0 | 0 | 0 | 2,669 |
| 1836 | 177,970 | 0 | 80,731 | 88,854 | 0 | 0 | 0 | 8,385 |
| 1837 | ...... | ...... | ...... | ...... | 0 | 0 | 0 | 0 |
| 1838 | 129,384 | 65,700 | 50,730 | 12,953 | 0 | 0 | 0 | 0 |
| 1839 | 154,248 | 65,200 | 50,730 | 38,317 | 0 | 0 | 0 | 0 |
| 1840 | 176,389 | 60,450 | 64,231 | 44,628 | 0 | 0 | 7,080 | 0 |
| 1841 | 204,876 | 72,750 | 91,231 | 33,665 | 0 | 0 | 7,230 | 0 |
| 1842 | 232,437 | 59,500 | 151,006 | 7,245 | 2,986 | 0 | 11,700 | 0 |
| 1843 | ...... | ...... | ...... | ...... | ...... | 0 | ...... | 0 |
| 1844 | 264,963 | 139,900 | 81,500 | 22,070 | 5,347 | 0 | 16,145 | 0 |
| 1845 | 386,801 | 229,200 | 111,500 | 34,443 | 0 | 0 | 11,657 | 0 |

(No data for years 1846–1855)

| Year | Total Assets | Mortgage Loans | Total Bonds | Commercial Bank Deposits | Cash | Call Loans | Building | Other |
|------|------|------|------|------|------|------|------|------|
| 1856 | 2,819,303 | 1,008,853 | 1,291,582 | 439,565[a] | ..... | ..... | 79,303 | 0 |
| 1857 | 3,311,934 | 1,277,186 | 1,176,852 | 778,593[a] | ..... | ..... | 79,303 | 0 |
| 1858 | 3,440,986 | 1,513,081 | 1,396,637 | 451,965 | ..... | 0 | 79,303 | 0 |
| 1859 | 3,678,180 | 1,634,191 | 1,482,700 | 450,519 | 31,468 | 0 | 79,303 | 0 |
| 1860 | 3,973,707 | 1,457,691 | 2,050,000 | 356,432 | 30,282 | 0 | 79,303 | 0 |
| 1861 | 4,092,195 | 1,458,816 | 2,163,300 | 384,883 | 35,196 | 0 | 50,000 | 0 |

Sources: Compiled from the *Annual Reports of the Trustees of the Greenwich Savings Bank,* in *New York State Senate Documents,* 1834–1836, 1838–1842, 1844–1845; *Banking Department Reports on Savings Banks* in *New York State Senate Documents,* 1856–1857 and *New York State Assembly Documents,* 1858–1861.

[a]Includes cash and call loans.

**Table C-6**  Geographical Itemization of Bonds, Greenwich Savings Bank

| Year | New York State | New York City | United States | Other States | Other Cities |
|---|---|---|---|---|---|
| 1834 | $    0 | $    0 | $0 | $    0 | $0 |
| 1835 | 0 | 0 | 0 | 35,000 | 0 |
| 1836 | 45,731 | 0 | 0 | 35,000 | 0 |
| 1837 | . . . . . | . . . . . | . . . | . . . . . | 0 |
| 1838 | 35,730 | 0 | 0 | 15,000 | 0 |
| 1839 | 35,730 | 0 | 0 | 15,000 | 0 |
| 1840 | 29,731 | 19,500 | 0 | 15,000 | 0 |
| 1841 | 29,731 | 46,500 | 0 | 15,000 | 0 |
| 1842 | 39,731 | 96,275 | 0 | 15,000 | 0 |
| 1843 | . . . . . | . . . . . | 0 | 0 | 0 |
| 1844 | 44,000 | 37,500 | 0 | 0 | 0 |
| 1845 | 44,000 | 67,500 | 0 | 0 | 0 |

(No data for remaining years)

Sources: See Table C-5.

**Table C-7**  Bowery Savings Bank

| Year | Total Assets | Mortgage Loans | Total Bonds | Commercial Bank Deposits | Cash | Call Loans | Building | Other |
|------|------|------|------|------|------|------|------|------|
| 1835 | $ 65,531 | $ 0 | $ 0 | $ 65,531 | $ 0 | $ 0 | $ 0 | $0 |
| 1836 | 256,858 | 242,875 | 0 | 13,983 | 0 | 0 | 0 | 0 |
| 1837 | 353,838 | 306,475 | 0 | 23,244 | 0 | 0 | 0 | 0 |
| 1838 | 301,931 | 236,225 | 28,000 | 13,526 | 0 | 0 | 24,119 | 0 |
| 1839 | 437,572 | 252,425 | 110,144 | 46,948 | 0 | 0 | 24,180 | 0 |
| 1840 | 505,391 | 297,540 | 154,600 | 29,071 | 0 | 0 | 28,055 | 0 |
| 1841 | 665,457 | 312,950 | 262,000 | 66,327 | 0 | 0 | 24,180 | 0 |
| 1842 | 816,216 | 325,400 | 335,533 | 126,803 | 0 | 0 | 28,480 | 0 |
| 1843 | 850,454 | 337,500 | 357,923 | 126,551 | 0 | 0 | 28,480 | 0 |
| 1844 | 1,081,475 | 335,165 | 538,021 | 183,609 | 0 | 0 | 24,680 | 0 |
| 1845 | 1,494,360 | 387,715 | 872,581 | 209,383 | 0 | 0 | 24,680 | 0 |
| 1846 | 1,881,080 | 666,345 | 1,006,181 | 183,874 | 0 | 0 | 24,680 | 0 |
| 1847 | 2,103,605 | 784,795 | 1,065,681 | 228,949 | 0 | 0 | 24,180 | 0 |
| 1848 | 2,439,289 | 935,245 | 1,327,281 | 152,582 | 0 | 0 | 24,180 | 0 |
| 1849 | 2,536,402 | 914,852 | 1,367,623 | 229,747 | 0 | 0 | 24,180 | 0 |
| 1850 | 2,928,469 | 950,671 | 1,530,364 | 423,254 | 0 | 0 | 24,180 | 0 |
| 1851 | 3,851,015 | 1,537,655 | 1,715,087 | 574,093 | 0 | 0 | 24,180 | 0 |
| 1852 | 4,289,608 | 2,144,144 | 1,666,032 | 455,252 | 0 | 0 | 24,180 | 0 |
| 1853 | 4,379,527 | 2,180,019 | 1,794,932 | 308,958 | 0 | 0 | 95,618 | 0 |
| 1854 | 5,270,519 | 2,378,414 | 2,119,232 | 466,977 | 175,188 | 5,000 | 125,708 | 0 |
| 1855 | 5,295,197 | 2,551,200 | 1,746,432 | 339,628 | 391,806 | 137,300 | 128,831 | 0 |
| 1856 | 5,749,523 | 2,568,400 | 2,327,332 | 593,175 | 131,785 | 0 | 128,831 | 0 |
| 1857 | 7,000,400 | 2,673,800 | 3,167,583 | 893,205 | 129,678 | 0 | 136,134 | 0 |
| 1858 | 7,256,563 | 3,109,200 | 3,116,583 | 158,509 | 505,997 | 225,000 | 141,274 | 0 |
| 1859 | 8,274,445 | 3,384,250 | 4,265,659 | 65,970 | 458,566 | 0 | 100,000 | 0 |
| 1860 | 10,020,791 | 3,704,000 | 5,618,159 | 124,254 | 474,378 | 0 | 100,000 | 0 |
| 1861 | 10,844,104 | 4,198,150 | 6,076,859 | 114,656 | 354,439 | 0 | 100,000 | 0 |

Sources: Compiled from Secretary's Minutes, Bowery Savings Bank, vols. 1–2, 1834–1862.

Table C-8    Geographical Itemization of Bonds, Bowery Savings Bank

| Year | New York State | New York City | United States | Other States | Other Cities |
|------|---------------|---------------|---------------|--------------|--------------|
| 1835 | $      0 | $       0 | $       0 | $       0 | $      0 |
| 1836 | 0 | 0 | 0 | 0 | 0 |
| 1837 | 0 | 0 | 0 | 0 | 0 |
| 1838 | 0 | 28,000 | 0 | 0 | 0 |
| 1839 | 0 | 70,000 | 40,144 | 0 | 0 |
| 1840 | 0 | 123,600 | 31,000 | 0 | 0 |
| 1841 | 0 | 175,600 | 35,000 | 51,400 | 0 |
| 1842 | 97,533 | 165,600 | 0 | 72,400 | 0 |
| 1843 | 107,533 | 167,940 | 10,050 | 72,400 | 0 |
| 1844 | 271,313 | 174,308 | 20,000 | 72,400 | 0 |
| 1845 | 300,313 | 181,468 | 260,000 | 130,800 | 0 |
| 1846 | 445,913 | 199,468 | 160,000 | 200,800 | 0 |
| 1847 | 445,413 | 239,468 | 180,000 | 200,800 | 0 |
| 1848 | 445,413 | 205,468 | 295,000 | 381,400 | 0 |
| 1849 | 406,755 | 199,468 | 365,000 | 396,400 | 0 |
| 1850 | 367,196 | 398,968 | 365,000 | 399,200 | 0 |
| 1851 | 399,200 | 596,968 | 365,000 | 353,918 | 0 |
| 1852 | 344,964 | 545,968 | 411,900 | 363,200 | 0 |
| 1853 | 259,363 | 760,468 | 411,900 | 363,200 | 0 |
| 1854 | 259,363 | 1,154,768 | 271,900 | 363,200 | 70,000 |
| 1855 | 259,363 | 1,028,868 | 0 | 363,200 | 95,000 |
| 1856 | 259,363 | 1,333,668 | 294,500 | 341,800 | 98,000 |
| 1857 | 253,863 | 1,786,319 | 677,000 | 352,400 | 98,000 |
| 1858 | 585,863 | 1,887,619 | 88,700 | 456,400 | 98,000 |
| 1859 | 772,939 | 1,887,619 | 1,000,700 | 506,400 | 98,000 |
| 1860 | 895,939 | 1,793,119 | 2,221,700 | 559,400 | 148,000 |
| 1861 | 800,939 | 1,894,819 | 2,673,700 | 559,400 | 148,000 |

Sources: See Table C-7.

**Table C-9**  East River Savings Institution

| Year | Total Assets | Mortgage Loans | Total Bonds | Commercial Bank Deposits | Cash | Call Loans | Building |
|---|---|---|---|---|---|---|---|
| 1849–1854 | ...... | ...... | ...... | ...... | ..... | ..... | ..... |
| 1855 | $ 370,082 | ...... | ...... | ...... | ..... | ..... | ..... |
| 1856 | 364,161 | $222,685 | $ 44,000 | $ 57,476[a] | ..... | ..... | $40,000 |
| 1857 | 578,662 | 249,385 | 118,011 | 171,230[a] | ..... | ..... | 40,037 |
| 1858 | 662,589 | 305,125 | 279,600 | 30,181 | $ 7,647 | ..... | 40,037 |
| 1859 | 829,570 | 251,099 | 401,600 | 86,001 | 6,200 | $30,000 | 54,671 |
| 1860 | 1,023,825 | 269,245 | 554,600 | 69,708 | 7,117 | 89,000 | 34,154 |
| 1861 | 1,210,152[b] | 460,065 | 510,000 | 161,674 | 11,272 | 20,000 | 47,201 |

Sources: Compiled from *Banking Department Reports on Savings Banks* in *New York State Senate Documents, 1856–1857,* and *New York State Assembly Documents, 1858–1861.*

[a]Includes cash and call loans.

[b]The total asset figure is $60 less than the sum of the itemized assets reported.

Table C-10  Dry Dock Savings Institution

| Year | Total Assets | Mortgage Loans | Total Bonds | Commercial Bank Deposits | Cash | Call Loans | Building | Other |
|------|-------------|----------------|-------------|--------------------------|------|-----------|----------|-------|
| 1849 | $ 17,755 | $ 5,000 | $ 0 | $ 12,755 | $ 0 | $ 0 | $ 0 | $0 |
| 1850 | 83,076 | 56,800 | 10,000 | 16,276 | 0 | 0 | 0 | 0 |
| 1851 | 165,574 | 143,800 | 0 | 21,774 | 0 | 0 | 0 | 0 |
| 1852 | 302,513 | 260,000 | 0 | 38,791 | 0 | 0 | 3,721 | 0 |
| 1853 | 380,365 | 287,400 | 0 | 92,965 | 0 | 0 | 0 | 0 |
| 1854 | 591,024[a] | 510,850 | 0 | 69,174 | 10,000 | 0 | 0 | 0 |
| 1855 | 647,254 | 601,100 | 22,750 | 15,554 | 7,850 | 10,000 | 0 | 0 |
| 1856 | 726,910 | 528,950 | 50,000 | 129,511 | 13,046 | 0 | 5,403 | 0 |
| 1857 | 929,365 | 600,134 | 138,000 | 69,287 | 11,542 | 105,000 | 5,403 | 0 |
| 1858 | 972,137 | 568,884 | 230,000 | 29,923 | 12,620 | 127,195 | 3,515 | 0 |
| 1859 | 1,169,402 | 568,450 | 225,000 | 273,410 | 6,500 | 50,000 | 46,042 | 0 |
| 1860 | 1,566,515 | 584,250 | 592,500 | 188,184 | 6,500 | 140,000 | 55,081 | 0 |
| 1861 | 2,026,929[b] | 771,070 | 812,500 | 189,586 | 96,192 | 120,500 | 55,081 | 0 |

Sources: Compiled from Secretary's Minutes, Dry Dock Savings Institution, vol. 1, 1848-1862; Minutes of the Funding Committee, Dry Dock Savings Institution, 1848-1862.

[a]The total asset figure is $9,000 less than the sum of the itemized assets reported.

[b]The total asset figure is $18,000 less than the sum of the itemized assets reported.

Table C-11    Geographical Itemization of Bonds, Dry Dock Savings
Institution

| Year | New York State | New York City | United States | Other States | Other Cities |
|---|---|---|---|---|---|
| 1849 | $0 | $    0 | $    0 | $0 | $    0 |
| 1850 | 0 | 10,000 | 0 | 0 | 0 |
| 1851 | 0 | 0 | 0 | 0 | 0 |
| 1852 | 0 | 0 | 0 | 0 | 0 |
| 1853 | 0 | 0 | 0 | 0 | 0 |
| 1854 | 0 | 0 | 0 | 0 | 0 |
| 1855 | 0 | 0 | 0 | 0 | 22,750 |
| 1856 | 0 | 0 | 0 | 0 | 50,000 |
| 1857 | 0 | 88,000 | 0 | 0 | 50,000 |
| 1858 | 0 | 180,000 | 0 | 0 | 50,000 |
| 1859 | 0 | 0 | 175,000 | 0 | 50,000 |
| 1860 | 0 | 330,000 | 200,000 | 0 | 62,500 |
| 1861 | 0 | 500,000 | 250,000 | 0 | 62,500 |

Sources: See Table C-10.

**Table C-12** Institution for the Savings of Merchants' Clerks

| Year | Total Assets | Mortgage Loans | Total Bonds | Commercial Bank Deposits | Cash | Call Loans | Building |
|---|---|---|---|---|---|---|---|
| 1849-1855 | ..... | ..... | ..... | ..... | ..... | ..... | ..... |
| 1856 | $ 960,041 | $446,150 | $ 392,307 | $ 64,249[a] | ..... | ..... | $57,335 |
| 1857 | 1,157,539 | 538,900 | 443,252 | 117,837[a] | ..... | ..... | 57,546 |
| 1858 | 1,202,287 | 657,800 | 464,173 | 22,425 | ..... | ..... | 57,889 |
| 1859 | 1,529,810 | 727,450 | 635,152 | 100,994 | ..... | $ 2,000 | 64,214 |
| 1860 | 1,858,744 | 829,550 | 824,814 | 111,972 | ..... | 28,000 | 64,408 |
| 1861 | 2,149,231 | 974,350 | 1,005,045 | 79,242 | ..... | 26,000 | 64,594 |

Sources: Compiled from *Banking Department Reports on Savings Banks* in *New York State Senate Documents*, 1856–1857, and *New York State Assembly Documents*, 1858–1861.
[a] Includes cash and call loans.

**Table C-13** Emigrant Industrial Savings Bank

| Year | Total Assets | Mortgage Loans | Total Bonds | Commercial Bank Deposits | Cash | Call Loans | Building |
|---|---|---|---|---|---|---|---|
| 1852-1855 | ..... | ..... | ..... | ..... | ..... | ..... | ..... |
| 1856 | $1,039,017 | $436,170 | $ 393,300 | $159,547[a] | ..... | ..... | $ 50,000 |
| 1857 | 1,371,274 | 419,266 | 496,100 | 405,908[a] | ..... | ..... | 50,000 |
| 1858 | 1,409,530 | 553,777 | 545,939 | 61,798 | $19,465 | $173,106 | 55,445 |
| 1859 | 1,695,951 | 752,253 | 651,546 | 123,184 | 24,865 | 61,375 | 82,729 |
| 1860 | 2,202,093 | 777,542 | 915,526 | 119,821 | 25,669 | 252,310 | 111,226 |
| 1861 | 2,657,733 | 968,133 | 1,106,476 | 163,174 | 36,061 | 271,250 | 112,640 |

Sources: Compiled from *Banking Department Reports on Savings Banks* in *New York State Senate Documents*, 1856–1857, and *New York State Assembly Documents*, 1858–1861.
[a] Includes cash and call loans.

**Table C-14**  Manhattan Savings Institution

| Year | Total Assets | Mortgage Loans | Total Bonds | Commercial Bank Deposits | Cash | Call Loans | Building |
|---|---|---|---|---|---|---|---|
| 1852[a] | ...... | ...... | ........ | ...... | ...... | $149,450 | ..... |
| 1856 | $1,321,430 | $ 691,453 | $ 200,000 | $195,563 | $ 79,229 | 150,000 | $ 5,185 |
| 1857 | 1,426,702 | 724,984 | 131,409 | 234,416 | 130,984 | 200,000 | 4,910 |
| 1858 | 1,425,597 | 862,052 | 256,790 | 139,104 | 20,265 | 138,550 | 8,837 |
| 1859 | 1,839,785 | 829,554 | 699,356 | 198,461 | 47,015 | 57,000 | 8,399 |
| 1860 | 2,342,004 | 969,161 | 1,131,980 | 159,951 | 33,941 | 27,535 | 19,436 |
| 1861 | 2,881,313 | 1,019,142 | 1,419,615 | 234,800 | 54,603 | 131,020 | 22,132 |

Sources: Compiled from *Banking Department Reports on Savings Banks* in *New York State Senate Documents*, 1856–1857, and *New York State Assembly Documents*, 1858–1861; Secretary's Minutes, Manhattan Savings Institution, vol. 1, 1851–1852.

[a] No data for 1853–55.

**Table C-15** Broadway Savings Institution

| Year | Total Assets | Mortgage Loans | Total Bonds | Commercial Bank Deposits | Cash | Call Loans | Building |
|------|-------------|----------------|-------------|--------------------------|------|------------|----------|
| 1853 | $ 214,284 | $ 75,300 | $ 0 | $ 37,909 | $ 0 | $ 99,100 | $0 |
| 1854 | 442,297 | 186,700 | 69,267 | 51,741 | 15,016 | 112,575 | 0 |
| 1855 | 552,775 | 282,500 | 154,000 | 43,381 | 41,646 | 21,272 | 0 |
| 1856 | 590,866 | 295,575 | 144,000 | 43,878 | 17,652 | 89,761 | 0 |
| 1857 | 720,218 | 375,550 | 118,000 | 235,668[a] | ...... | ...... | 0 |
| 1858 | 689,920[b] | 404,400 | 134,000 | 82,723 | 28,342 | 40,000 | 0 |
| 1859 | 872,968[c] | 360,650 | 360,100 | 82,169 | 71,609 | 52,440 | 0 |
| 1860 | 1,010,897 | 449,150 | 272,100 | 75,587 | 82,120 | 131,940 | 0 |
| 1861 | 1,148,794 | 487,500 | 289,100 | 92,662 | 160,155 | 119,377 | 0 |

Sources: Compiled from *Banking Department Reports on Savings Banks* in *New York State Senate Documents*, 1865–1857, and *New York State Assembly Documents*, 1858–1861; Trustees' Minutes, Broadway Savings Institution, vol. 1, 1851–1862.

[a] Includes cash and call loans.

[b] The total asset figure is $455 larger than the sum of the itemized reported assets.

[c] The total asset figure is $54,000 less than the sum of the itemized assets. This inconsistency may be due to a printing error in the cash figure reported as $71,609. If this is changed to $17,609, the sum of assets would equal the total figure reported.

**Table C-16**  Irving Savings Institution

| Year | Total Assets | Mortgage Loans | Total Bonds | Commercial Bank Deposits | Cash | Call Loans | Building |
|---|---|---|---|---|---|---|---|
| 1852–1855 | ...... | ...... | ...... | ...... | ...... | ...... | ...... |
| 1856 | $ 456,902 | $228,667 | 0 | $204,304ᵃ | ...... | ...... | $23,931 |
| 1857 | 575,243 | 278,777 | $135,600 | 136,935ᵃ | ...... | ...... | 23,931 |
| 1858 | 600,817 | 327,168 | 81,100 | 27,699 | $ 45,850 | $ 95,000 | 24,000 |
| 1859 | 736,323 | 409,828 | 83,400 | 49,050 | 45,045 | 125,000 | 24,000 |
| 1860 | 912,226 | 467,600 | 325,800 | 49,455 | 44,946 | 425 | 24,000 |
| 1861 | 1,109,421 | 542,100 | 363,800 | 46,499 | 133,022 | 0 | 24,000 |

Sources: Compiled from Banking Department Reports on Savings Banks in New York State Senate Documents, 1856–1857, and New York State Assembly Documents, 1858–1861.

ᵃIncludes cash and call loans.

**Table C-17**  Mechanics' and Traders' Savings Institution

| Year | Total Assets | Mortgage Loans | Total Bonds | Commercial Bank Deposits | Cash | Call Loans | Building |
|---|---|---|---|---|---|---|---|
| 1853–1855 | ...... | ...... | ...... | ...... | ...... | ...... | ...... |
| 1856 | $287,512 | $188,800 | $ 75,750 | $22,962ᵃ | ...... | ...... | ...... |
| 1857 | 314,620 | 190,200 | 105,000 | 17,420ᵃ | ...... | ...... | $2,000 |
| 1858 | 319,606 | 200,400 | 13,000 | 27,446 | $2,944 | $53,600 | 2,500 |
| 1859 | 372,417 | 176,350 | 95,718 | 45,340 | 3,753 | 26,000 | 2,500 |
| 1860 | 443,635 | 183,700 | 176,452 | 67,672 | 3,879 | 6,400 | 2,500 |
| 1861 | 542,444 | 218,950 | 273,049 | 34,363 | 3,402 | 0 | 2,500 |

Sources: Compiled from Banking Department Reports on Savings Banks in New York State Senate Documents, 1856–1857 and New York State Assembly Documents, 1858–1861.

ᵃIncludes cash and call loans.

**Table C-18**  Mariners' Savings Institution

| Year | Total Assets | Mortgage Loans | Total Bonds | Commercial Bank Deposits | Cash | Call Loans | Building |
|---|---|---|---|---|---|---|---|
| 1854–1855 | ..... | ..... | ..... | ..... | ..... | ..... | ..... |
| 1856 | $130,005 | $ 71,200 | 0 | $58,805[a] | ..... | ..... | ..... |
| 1857 | 244,038 | 95,890 | $ 32,500 | 115,988[a] | ..... | ..... | $ 450 |
| 1858 | 293,505 | 124,257 | 91,890 | 25,855 | $ 2,503 | $ 48,550 | 450 |
| 1859 | 430,141 | 157,607 | 132,951 | 37,396 | 2,137 | 75,550 | 24,500 |
| 1860 | 611,322 | 200,357 | 172,871 | 51,606 | 12,946 | 148,542 | 25,000 |
| 1861 | 780,845 | 245,107 | 233,906 | 76,980 | 3,682 | 196,169 | 25,000 |

Sources: Compiled from *Banking Department Reports on Savings Banks* in *New York State Senate Documents*, 1856–1857, and *New York State Assembly Documents*, 1858–1861.

[a] Includes cash and call loans.

**Table C-19**  Sixpenny Savings Bank

| Year | Total Assets | Mortgage Loans | Total Bonds | Commercial Bank Deposits | Cash | Call Loans | Building |
|---|---|---|---|---|---|---|---|
| 1854–1855 | ..... | ..... | ..... | ..... | ..... | ..... | ..... |
| 1856 | $ 76,134 | $ 73,595 | $ 0 | $ 2,539[a] | ..... | ..... | ..... |
| 1857 | 78,511 | 72,554 | 0 | 5,957[a] | ..... | ..... | ..... |
| 1858 | 84,817 | 43,428 | 0 | 5,100 | $3,803 | $0 | $29,080 |
| 1859 | 113,548 | 43,428 | 7,303 | 22,749 | 4,327 | 0 | 30,058 |
| 1860 | 146,965[b] | 50,275 | 40,421 | 16,334 | 5,203 | 0 | 30,058 |
| 1861 | 178,543 | 120,233 | 14,000 | 33,989 | 4,138 | 0 | 0 |

Sources: Compiled from *Banking Department Reports on Savings Banks* in *New York State Senate Documents*, 1856–1857, and *New York State Assembly Documents*, 1858–1861.

[a] Includes cash and call loans.

[b] The total asset figure is $529 less than the sum of the itemized assets reported.

**Table C-20**  Rose Hill Savings Bank

| Year | Total Assets | Mortgage Loans | Total Bonds | Commercial Bank Deposits | Cash | Call Loans | Building |
|---|---|---|---|---|---|---|---|
| 1855 | ...... | ...... | ...... | | | | |
| 1856 | $ 20,342 | $ 0 | $ 0 | $20,342[a] | ..... | ..... | $0 |
| 1857 | 20,882 | 0 | 0 | 20,882[a] | ..... | ..... | 0 |
| 1858 | 35,306 | 20,000 | 10,000 | 2,978 | $ 0 | $ 0 | 0 |
| 1859 | 72,285 | 37,000 | 4,000 | 1,349 | 931 | 26,829 | 0 |
| 1860 | 108,493 | 32,000 | 4,000 | 4,846 | 8,558 | 57,000 | 0 |
| 1861 | 123,539 | 32,000 | 0 | 56,276 | 370 | 33,200 | 0 |

Sources: Compiled from *Banking Department Reports on Savings Banks* in *New York State Assembly Documents*, 1858–1861, and *New York State Senate Documents*, 1856–1857.
[a] Includes cash and call loans.

**Table C-21**  Bloomingdale Savings Bank

| Year | Total Assets | Mortgage Loans | Total Bonds | Commercial Bank Deposits | Cash | Call Loans | Building |
|---|---|---|---|---|---|---|---|
| 1855 | ...... | ...... | ...... | | | | |
| 1856 | $ 1,237 | $ 0 | $ 0 | $ 1,237[a] | ..... | ..... | $0 |
| 1857 | 2,234 | 0 | 0 | 2,234[a] | ..... | ..... | 0 |
| 1858 | 1,508 | 0 | 0 | 158 | $ 424 | $ 0 | 0 |
| 1859 | 57,599 | 20,038 | 0 | 4,753 | 15,608 | 16,700 | 0 |
| 1860 | 126,328 | 57,450 | 10,000 | 7,382 | 5,866 | 45,630 | 0 |
| 1861 | 304,577 | 100,450 | 79,468 | 19,075 | 8,451 | 87,134 | 0 |

Sources: Compiled from *Banking Department Reports on Savings Banks* in *New York State Assembly Documents*, 1858–1861, and *New York State Senate Documents*, 1856–1857.
[a] Includes cash and call loans.

**Table C-22** Union Dime Savings Institution

| Year | Total Assets | Mortgage Loans | Total Bonds | Commercial Bank Deposits | Cash | Call Loans | Building |
|---|---|---|---|---|---|---|---|
| 1860 | $ 62,013 | $ 29,255 | $15,000 | $14,885 | $2,090 | $0 | $783 |
| 1861 | 255,595 | 219,050 | 0 | 32,150 | 4,395 | 0 | 0 |

Sources: Compiled from Banking Department Reports on Savings Banks in New York State Assembly Documents, 1860–1861.

**Table C-23** German Savings Bank

| Year | Total Assets | Mortgage Loans | Total Bonds | Commercial Bank Deposits | Cash | Call Loans | Building |
|---|---|---|---|---|---|---|---|
| 1860 | $239,955[a] | $ 48,700 | $130,000 | $52,328 | $ 6,508 | $ 0 | $2,154 |
| 1861 | 762,588 | 210,000 | 447,109 | 72,092 | 22,050 | 10,000 | 1,338 |

Sources: Compiled from Banking Department Reports on Savings Banks in New York State Assembly Documents, 1860–1861.
[a]The total asset figure is $265 larger than the sum of the itemized assets reported.

# APPENDIX D

## Total Amount on Deposit and Number of Accounts in All New York City Mutuals, 1 January 1820-1861[a]

Table D-1

| Year | Number of Accounts | Amount on Deposit |
|------|--------------------|-----------------|
| 1820 | 1,481 | $    148,194 |
| 1821 | 2,684 | 413,433 |
| 1822 | 4,116 | 659,846 |
| 1823 | 5,383 | 863,465 |
| 1824 | 7,002 | 1,085,069 |
| 1825 | 9,043 | 1,388,716 |
| 1826 | 9,564 | 1,409,592 |
| 1827 | 10,501 | 1,600,392 |
| 1828 | 12,249 | 1,867,073 |
| 1829 | 13,420 | 1,923,054 |
| 1830 | 14,774 | 2,075,551 |
| 1831 | 16,506 | 2,383,320 |
| 1832 | 18,492 | 2,805,495 |
| 1833 | 19,421 | 2,835,218 |
| 1834 | 22,380 | 3,270,487 |
| 1835 | 24,299 | 3,355,509 |
| 1836 | 28,149 | 4,168,761 |
| 1837 | 29,749 | 4,186,089 |
| 1838 | 26,668 | 3,236,391 |
| 1839 | 29,267 | 3,682,447 |
| 1840 | 30,844 | 3,925,733 |
| 1841 | 32,460 | 4,418,849 |
| 1842 | 34,313 | 4,960,896 |
| 1843 | 34,033 | 4,717,038 |
| 1844 | 36,620 | 5,439,842 |
| 1845 | 42,552 | 6,892,534 |
| 1846 | 45,264 | 8,260,221 |
| 1847 | 47,349 | 9,031,064 |
| 1848 | 50,748 | 10,651,827 |
| 1849 | 62,510 | 11,621,705 |
| 1850 | 67,859 | 13,484,961 |
| 1851 | 79,325 | 17,031,259 |
| 1852 | 88,893 | 19,572,078 |
| 1853 | 98,131 | 22,105,796 |
| 1854 | 118,362 | 26,160,671 |
| 1855 | 122,453 | 26,155,318 |
| 1856 | 132,917 | 28,220,572 |

Table D-1    (Continued)

| Year | Number of Accounts | Amount on Deposit |
|------|--------------------|--------------------|
| 1857 | 151,510 | 32,567,386 |
| 1858 | 154,569 | 32,848,904 |
| 1859 | 170,433 | 37,023,202 |
| 1860 | 196,079 | 43,710,507 |
| 1861 | 216,755 | 49,236,585 |

Source: Appendix B.

[a] The reader should refer to Appendix B to ascertain for which banks there are data in specific years.

# Cumulative Assets of All New York City Mutuals, 1 January 1820-1861[a]

Table E-1 Total Assets

| Year | Total Assets | Mortgage Loans | Total Bonds | Commercial Bank Deposits | Cash | Call Loans | Building | Other |
|------|------|------|------|------|------|------|------|------|
| 1820 | $ 147,912 | $ 0 | $ 147,912 | $ 0 | $ 0 | $ 0 | $ 0 | $ 0 |
| 1821 | 535,683 | 0 | 535,683 | 0 | 0 | 0 | 0 | 0 |
| 1822 | 744,480 | 0 | 701,745 | 42,735 | 0 | 0 | 0 | 0 |
| 1823 | 865,238 | 0 | 722,435 | 142,803 | 0 | 0 | 0 | 0 |
| 1824 | 1,098,477 | 0 | 1,005,582 | 92,895 | 0 | 0 | 15,846 | 0 |
| 1825 | 1,381,637 | 0 | 1,122,847 | 242,944 | 0 | 0 | 22,287 | 0 |
| 1826 | 1,420,327 | 0 | 1,367,690 | 30,350 | 0 | 0 | 22,293 | 0 |
| 1827 | 1,611,044 | 0 | 1,483,863 | 104,888 | 0 | 0 | 22,293 | 0 |
| 1828 | 1,878,397 | 0 | 1,721,807 | 134,297 | 0 | 0 | 22,293 | 0 |
| 1829 | 1,948,325 | 0 | 1,920,307 | 5,724 | 0 | 0 | 22,293 | 0 |
| 1830 | 2,098,394 | 0 | 1,920,307 | 155,794 | 0 | 0 | 22,293 | 0 |
| 1831 | 2,426,594 | 60,000 | 2,294,199 | 50,102 | 0 | 0 | 22,293 | 0 |
| 1832 | 2,764,001 | 60,000 | 2,500,133 | 181,574 | 0 | 0 | 22,293 | 0 |
| 1833 | 2,838,317 | 50,000 | 2,513,528 | 252,496 | 0 | 0 | 22,293 | 0 |
| 1834 | 3,240,309 | 40,000 | 2,367,765 | 810,302 | 0 | 0 | 22,243 | 0 |
| 1835 | 3,347,292 | 50,000 | 2,427,694 | 844,688 | 0 | 0 | 22,243 | 2,669 |
| 1836 | 4,105,240 | 343,875 | 3,145,689 | 585,047 | 0 | 0 | 22,243 | 8,385 |

**Table E-1** (Continued)

| Year | Total Assets | Mortgage Loans | Total Bonds | Commercial Bank Deposits | Cash | Call Loans | Building | Other |
|------|------|------|------|------|------|------|------|------|
| 1837 | $ 3,957,300 | $ 507,475 | $ 3,248,808 | $ 154,655 | $ 0 | $ 0 | $ 46,362 | $ 0 |
| 1838 | 3,181,119 | 460,925 | 2,461,922 | 192,464 | 0 | 0 | 46,686 | 19,122 |
| 1839 | 3,752,530 | 748,582 | 2,561,519 | 371,292 | 0 | 0 | 51,116 | 20,020 |
| 1840 | 4,052,875 | 944,947 | 2,818,417 | 203,863 | 0 | 0 | 54,636 | 31,013 |
| 1841 | 4,603,371 | 972,657 | 3,067,025 | 478,172 | 0 | 0 | 54,786 | 30,731 |
| 1842 | 5,234,685 | 957,857 | 3,648,325 | 531,167 | 2,986 | 0 | 63,556 | 30,792 |
| 1843 | 4,838,178 | 893,457 | 3,464,160 | 401,081 | 0 | 0 | 51,856 | 27,624 |
| 1844 | 5,815,390 | 978,480 | 4,313,742 | 402,931 | 5,347 | 0 | 64,201 | 50,688 |
| 1845 | 7,292,308 | 1,110,015 | 5,639,808 | 372,175 | 0 | 0 | 94,113 | 76,194 |
| 1846 | 8,165,035 | 1,542,713 | 6,076,762 | 426,126 | 0 | 0 | 64,985 | 54,449 |
| 1847 | 8,993,411 | 1,872,209 | 6,338,637 | 608,563 | 3,336 | 0 | 92,968 | 77,698 |
| 1848 | 10,551,563 | 2,222,513 | 7,494,111 | 619,779 | 0 | 0 | 112,558 | 102,601 |
| 1849 | 11,553,613 | 2,490,767 | 8,154,789 | 670,493 | 0 | 0 | 112,456 | 125,107 |
| 1850 | 9,326,225 | 3,164,189 | 6,691,451 | 1,000,193 | 0 | 0 | 54,180 | 73,211 |
| 1851 | 10,943,102 | 4,474,373 | 6,865,474 | 1,341,191 | 0 | 0 | 54,180 | 73,854 |
| 1852 | 17,412,103 | 6,341,631 | 9,728,877 | 1,023,335 | 0 | 149,450 | 184,307 | 133,953 |
| 1853 | 18,665,228 | 7,123,212 | 9,810,890 | 1,237,183 | 0 | 99,100 | 258,506 | 134,363 |
| 1854 | 21,150,146 | 8,696,447 | 10,455,772 | 1,321,140 | 200,204 | 127,575 | 286,865 | 64,144 |
| 1855 | 21,344,409 | 9,694,583 | 9,283,441 | 961,438 | 441,302 | 158,572 | 359,688 | 65,325 |
| 1856 | 29,887,559 | 12,987,581 | 12,900,314 | 2,556,407 | 241,712 | 239,761 | 695,468 | 266,296 |
| 1857 | 34,248,933 | 13,912,759 | 14,762,894 | 4,065,973 | 272,204 | 305,000 | 660,204 | 279,488 |
| 1858 | 34,935,014 | 15,400,207 | 15,034,594 | 1,950,321 | 649,860 | 901,001 | 703,371 | 268,832 |
| 1859 | 38,725,168 | 15,750,383 | 18,908,665 | 2,037,560 | 718,024 | 522,894 | 810,531 | 0 |
| 1860 | 45,524,027 | 16,466,994 | 24,445,167 | 1,850,365 | 750,003 | 926,782 | 839,965 | 234,692 |
| 1861 | 51,333,270 | 18,476,066 | 27,526,485 | 2,388,797 | 927,428 | 1,014,650 | 773,428 | 226,422 |

Source: Appendix C

<sup></sup>ªThe reader should refer to Appendix C to ascertain for which banks there are data in specific years.

Table E-2   Geographical Itemization of Bonds, All Banks

| Year | New York State | New York City | United States | Other States | Other Cities |
|------|------|------|------|------|------|
| 1820 | $   97,912 | $   50,000 | $   0 | $   0 | $   0 |
| 1821 | 475,465 | 60,218 | 0 | 0 | 0 |
| 1822 | 581,515 | 120,230 | 0 | 0 | 0 |
| 1823 | 581,515 | 151,713 | 0 | 0 | 0 |
| 1824 | 783,087 | 140,900 | 70,782 | 0 | 0 |
| 1825 | 940,507 | 151,300 | 31,039 | 0 | 0 |
| 1826 | 940,507 | 151,300 | 275,882 | 0 | 0 |
| 1827 | 1,090,507 | 151,300 | 242,055 | 0 | 0 |
| 1828 | 1,090,507 | 151,300 | 200,000 | 280,000 | 0 |
| 1829 | 1,090,507 | 349,800 | 200,000 | 280,000 | 0 |
| 1830 | 1,090,507 | 349,800 | 200,000 | 280,000 | 0 |
| 1831 | 1,150,086 | 355,314 | 200,000 | 588,799 | 0 |
| 1832 | 1,150,086 | 319,918 | 72,100 | 958,029 | 0 |
| 1833 | 1,166,424 | 319,918 | 79,846 | 947,340 | 0 |
| 1834 | 619,264 | 119,918 | 81,243 | 1,547,340 | 0 |
| 1835 | 619,264 | 119,918 | 68,247 | 1,620,265 | 0 |
| 1836 | 656,438 | 413,200 | 66,000 | 2,010,052 | 0 |
| 1837 | 610,556 | 713,200 | 0 | 1,925,052 | 0 |
| 1838 | 582,614 | 701,200 | 0 | 1,178,108 | 0 |
| 1839 | 600,067 | 743,200 | 40,144 | 1,178,108 | 0 |
| 1840 | 604,009 | 816,300 | 145,000 | 1,253,108 | 0 |
| 1841 | 612,768 | 895,300 | 235,000 | 1,323,957 | 0 |
| 1842 | 751,542 | 825,075 | 716,200 | 1,355,508 | 0 |
| 1843 | 741,811 | 731,140 | 644,750 | 1,346,459 | 0 |
| 1844 | 1,111,405 | 1,208,878 | 657,000 | 1,336,459 | 0 |
| 1845 | 1,340,116 | 1,792,553 | 1,175,331 | 1,331,808 | 0 |
| 1846 | 1,728,490 | 2,194,615 | 726,400 | 1,427,258 | 0 |
| 1847 | 1,716,420 | 2,244,195 | 950,764 | 1,427,258 | 0 |
| 1848 | 625,216 | 350,048 | 730,364 | 1,813,758 | 0 |
| 1849 | 1,458,286 | 2,314,081 | 2,524,664 | 1,857,758 | 0 |
| 1850 | 1,071,892 | 2,366,601 | 1,912,300 | 1,340,658 | 0 |
| 1851 | 976,096 | 2,569,101 | 2,024,900 | 1,295,376 | 0 |
| 1852 | 1,130,878 | 2,895,185 | 3,206,400 | 2,496,414 | 0 |
| 1853 | 950,225 | 3,554,555 | 2,259,250 | 3,046,859 | 0 |
| 1854 | 809,047 | 4,038,155 | 2,055,050 | 3,414,252 | 7,000 |
| 1855 | 878,847 | 3,841,355 | 781,150 | 3,460,338 | 167,750 |
| 1856 | 1,164,536 | 4,796,055 | 643,850 | 3,556,953 | 198,000 |
| 1857 | 1,258,411 | 5,020,568 | 1,623,450 | 3,905,740 | 198,000 |
| 1858 | 2,404,635 | 4,893,568 | 144,700 | 4,120,561 | 198,000 |
| 1859 | 2,624,797 | 3,847,380 | 3,603,100 | 4,081,561 | 198,000 |
| 1860 | 3,461,797 | 4,268,794 | 5,901,950 | 3,928,561 | 260,500 |
| 1861 | 3,269,433 | 4,902,322 | 7,320,800 | 3,853,561 | 275,500 |

Source: Appendix C.

APPENDIX F

# Balances in Commercial Banks
# on 1 January

**Table F-1**  Balances in Commercial Banks on 1 January, Bank for Savings

| Year | Commercial Bank | Amount | Total | Interest and Terms (%)[a] |
|------|-----------------|--------|-------|---------------------------|
| 1822 | Mechanics' Bank | $ 42,735 | | 5 |
| 1823 | Mechanics' Bank | 142,803 | | 5 |
| 1824 | Mechanics' Bank | 92,895 | | 5 |
| 1825 | Mechanics' Bank | 242,944 | | 5 |
| 1826 | Mechanics' Bank | 30,350 | | 5 |
| 1827 | Mechanics' Bank | 104,888 | | 5 |
| 1828 | Mechanics' Bank | 134,297 | | 5 |
| 1829 | Mechanics' Bank | 5,724 | | 5 |
| 1830 | Mechanics' Bank | 155,794 | | 5 |
| 1831 | Mechanics' Bank | 46,777 | | 5 |
| 1832 | Mechanics' Bank | 160,632 | | 5 |
| 1833 | Mechanics' Bank | 230,079 | | 5 |
| 1834 | Mechanics' Bank | 310,661 | | 5 |
| | Bank of America | 100,000[b] | | |
| | Bank of New York | 300,000[b] | $710,661 | |
| 1835 | Mechanics' Bank | 279,657 | | 5 |
| | Bank of America | 100,000[b] | | |
| | Bank of New York | 300,000[b] | 679,657 | |
| 1836 | Union Bank | 166,787 | | ... |
| | Bank of New York | 300,000[b] | 466,787 | |
| 1837 | Union Bank | 121,851 | | ... |
| 1838 | Union Bank | 165,985 | | ... |
| 1839 | Union Bank | 254,336 | | ... |
| 1840 | Union Bank | $113,723 | | ... |
| 1841 | Union Bank | 351,119 | | ... |
| 1842 | Union Bank | 364,174 | | ... |
| 1843 | Union Bank | 242,027 | | ... |
| 1844 | Union Bank | 151,483 | | ... |
| 1845 | Union Bank | 84,101 | | ... |
| 1846 | Union Bank | 178,753 | | ... |
| 1847 | Union Bank | 301,176 | | ... |
| 1848 | Manhattan Company Bank | 360,022 | | ... |
| 1849 | Manhattan Company Bank | 257,400 | | ... |
| 1850 | Manhattan Company Bank | 560,663 | | 2.5 to 4[c] |
| 1851 | Manhattan Company Bank | 745,324 | | 2.5 to 4 |
| 1852 | Manhattan Company Bank | 347,030 | | 2.5 to 4 |

Table F-1   (Continued)

| Year | Commercial Bank | Amount | Total | Interest and Terms (%) |
|------|-----------------|--------|-------|------------------------|
| 1853 | Manhattan Company Bank | 420,733 | | 2.5 to 4 |
| 1854 | Manhattan Company Bank | . . . . . . . | | 2.5 to 4 |
| | Bank of Commerce | . . . . . . . | $380,422 | 2.5 to 4 |
| 1855 | Manhattan Company Bank | 167,694 | | 2.5 to 4 |
| | Bank of Commerce | 120,153 | 287,847 | 2.5 to 4 |
| 1856 | Manhattan Company Bank | 169,143 | | 2.5 to 4 |
| | Bank of Commerce | 140,000 | 309,143 | 2.5 to 4 |
| 1857 | Manhattan Company Bank | 204,588 | | 2.5 to 4 |
| | Bank of Commerce | 220,000 | 424,588 | 2.5 to 4 |
| 1858 | Manhattan Company Bank | 166,638 | | 2.5 to 4 |
| | Bank of Commerce | 200,000 | 366,638 | 2.5 to 4 |
| 1859 | Manhattan Company Bank | 75,337 | | 2.5 to 4 |
| | Bank of Commerce | 50,033 | 125,369 | 2.5 to 4 |
| 1860 | Manhattan Company Bank | . . . . . . . | | . . . |
| | Bank of Commerce | . . . . . . . | 49,858 | . . . |
| 1861 | Manhattan Company Bank | . . . . . . . | | . . . |
| | Bank of Commerce | . . . . . . . | | . . . |
| | Bank of New York | . . . . . . . | 264,053 | . . . |

Sources: Compiled from Minutes, Bank for Savings, 1819-1861.

[a] All deposits are demand deposits except where noted otherwise.

[b] Time deposit for which there is no interest information.

[c] In the 1850s, Bank for Savings received from 2.5% to 4% from the Bank of Commerce and Manhattan Company Bank on their balances.

Table F-2   Balances in Commercial Banks on 1 January, Seamen's Bank for Savings

| Year | Commercial Bank | Amount | Total | Interest and Terms (%) |
|------|-----------------|--------|-------|------------------------|
| 1830 | Fulton Bank | $      0 | | 5 |
| 1831 | Fulton Bank | 3,325 | | 5 |
| 1832 | Fulton Bank | 20,942 | | 5 |
| 1833 | Fulton Bank | 22,417 | | 5 |
| 1834 | Fulton Bank | 27,851 | | 5 |
| 1835 | Fulton Bank | 17,011 | | 5 |
| 1836 | Fulton Bank | 15,423 | | 5 |
| 1837 | Fulton Bank | 9,560 | | 5 |
| 1838 | Fulton Bank | . . . . . . . | | 5 |
| 1839 | Mechanics' Bank | 31,691 | | 5 |
| 1840 | Leather Manufacturers' Bank | 16,441 | | . . . |
| 1841 | Leather Manufacturers' Bank | 27,061 | | . . . |
| 1842 | Leather Manufacturers' Bank | 32,945 | | . . . |
| 1843 | Leather Manufacturers' Bank | 32,903 | | . . . |

Table F-2    (Continued)

| Year | Commercial Bank | Amount | Total | Interest and Terms (%) |
|------|-----------------|--------|-------|------------------------|
| 1844 | Leather Manufacturers' Bank | 45,769 | | ... |
| 1845 | Leather Manufacturers' Bank | 44,248 | | 3[a] |
| 1846 | Leather Manufacturers' Bank | 63,499 | | ... |
| 1847 | Leather Manufacturers' Bank | 78,438 | | ... |
| 1848 | Leather Manufacturers' Bank | 107,175 | | ... |
| 1849 | Leather Manufacturers' Bank | 170,591 | | ... |
| 1850 | Leather Manufacturers' Bank | ....... | | ... |
| 1851 | Leather Manufacturers' Bank | ....... | | ... |
| 1852 | Leather Manufacturers' Bank | $179,862 | | ... |
| | Bank of Commerce | 2,400 | $182,262 | ... |
| 1853 | Leather Manufacturers' Bank | 176,618 | | ... |
| | Bank of Commerce | 200,000 | 376,618 | ... |
| 1854 | Leather Manufacturers' Bank | 98,082 | | ... |
| | Bank of Commerce | 245,744 | 352,826 | .. |
| 1855 | Leather Manufacturers' Bank | 55,796 | | ... |
| | Bank of Commerce | 219,232 | 275,028 | ... |
| 1856 | Leather Manufacturers' Bank | ....... | | ... |
| | Bank of Commerce | ....... | 254,111 | ... |
| 1857 | Leather Manufacturers' Bank | 59,716 | | ... |
| | Bank of Commerce | 376,109 | 435,825 | ... |
| 1858 | Leather Manufacturers' Bank | 67,138 | | ... |
| | Bank of Commerce | 450,681 | 517,819 | ... |
| 1859 | Leather Manufacturers' Bank | 54,827 | | ... |
| | Bank of Commerce | 316,019 | 370,846 | ... |
| 1860 | Leather Manufacturers' Bank | 61,426 | | ... |
| | Bank of Commerce | 268,664 | 330,090 | ... |
| 1861 | Leather Manufacturers' Bank | 133,054 | | ... |
| | Bank of Commerce | 199,589 | 332,643 | ... |

Sources: Compiled from Secretary's Minutes, Seamen's Bank for Savings, vols. 1 and 2, 1829–1861.

[a] As of January 1845 the rate of interest was *reduced* to 3% on the average monthly balance.

**Table F-3**   Balances in Commercial Banks on 1 January, Greenwich
Savings Bank

| Year | Commercial Bank | Amount | Total | Interest and Terms (%) |
|------|-----------------|--------|-------|------------------------|
| 1834 | Greenwich Bank | $71,790 | | 5 |
| 1835 | Greenwich Bank | 82,489 | | 5 |
| 1836 | Greenwich Bank | 48,854 | | 5 |
| | Commercial Bank | 40,000 | $ 88,854 | 5 |
| 1837 | Greenwich Bank | . . . . . | | . . . |
| | Commercial Bank | . . . . . | . . . . . | . . . |
| 1838 | Greenwich Bank | 7,957 | | . . . |
| | Commercial Bank | 5,000 | 12,953 | . . . |
| 1839 | Greenwich Bank | 33,317 | | . . . |
| | Commercial Bank | 5,000 | 38,317 | . . . |
| 1840 | Greenwich Bank | 39,628 | | 5 |
| | Commercial Bank | 5,000 | 44,628 | 5 |
| 1841 | Greenwich Bank | 28,665 | | 5 |
| | Commercial Bank | 5,000 | 33,665 | 5 |
| 1842 | Greenwich Bank | 7,245 | | . . . |
| | Commercial Bank | . . . . . | | . . . |
| 1843 | . . . | . . . . . | | . . . |
| 1844 | Greenwich Bank | 22,070 | | . . . |
| 1845 | Greenwich Bank | 34,443 | | . . . |
| | (no data 1846 to 1857) | | | |
| 1858 | Greenwich Bank & | . . . . . | . . . | |
| | Others | . . . . . | 451,965 | . . . |
| 1859 | Greenwich Bank & | . . . . . | | . . . |
| | Others | . . . . . | 450,519 | . . . |
| 1860 | Greenwich Bank & | . . . . . | | . . . |
| | Others | . . . . . | 356,432 | . . . |
| 1861 | Greenwich Bank & | . . . . . | | . . . |
| | Others | . . . . . | 384,883 | . . . |

Sources: Compiled from the *Annual Reports* in *New York State Senate Documents*, 1834-1836,
1837-1842, 1844-1845, and *New York State Assembly Documents*, 1858-1861.

**Table F-4**   Balances in Commercial Banks on 1 January, Bowery Savings
Bank

| Year | Commercial Bank | Amount | Total | Interest and Terms (%) |
|------|-----------------|--------|-------|------------------------|
| 1835 | Butchers' and Drovers' Bank | $ 64,651 | | 5 |
| 1836 | Butchers' and Drovers' Bank | 13,983 | | 0 |
| 1837 | Butchers' and Drovers' Bank | 23,246 | | 0 |
| 1838 | Butchers' and Drovers' Bank | 13,526 | | 0 |
| 1839 | Butchers' and Drovers' Bank | 46,948 | | 0 |
| 1840 | Butchers' and Drovers' Bank | 29,071 | | 0 |
| 1841 | Butchers' and Drovers' Bank | 41,327 | | 0 |
| | Butchers' and Drovers' Bank | 25,000[a] | $ 66,327 | |
| 1842 | Butchers' and Drovers' Bank | 126,803 | | 0 |
| 1843 | Butchers' and Drovers' Bank | 126,551 | | 0 |
| 1844 | Butchers' and Drovers' Bank | 183,609 | | 0 |
| 1845 | Butchers' and Drovers' Bank | 209,383 | | b |
| 1846 | Butchers' and Drovers' Bank | 183,874 | | b |
| 1847 | Butchers' and Drovers' Bank | 228,949 | | c |
| 1848 | Butchers' and Drovers' Bank | 152,582 | | c |
| 1849 | Butchers' and Drovers' Bank | 229,747 | | c |
| 1850 | Butchers' and Drovers' Bank | 423,254 | | c |
| 1851 | Butchers' and Drovers' Bank | 574,093 | | c |
| 1852 | Butchers' and Drovers' Bank | 250,841 | | d |
| | Bowery Bank | 51,109 | | e |
| | Broadway Bank | 51,108 | | e |
| | Pacific Bank | 51,097 | | e |
| | Mercantile Bank | 51,097 | 455,352 | e |
| 1853 | Butchers' and Drovers' Bank | $225,765 | | d |
| | Bowery Bank | 31,375 | | e |
| | Broadway Bank | 31,375 | | e |
| | Pacific Bank | 20,444 | $308,958 | e |
| 1854 | Butchers' and Drovers' Bank | 72,551 | | d |
| | Bowery Bank | 36,378 | | e |
| | Broadway Bank | 61,200 | | e |
| | Pacific Bank | 43,115 | | e |
| | Tradesmen's Bank | 40,893 | | e |
| | Continental Bank | 152,838 | | e |
| | Fulton Bank | 60,000 | 466,977 | e |
| 1855 | Butchers' and Drovers' Bank | 63,535 | | d |
| | Bowery Bank | 26,058 | | e |
| | Broadway Bank | 42,413 | | e |
| | Pacific Bank | 30,390 | | e |
| | Tradesmen's Bank | 28,075 | | e |
| | Continental Bank | 94,874 | | e |
| | Fulton Bank | 42,611 | | e |
| | Manhattan Company Bank | 11,668 | 339,628 | e |
| 1856 | Butchers' and Drovers' Bank | 83,116 | | d |
| | Bowery Bank | 35,611 | | e |
| | Broadway Bank | 30,611 | | e |

Table F-4    (Continued)

| Year | Commercial Bank | Amount | Total | Interest and Terms (%) |
|------|-----------------|--------|-------|------------------------|
| 1856 | Pacific Bank | 42,849 | | e |
| | Tradesmen's Bank | 61,200 | | e |
| | Continental Bank | 152,048 | | e |
| | Fulton Bank | 61,200 | | e |
| | Manhattan Bank | 131,784 | 593,175 | e |
| 1857 | Butchers' and Drovers' Bank | $ 76,133 | | d |
| | Bowery Bank | 35,704 | | e |
| | Broadway Bank | 60,929 | | e |
| | Pacific Bank | 42,841 | | e |
| | Tradesmen's Bank | 61,200 | | e |
| | Continental Bank | 152,588 | | e |
| | Fulton Bank | 61,200 | | e |
| | Manhattan Bank | 202,207 | | e |
| | Mechanics' and Traders' Bank | 20,400 | | e |
| | Market Bank | 100,000 | | e |
| | Park Bank | 80,000 | $893,205 | e |
| 1858 | Butchers' and Drovers' Bank | 55,217 | | ... |
| | Broadway Bank | 12,905 | | ... |
| | Pacific Bank | 12,733 | | ... |
| | Continental Bank | 20,561 | | ... |
| | Fulton Bank | 45,345 | | ... |
| | Park Bank | 11,746 | 158,509 | ... |
| 1859 | Butchers' and Drovers' Bank | 65,970 | | ... |
| 1860 | Butchers' and Drovers' Bank | 79,253 | | ... |
| | Mechanics' and Traders' Bank | 45,000 | 124,254 | ... |
| 1861 | Butchers' and Drovers' Bank | 68,656 | | ... |
| | Mechanics' and Traders' Bank | 46,000 | 114,656 | ... |

Sources: Compiled from Secretary's Minutes, Bowery Savings Bank, vols. 1 and 2, 1834–1861.

[a] Time deposit receiving interest; rate of interest unknown.

[b] 4% on first $40,000; no interest on the balance in excess of $40,000.

[c] 3% on first $100,000; no interest on the balance in excess of $100,000.

[d] 4% on first $100,000; 3% on balance in excess of $100,000.

[e] Time deposit received 4%; ten days' notice required on withdrawals over $10,000.

**Table F-5**    Balances in Commercial Banks on 1 January, Dry Dock Savings Institution

| Year | Commercial Bank | Amount | Total | Interest and Terms (%) |
|------|-----------------|--------|-------|------------------------|
| 1849 | Bowery Bank | $ 12,755 | | 6 |
| 1850 | Bowery Bank | 16,276 | | 4 |
| 1851 | Bowery Bank | 21,774 | | . . . |
| 1852 | Bowery Bank | 38,791 | | . . . |
| 1853 | Bowery Bank | 92,965 | | . . . |
| 1854 | Bowery Bank | 59,174 | | . . . |
| | Citizen's Bank | 5,000 | | . . . |
| | Pacific Bank | 5,000 | $ 69,174 | . . . |
| 1855 | Bowery Bank | 9,164 | | . . . |
| | Oriental Bank | 6,390 | 15,554 | . . . |
| 1856 | Broadway Bank | 40,000 | | . . . |
| | Pacific Bank | 30,000 | | . . . |
| | Citizen's Bank | 30,000 | | . . . |
| | Oriental Bank | 29,511 | 129,511 | . . . |
| 1857 | Pacific Bank | 20,000 | | 5 |
| | Oriental Bank | 39,287 | | 5 |
| | Shoe & Leathers' Bank | 10,000 | 69,287 | 5 |
| 1858 | Broadway Bank | 2,000 | | . . . |
| | Citizen's Bank | 3,000 | | . . . |
| | Oriental Bank | 24,922 | 29,922 | . . . |
| 1859 | Broadway Bank | 221,000 | | . . . |
| | Oriental Bank | 52,410 | 273,410 | . . . |
| 1860 | Broadway Bank | 90,000 | | . . . |
| | Oriental Bank | 98,184 | 188,183 | . . . |

Sources: Compiled from Secretary's Minutes, Dry Dock Savings Institution, vol. 1, 1848–1860.

**Table F-6**   Balances in Commercial Banks on 1 January, Manhattan
Savings Institution

| Year | Commercial Bank | Amount | Total | Interest and Terms (%) |
|---|---|---|---|---|
| 1852 | Bowery Bank | ... | | 4 |
| | Citizen's Bank | ... | | 4 |
| 1853 | Bowery Bank | ... | | 4 |
| | Citizen's Bank | ... | | 4 |
| 1854 | Bowery Bank | ... | | 4 |
| | Citizen's Bank | ... | | 4 |
| 1855 | Bowery Bank | ... | | 4 |
| | Citizen's Bank | ... | | 4 |
| 1856 | Bowery Bank | ... | | 4 |
| | Citizen's Bank | ... | $195,563 | 4 |
| 1857 | Bank of North America | $50,000 | | 5.5[a] |
| | Bank of North America & | ..... | | 5 |
| | Others | ..... | 234,416 | 5 |
| 1858 | Bank of North America | 50,000 | | 5.5[a] |
| | Bank of North America & | ..... | | 5 |
| | Others | ..... | 139,104 | 5 |
| 1859 | Shoe and Leathers' Bank | ..... | | 5[a] |
| | St. Nicholas Bank | ..... | 198,416 | 4 |
| 1860 | Shoe and Leathers' Bank | ..... | | 5[a] |
| | St. Nicholas Bank | ..... | 159,951 | 4 |
| 1861 | Shoe and Leathers' Bank | ..... | | ... |
| | St. Nicholas Bank | ..... | | ... |
| | Mfrs.' and Merchants' Bank | ..... | | ... |
| | Importers' and Traders' Bank | ..... | 234,800 | ... |

Sources: Compiled from Secretary's Minutes, Manhattan Savings Institution, vol. 1, 1851–1862; Minutes of the Finance Committee, Manhattan Savings Institution, 1851–1859.
[a]Time deposit.

**Table F-7**   Balances in Commercial Banks on 1 January, Broadway Savings
Institution

| Year | Commercial Bank | Amount | Total | Interest and Terms (%) |
|---|---|---|---|---|
| 1853 | Broadway Bank | $37,909 | | ... |
| 1854 | Broadway Bank | 51,741 | | ... |
| 1855 | Broadway Bank | 43,381 | | ... |
| 1856 | Broadway Bank | 43,878 | | ... |
| 1857 | Broadway Bank | ... | | ... |
| 1858 | Broadway Bank | 82,723 | | ... |
| 1859 | Broadway Bank | 82,169 | | ... |
| 1860 | Broadway Bank | 75,587 | | ... |
| 1861 | Broadway Bank | 92,662 | | ... |

Sources: Compiled from Trustees' Minutes, Broadway Savings Institution, vol. 1, 1852–1861.

# Notes

CHAPTER 1

1. Peter L. Payne and Lance E. Davis, *The Savings Bank of Baltimore, 1818-1866*, p. 22.

2. Emerson W. Keyes, *A History of Savings Banks in the United States*, 1: 46.

3. National Association of Mutual Savings Banks, *National Fact Book* (May 1969), 6.

4. United States Bureau of the Census, *Historical Statistics of the United States, Colonial Times to 1957*, p. 676.

5. Lance E. Davis, Jonathan R. T. Hughes, and Duncan M. McDougall, *American Economic History*, p. 202.

6. Keyes, *Savings Banks in the United States*, 1: 15-18; H. Oliver Horne, *A History of Savings Banks*, pp. 1-8, 31-32.

7. Horne, *Savings Banks*, pp. 50, 80-81.

8. Raymond A. Mohl, *Poverty in New York, 1783-1825*, pp. 250, 304.

9. John Pintard, *Letters from John Pintard to His Daughter*, 1: 7.

10. Charles E. Knowles, *History of the Bank for Savings in the City of New York, 1819-1929*, pp.13-16; Fritz Redlich, *The Molding of American Banking*, pt. 1, pp. 209-11.

11. Minutes of the Directors of the Savings Bank of New York, 29 November 1816, pp. 2-4; the *New York Evening Post*, 2 December 1816, p. 4.

12. Knowles, *Bank for Savings*, pp. 23-28; Minutes of the Savings Bank of New York, 17 December 1816, pp. 7-11.

13. Emerson W. Keyes, *Savings Banks in the United States*, 2: 356-57; Payne and Davis, *Baltimore*, pp. 17-18.

14. Knowles reproduces the bank's Act of Incorporation in *Bank for Savings*, pp. 164-68.

15. Italics added. Minutes of the Savings Bank of New York, 29 November 1816, p. 3.

16. Payne and Davis, *Baltimore*, p. 27; Keyes, *Savings Banks in the United States*, 1: 42; James M. Willcox, *A History of the Philadelphia Saving Fund Society, 1816-1916*, pp. 157, 161-63, 208-18.

17. Minutes of the Savings Bank of New York, 29 November 1816, p. 2.

18. Keyes, *Savings Banks in the United States*, 1: 311-12.

19. Minutes of the Trustees of the Bank for Savings in the City of New York, vol. 1, 5 April 1819, p. 16.

20. Bray Hammond, *Banks and Politics in America*, p. 161.

21. Ibid., pp. 144-53; J. Van Fenstermaker, *The Development of American Commercial Banking, 1782-1837*, pp. 159-61; Alvin Kass, *Politics in New York State, 1800-1830*, pp. 93-132.

22. Keyes, *Savings Banks in the United States*, 1: 314, 330.

23. Ibid., pp. 319-21; Mohl, *Poverty*, pp. 245-46; David M. Schneider, *The History of Public Welfare in New York State, 1609-1866*, 1: 212-14; Pintard, *Letters*, 1: 151-52, 157-60.

24. Pintard, *Letters*, 1: 205-6; Redlich, *Molding*, pt. 1, p. 213; Knowles, *Bank for Savings*, p. 36.

25. Keyes, *Savings Banks in the United States*, 1: 323-25.

26. Ibid., pp. 333-40.

27. Pintard, *Letters*, 1: 205.

28. Minutes of the Savings Bank of New York, 24 December 1816, p. 14.

29. Payne and Davis, *Baltimore*, p. 30.

30. Nathan Miller, *The Enterprise of a Free People*, p. 89. Eddy was a governor and for a while president of the New York Hospital, a member of the New York Manumission Society, a founder and trustee of the Free School Society, a founder and director of the American Bible Society, a manager of the Society for the Reformation of Juvenile Delinquents, an active campaigner for more humane prisons, a member of the Society for the Prevention of Pauperism, and a member of the Committee for the Improvement of Indians. His house was a "wigwam to the travelling Indians .... He sometimes had a dozen Indians ... in the house at once." Samuel L. Knapp, *The Life of Thomas Eddy*, pp. 12, 14, 55, 100-101.

31. Pintard, *Letters*, 1: 97.

32. Ibid., 1: 157, 1: 206, 3: 88. Pintard was not alone in believing that savings banks instigated a moral revolution among the poor, causing them to change significantly their consumption-saving behavior. This observed change in behavior, assuming it was not merely a figment of Pintard's imagination, need not have resulted from any change in saver morality (a change in taste which would be depicted by a change in the shape of an individual's indifference curves). Mutuals offered savers small-denomination, highly liquid, relatively low-risk, interest-bearing debt in the form of passbook balances for which there were few if any close substitutes throughout much of the antebellum period. Thus the emergence of mutuals probably led to a significant increase in the real rate of interest that many individuals could have expected to earn on their savings. See Donald V. T. Bear, "The Relationship of Saving to the Rate of Interest, Real Income and Expected Future Prices," *Review of Economics and Statistics* 43, no. 1 (February 1961): 27-35; Milton Friedman, *A Theory of the Consumption Function*, pp. 7-9.

33. Pintard, *Letters*, 1: 97-98.

34. Secretary's Minutes, Seamen's Bank for Savings, vol. 1, n.d., p. 6; "Act of Incorporation," 31 January 1829, Article VI; Herbert Manchester, *A Century of Service, The Seamen's Bank for Savings, 1829-1929*, p. 22.

35. For example, in 1831 The Seamen's Fund and Retreat paid $100 and the Marine Merchants' Association paid $40 toward the bank's rent. Minutes, Seamen's Bank for Savings, vol. 1, 2 November 1831, p. 44.

36. Andrew Mills, *That's My Bank*, p. 21.

37. Dorcas Elisabeth Campbell, *The First Hundred Years*, p. 14.

38. William H. Bennett, "A Chronological History of the Emigrant Industrial Savings Bank," in the archives of the Emigrant Savings Bank, p. 1; Robert Ernst, *Immigrant Life in New York City, 1825-1863*, p. 137.

39. For an example of the problems of specifying the objectives of mutual trustees in a more modern context see: Donald D. Hester and Kenneth E. Scott, *Conversion of Mutual Savings and Loan Associations to Stock Form*, p. 36.

40. Myers, *History of the Great American Fortunes*.

41. Keyes, *Savings Banks in the United States*, 1: 356.

42. Ibid., 1: 361. This law was seldom, if ever, enforced in the antebellum years.

43. Ibid., 2: 195.


CHAPTER 2

1. Lance E. Davis and Peter L. Payne, "From Benevolence to Business: The Story of Two Savings Banks," *Business History Review* 32 (Winter 1958): 393.

2. Charles E. Knowles, *History of the Bank for Savings in the City of New York, 1819-1929*, pp. 44, 164-68, 71, 180-81; Minutes of the Trustees of the Bank for Savings in the City of New York, vol. 1, 1 July 1819, p. 43 (hereafter cited as Minutes, Bank for Savings).

3. On 19 September 1819 John Pintard noted that he had attended "to the rec[eip]t of deposits having taken in $4,645, a great deal of w[hic]h in small silver & sums, w[hic]h makes it very troublesome, & then to lug all this specie to the Mechanics'

Bank, for no one is trusted to lodge the money but a Trustee." John Pintard, *Letters from John Pintard to His Daughter*, 1: 228.

4. Knowles, *Bank for Savings*, pp. 173-74.

5. Pintard, *Letters*, 1: 206, 211, 228, 250, 257, 260. The following excerpts from Pintard's *Letters* offer some insight as to the amount of time and effort he contributed. "Last Sat[urda]y I rose [at] 1/2 p[ast] 4, was at my desk (meal & marketing 1 hour excepted) till past 3, was at the Bank from 4 to 11, & returned home after 17 hours [of] constant work, battered down. . . ." "Attending at the Savings Bank last night & sitting up late, I did not rise till after 6, when after dressing . . . I drew up as usual the Report of our deposits with a few obvious & timely reflections, w[hic]h I c[oul]d not copy fair until after breakfast & was detained too late to get to Church." Ibid., 1: 206 and 1: 221.

6. Ibid., 1: 206, 219.

7. The exception to this observation was the Greenwich Savings Bank, which originally had only one trustee on its attending committee but increased the number to two members. James H. Collins, *Ninety Years of the Greenwich Savings Bank*, p. 21.

8. Pintard, *Letters*, 3: 212.

9. Allan Nevins and Milton H. Thomas, eds., *The Diary of George Templeton Strong*, 2: 241; De Coursey Fales, *Some Historical Notes of the Early Days of the Bank for Savings in the City of New York*, p. 30.

10. *The Charter and By-Laws of the Bank for Savings in the City of New York*, 1857, pp. 3-4.

11. Minutes, Bank for Savings, vol. 7, 10 June 1857, p. 57; Knowles, *Bank for Savings*, p. 181.

12. Ibid., pp. 109-10; Seamen's Bank for Savings, *One Hundred Fifteen Years of Service, 1829-1944*, p. 9; Najah Taylor, "Autobiography of Najah Taylor," n.d., no page, Records of the Bank for Savings.

13. Nevins and Thomas, *Strong*, 3: 104.

14. Stephen C. Massett, "*Drifting About*," pp. 29-32.

15. This gradual transition of trustee responsibility has not been appreciated by some writers: "During the early months of its existence the trustees of The Bank for Savings elected officers from among their own number, performed the bookkeeping, and jointly formed the 'attending committees' that handled the daily transactions. As the Bank grew, however, full-time personnel were hired and the trustees' role became more and more supervisory. In less than ten years, the managerial functions had been turned over entirely to trustee-appointed, salaried officers." Allen Teck, *Mutual Savings Banks and Savings and Loan Associations*, p. 13. Teck does not cite what sources led him to this mistaken conclusion.

16. Bayard Tuckerman, ed., *The Diary of Philip Hone, 1825-1851*, 2: 82.

17. Nevins and Thomas, *Strong*, 2: 421.

18. Williamson has suggested that firm managers attempt to maximize their own utility, which he argues is a function of staff, emoluments, and discretionary profits. It is suggested above that at least some trustees' utility was a function of less mundane and less selfish desires. Oliver E. Williamson, "Managerial Discretion and Business Behavior," *American Economic Review*, 53 (December 1963): 1032-57. For a discussion of responsibility and integrity as ends in themselves to antebellum businessmen see Paul Goodman, "Ethics and Enterprise: The Values of a Boston Elite, 1800-1860," *American Quarterly*, 18, no. 3 (Fall 1966): 437-51.

19. *By-Laws of the Bowery Savings Bank*, 1839, Articles XXIII and XXIV. *By-Laws of the Bank for Savings*, 1832, Articles XXIII, XXIV, and XXV.

20. Secretary's Minutes, Seamen's Bank for Savings, vol. 1, 19 February 1851, pp. 22-24.

21. William Dana Orcott, *The Miracle of Mutual Savings*, p. 44; Secretary's Minutes, Bowery Savings Bank, vol. 1, 12 May 1858, p. 569; Emerson W. Keyes, *A History of Savings Banks in the United States*, 2: 8.

22. Andrew Mills, *That's My Bank*, p. 55; Dorcas Elisabeth Campbell, *The First Hundred Years*, p. 60.

23. Davis and Payne, "From Benevolence to Business," pp. 386-87.

24. Peter L. Payne and Lance E. Davis, *The Savings Bank of Baltimore, 1818-1866*, pp. 47-48.

25. Ibid., p. 49. The New York experience suggests that the rapid transfer of responsibilities in Baltimore may have been more a function of convenience than of necessity.

26. Davis and Payne, "From Benevolence to Business," pp. 395-96.

27. Payne and Davis recognized the important link between a mutual's hours and its form of management when they noted in their treatment of the Savings Bank of Baltimore that "it was probably not until 1841, however, when the Bank first opened every day instead of twice a week, that professional officers began making the bulk of administrative decisions." Payne and Davis, *Baltimore*, p. 50.

28. Not until 1857 did these hours appear in the bank's bylaws and not until the mid-1850s were they regularly listed in public notices and then with an explicit statement that no business would be transacted.

29. Emerson W. Keyes, *A History of Savings Banks in the State of New York*, pp. 172-73.

30. *New York Herald*, 10 May 1837, pp. 2-3; 2 June 1837, p. 2.

31. These were the bank's summer hours. From 31 March to 1 October the hours were reduced to 6 to 8 P.M. Trustees' Minutes, Broadway Savings Institution, vol. 1, n.d., no page.

32. Funding Committee Minutes, Broadway Savings Institution, 8 August 1854, no page.

33. Chap. 3 argues that the Bank for Savings (and to a lesser extent the Bowery) on numerous occasions rejected business accounts for ideological as well as practical reasons.

34. There is some question whether the entire amount or just that part over $500 received the lower rate of interest. A considerable amount of evidence supports both possibilities, and it is entirely possible that the practice changed over time and differed between banks. The only statistical evidence available is from the report of the Seamen's Bank for Savings for January 1845 and from a hypothetical example used by Keyes in arguing against paying differential rates. Both of these support the position taken above that the entire amount in accounts over $500 (or in some cases $1,000) received the lower rate. This issue is important to our understanding of both bank and depositor behavior. If a bank paid a lower rate on the entire account, then its trustees were obviously much more serious in their efforts to restrict account sizes than if they just paid the lower rate on the marginal amount over $500. Similarly, if the differential rate was calculated on an average and not a marginal basis, one would expect more depositors to split accounts or otherwise dispose of their savings in excess of $500. Keyes, *Savings Banks in the United States*, 1: 422; Report Book No. 2, July 1839 through January 1845, Seamen's Bank for Savings.

35. *Laws of the State of New York*, 1853, chap. 257, section 5.

36. The date of payment differed, but common dates were on or after the third Monday, or the twentieth.

37. No allowance for compounding was made in the above interest rate computations.

38. Knowles, *Bank for Savings*, pp. 112-18. A mutual's surplus is defined as its total assets minus its total liabilities. The bank was allowed only a 10 percent surplus.

39. Keyes, *Savings Banks in the United States*, 1: 438.

40. Minutes of the Finance Committee, Manhattan Savings Institution, 19 December 1854, no page.

41. In 1854 the Greenwich also adopted a policy of allowing grace periods and advertising its rates ahead of time. *New York Herald*, 30 June 1854, p. 7. The length of grace periods varied; the longest found was 15 days, offered by the Mariners' Savings Institution. Ibid., 6 July 1853, p. 3.

42. *Annual Report of the Superintendent of the Banking Department Relative to Savings Banks*, to the New York State Legislature, 20 March 1862, in *New York State Senate Documents*, vol. 5, no. 80, p. 5 (hereafter cited as *Banking Department Report on Savings Banks*).

43. It could be argued that it was relatively easy for the trustees of the Bank for Savings, the Seamen's, and the Bowery to shun competitive pressures. It is a common practice for well-known companies to remain aloof and charge new entries with using unprofessional methods. But these banks also avoided competing with each other. In 1861 when the Bowery surpassed the Bank for Savings in total assets there was no fanfare by the Bowery's trustees, nor gloom by the trustees of the Bank for Savings. In fact, there was no comment at all in the records of either bank or in newspapers. It will be argued in the next chapter that the growth of these three banks was adversely affected as a result of their policies.

44. Pintard, *Letters*, 3: 57-58, 4: 170; Orcutt, *Miracle*, p. 26.

45. In 1857 the Seamen's made substantial loans to the Brooklyn Savings Bank, the Bowery Savings Bank, the East River Savings Institution, and the South Brooklyn Savings Bank. Secretary's Minutes, Seamen's Bank for Savings, vol. 1, 10 October 1857, no page; 12 October 1857, no page.

46. The implicit assumption mutuals make here is that the increase in utility that depositors gained in safety from the surplus was greater than the marginal disutility of receiving a lower rate of interest.

47. A fourth reason why trustees might accumulate a surplus is for personal profit, but this is extremely unlikely. Today this is an important consideration, especially if conversion from mutual to stock form is in the offing. But in the antebellum years, given the laxity of government regulation, there were more direct and more profitable ways to profiteer if trustees were so inclined.

48. *Charter and Bylaws of the Bank for Savings*, 1832, p. 8; Minutes, Bank for Savings, vol. 3, 20 January 1836, p. 1172.

49. In 1839 a general law extended a 10 percent surplus limit to all savings banks in the state. Keyes, *Savings Banks in the United States*, 1: 431. It is interesting to note that all the early legislation in New York established maximum rather than minimum limits, which abound today.

50. For example, Minutes, Bank for Savings, vol. 7, 13 January 1858, p. 98.

51. Secretary's Minutes, Bowery Savings Bank, vol. 1, 8 March 1858, pp. 234-35; 8 November 1848, p. 245; 12 December 1859, p. 601.

52. Secretary's Minutes, Seamen's Bank for Savings, vol. 1, 8 March 1852, no page; 9 February 1853, no page.

53. The figures shown in Table 4 do not correspond to those listed in Keyes or in the annual reports to the state banking department. In 1860 these reports did not include the interest due to depositors on 1 January under the heading "amount due depositors." As a result the banks' liabilities are slightly understated, and their surpluses are greatly overstated—by as much as several hundred percent. When no independent data were available the amount due depositors (as listed in the annual reports) was adjusted upward by 2 percent to account for interest accrued to depositors. This procedure yielded very close approximations to a bank's true liabilities when tested on those mutuals for which we have complete data.

Taking a bank's surplus as a percentage of its assets is an arbitrary choice. An alternative would be to use deposits instead of assets in the denominator. Both assets and deposits were used in this context by the banks during the period under study. In the case of those mutuals with negligible surpluses it makes little difference which figure is used in the denominator. For those banks with larger surpluses, using assets instead of deposits understates the percentage surplus.

54. No mention of state intervention was found in the minute books for the Dry Dock, Manhattan, Broadway, and Mariners'. Bank-sponsored histories based on the minutes of the East River and Emigrant Industrial also fail to mention this subject.

55. Even the most enthusiastic founders of the Bank for Savings were not without some hope of personal gain through lower taxes and better state services.

56. Minutes of the Trustees, Mariners' Savings Institution, for August, September, October, and November 1853, and for July, August, September, and October 1855.

57. Ibid., 11 January 1855, no page.

58. This concept of firm behavior has only recently been integrated into the body of economic theory. Baumol has suggested that managers' salaries may be more closely

related to the size of a firm than to its profitability. As a result, Baumol argued, one might expect firms to maximize sales (subject to minimum profit constraints) rather than maximize profits. William J. Baumol, *Economic Theory and Operations Analysis*, pp. 47-51. A New York state senate committee identified this managerial motive as an important determinant of mutual behavior over a century before it crept into the theoretical literature. The senate committee was quite explicit: "The immediate officers are stimulated to increase the aggregate amount of business . . . [for] a variety of causes, among which the hope of increased salary. . . ." The committee's conclusion was probably based on its study of mutuals outside New York City, because the trustees of the four banks open in the city when the report was written still had a firm grip on day-to-day operation. Keyes, *Savings Banks in New York*, pp. 293-94.

59. Neil W. Chamberlain, *Enterprise and Environment*, p. 48.

CHAPTER 3

1. Previous writers never offered explicit definitions of the terms they relied on, such as "frugal workers," "indigent poor," or "industrious laborers," to describe mutual customers. Keyes defined "industrious and thrifty toilers" as steadily employed workers who, although poor were not hovering on the brink of pauperism. "Though poor they were independent, because their labor was in regular demand, and their impulse was to industry and thrift." Emerson W. Keyes, *A History of Savings Banks in the United States*, 2: 527.

2. Payne and Davis were obviously correct in the sense that no hypothesis can be proved, but the two alternatives that they presented suggest that they were asking wrong questions of Keyes's original hypothesis. Peter L. Payne and Lance E. Davis, *The Savings Bank of Baltimore*, p. 29. Also see Fritz Redlich, *The Molding of American Banking*, pt. 1, p. 228. None of the writers mentioned above hazarded a guess as to exactly how many years passed before this change from indigent poor to industrious toilers took place. More recently Professor Redlich has revised his position: "In a paper entitled 'The Trustee Savings Banks 1817-1861' in the *Journal of Economic History*, 21 (1961), p. 26 ff., Albert Fishlow has shown that English savings banks, established to assist the poor, actually became a boon for the lower middle classes. This article should inspire young American historians to make similar investigations into the early American savings banks, if the extant material permits. I would not dare make guesses in advance as to the result." Ibid., p. xv(a).

3. Davis and Payne, "From Benevolence to Business," p. 388.

4. For example: "The bank conveniently gathered the savings of laborers, seamstresses, chambermaids, cooks, clerks, nurses, boot cleaners, preachers of the gospel, and others of comparable income. . . ." Nathan Miller, *The Enterprise of a Free People*, p. 89. Also see Alan Teck, *Mutual Savings Banks and Savings and Loan Associations*, p. 11. One of the few scholars to question this traditional description of mutual customers is Herman Krooss in "Financial Institutions," in David T. Gilchrist, ed., *The Growth of the Seaport Cities, 1790-1825*, pp. 107-108.

5. It must be emphasized that these reports listed only new depositors. In 1868, at the request of the superintendent of banking, some of the state's mutuals supplied lists of all of their customers' occupations. A comparison of this list for the Bank for Savings with the bank's annual report for 1864 (the closest report I had to 1868) shows that the occupations of people opening accounts that year were proportionally representative of all the bank's customers four years later.

6. For a list of specific occupations in each category see Appendix A.

7. The occupation of the minor's father often was listed in the Original Test Book. In many cases a parent opened separate accounts for each member of the family.

8. John Pintard, *Letters from John Pintard to His Daughter*, 2: 340. Pintard was vice-president of this society and took a personal interest in his servants' savings habits. He undoubtedly felt that his cook's achievement reflected his wise counsel. Prior to the founding of the Bank for Savings, Pintard personally kept her savings and paid her 7 percent interest per annum. Ibid., 4: 185.

9. Minutes, Bank for Savings, vol. 1, 4 December 1824, pp. 393, 389-90.

10. The report listed only account numbers and balances. To find a person's occupation it was necessary to check the account numbers in the Original Test Book. The conclusion that the children and females who held these large balances were of middle- and upper-class families rests on more than the plausible inference that it would have been very improbable that the children, wives, and widows of the working class could have accumulated balances in excess of $500. Several threads of evidence support such an inference. First, it was bank policy to record the occupation of each depositor at the time the individual opened an account. If the females had been working as domestics or if the children had been working as chimney sweepers, it most probably would have been recorded. Since no occupations were listed for this elite group of depositors we can reasonably assume that the overwhelming majority were in fact not employed, thus increasing the probability that their balances represented gifts and inheritances rather than an accumulation of their own meager savings. Second, in a number of instances two or more children (or a wife and child) with the same last name owned consecutively numbered accounts with similar balances. In such cases the accounts most probably represented gifts. Finally, the occupations of nine of the fathers or husbands were listed. Five were clearly upper class (one M.D., one state Supreme Court justice, and three shipmasters); another was a pilot, a highly skilled and well-paying profession; two (a grocer and a clergyman) were in occupations that fall under the merchant/professional heading; the last individual was a rigger.

11. It must be emphasized that these data refer only to individual acts of deposit; they tell us nothing directly about the total sums in accounts, nor about the number of times any individual made deposits or withdrawals. For example, in 1829 there were 1,274 deposits made between $1 and $5; 1,690 between $5 and $10; and 2,200 between $10 and $20, etc. At the other end of the scale there was one deposit between $800 and $900, two between $900 and $1,000, and one between $1,000 and $2,000.

The figures given in Table 7 were estimated by using the following procedure. First, starting with the largest deposit size and working down, sum the number of acts of deposit until reaching 10 percent of the total number of deposits made that year. Second, take the mean of each deposit group (e.g., $950, $850, etc.) and multiply by the number of depositors in that group. Continue this process until the sum represents 10 percent of the deposits. The resulting figure is the estimate of the amount deposited by the largest 10 percent of the acts of deposit. Divide this figure by the total amount deposited that year to get the percentage of total deposits accounted for by the largest 10 percent of deposits. Repeat the same steps at the other end of the scale to arrive at the percentage of deposits accounted for by the smallest 50 percent of deposits.

12. Payne and Davis, *Baltimore*, p. 22.

13. Report Book No. 2, July 1839 through January 1845, Seamen's Bank for Savings.

14. Stanley Lebergott, *Manpower in Economic Growth*, pp. 530, 541-47.

15. Albert Fishlow, "The Trustee Savings Banks, 1817-1861," *Journal of Economic History* 21, no. 1 (March 1961): 29-32.

16. Allan Nevins and Milton H. Thomas, eds., *The Diary of George Templeton Strong*, 2: 363.

17. This statement assumes that the Bank for Savings' investments were large enough relative to the total market that the bank could not make all the investments it wanted at some constant market price. The next chapter argues that this was in fact the case.

18. *Laws of the State of New York*, 1853, chap. 257, section 5.

19. Charles E. Knowles, *History of the Bank for Savings in the City of New York, 1819-1829*, p. 164.

20. Minutes, Bank for Savings, vol. 1, 10 November 1819, p. 63.

21. Pintard, *Letters*, 1: 302; 2: 57-58.

22. Minutes, Bank for Savings, vol. 1, 12 October 1824, p. 393.

23. Pintard, *Letters*, 2: 164-65.

24. Ibid., 2:352 and 355.

25. Minutes, Bank for Savings, vol. 2, 16 May 1827, p. 554.

26. Transfer Book A-1, Bank for Savings, Account no. 447. Pilots were highly respected professionals. New York pilots had a privileged position in that they were

able to limit entry into the profession by requiring association licensing. Robert Albion, *The Rise of New York Port, 1815-1860*, pp. 214-16.

27. Deposit and Account Ledgers, 1829 and 1830, Bank for Savings.

28. Pintard, *Letters*, 3: 212.

29. Minutes, Bank for Savings, vol. 2, 14 December 1831, p. 850; 12 January 1831, p. 782.

30. Ibid., vol. 2, 13 April 1831, p. 803; 13 October 1830.

31. Ibid., vol. 3, 14 June 1837, p. 1341; vol. 5, 14 February 1849, p. 2326; vol. 7, 14 October 1857, p. 89; vol. 7, 14 October 1857, p. 89; vol. 7, 11 November 1857, p. 93.

32. Allan Nevins, ed., *The Diary of Philip Hone, 1828-1851*, p. 257. Hone noted that the day before the bank suspended payments it paid 375 withdrawals totaling $81,000.

33. Report Book No. 2, July 1839 through January 1845, Seamen's Bank for Savings; Secretary's Minutes, Seamen's Bank for Savings, vol. 1, 9 February 1853, no page. Herbert Manchester, who wrote a history of the Seamen's Bank for Savings in 1929, stated that "the next year [1852] a committee was appointed to consider the limiting of deposits, because previously some of the deposits had been as high as $50,000." Although it is possible that Manchester was correct, I found no record of any deposit of this size. The committee he referred to was probably a committee formed to study the impending legislation mentioned above. The sum "$50,000" appeared in the minutes quite frequently in the early 1850s because at almost every meeting the board recommended that the cash reserves be kept at that level. The cash reserves were deposited in a commercial bank, and it would have been easy for Manchester to misinterpret this as a deposit in the savings bank. Herbert Manchester, *A Century of Service*, p. 30.

34. The Bowery's original charter did not place a limit on deposits, but in 1835 the charter was amended to include a $3,000 limit.

35. Walter B. Smith and Arthur H. Cole, *Fluctuations in American Business, 1790-1860*, pp. 83, 126. Charts 27 and 44 show discount rates peaking in 1837, 1839, 1848, and 1857. Davis disputes the accuracy of the Bigelow series for 1848 used by Smith and Cole. Lance E. Davis, "The New England Textile Mills and the Capital Markets: A Study in Industrial Borrowing, 1840-1860," *Journal of Economic History* 20, no. 1 (March 1960): 1-30. For an analysis of this controversy and of interest rates in 1848 see Alan L. Olmstead, "Davis and Bigelow Revisited: Antebellum American Interest Rates," *Journal of Economic History* 34, no. 2 (June 1974): 483-91.

36. Secretary's Minutes, Bowery Savings Bank, vol. 1, 11 November 1839, p. 99; 11 October 1848, p. 243; 8 November 1848, p. 246; 14 October 1857, p. 523; 9 December 1857, pp. 520-31; 19 December 1857, p. 532.

37. Secretary's Minutes, Dry Dock Savings Institution, vol. 1, 20 December 1848, no page; Andrew Mills, *That's My Bank*, p. 109. The Dry Dock's original charter did not place a limit on account sizes.

38. The Emigrant Industrial had one account as large as $10,000 in 1857. Robert Ernst, *Immigrant Life in New York City, 1825-1863*, p. 133.

39. The legislation of 1853 supposedly limited account sizes in mutuals formed after that date to $1,000, but several charters written after 1853 allowed for larger accounts, and trustees could avoid this constraint by allowing a depositor to open trust accounts.

40. Emerson W. Keyes, *A History of Savings Banks in the State of New York*, pp. 142, 166.

41. Keyes, *Savings Banks in the United States*, 2: table opposite p. 568.

42. Henry A. Schenck, comp., *Manual of the Bowery Savings Bank*, p. 31.

43. *Banking Department Report on Savings Banks*, 3 March 1865, in *New York State Assembly Documents*, vol. 7, no. 127, p. 6.

44. Payne and Davis, *Baltimore*, pp. 32-36. The weekly limit on deposits was at different times placed at $20 (1817), $30 (1821), $10 (1822), $50 (1822), $20 (1839), and $10 (1863).

45. Redlich, *Molding*, pt. 1, pp. 224-25.

46. For example: "Because the small saver, 'is more concerned with the security of his money than with the rate of interest,' the amounts deposited at, and withdrawn from, the Savings Bank of Baltimore were highly susceptible to panics." Payne and Davis, *Baltimore*, p. 82. Payne and Davis do not perform any tests to determine the responsiveness of savers to interest differentials.

47. There is evidence that some early mutuals informed their customers before lowering dividend rates, but not before raising them.

48. Dorcas Elisabeth Campbell, *The First Hundred Years*, pp. 45-46.

49. *New York Times*, 15 January 1856, p. 7.

50. These data are available for the Bank for Savings, the Seamen's, the Bowery, the Greenwich, the Dry Dock, and the Broadway.

51. There were no data for July and August of 1832.

52. This is of course the type of price discrimination that banks and utility companies use today.


CHAPTER 4

1. This means that they were managing the mutual to maximize the return on its portfolio given legal constraints. It should not be construed to mean that they were trying to profit personally from their position.

2. J. Van Fenstermaker, *The Development of American Commercial Banking: 1782-1837*, pp. 16-17.

3. Nathan Miller, *The Enterprise of a Free People*; Harry N. Scheiber, *Ohio Canal Era*.

4. Miller, *Enterprise*, pp. 2, 63-67, 77-82; John Pintard, *Letters from John Pintard to His Daughter*, 1: 97.

5. A. Robert Sadov and Gary Fromm, "Financing Transport Investment," in Gary Fromm, ed., *Transport Investment and Economic Development*, p. 225.

6. Charles E. Knowles, *History of the Bank for Savings in the City of New York, 1819-1929*, p. 164.

7. Minutes, Bank for Savings, vol. 1, 10 November 1819, p. 63.

8. Knowles, *Bank for Savings*, p. 178.

9. *Charter and By-Laws of the Bank for Savings in the City of New York*, 1832, p. 6.

10. The Case I assumption—that the bank must invest all its assets in New York debt—is made for clarity of exposition and is not historically accurate. In 1819 the bank could also invest in United States debt. If this assumption were relaxed to fit historical reality, $d_1d_1$ (figure 4) would not be perfectly inelastic, but would still be relatively inelastic compared to $d_2d_2$—the demand curve under the free-choice case (II). The market demand curve $D_2D_2$ would not be as far to the left nor would it be as elastic as shown in Figure 5.

11. Minutes, Bank for Savings, vol. 1, 1819, p. 44; 8 March 1820, p. 88; 14 February 1821, p. 149; Knowles, *Bank for Savings*, p. 178.

12. Margaret G. Myers, *The New York Money Market*, 1: 23.

13. Minutes, Bank for Savings, vol. 1, 12 July 1820, pp. 116-18; 1 January 1821, p. 145.

14. Ibid., vol. 1, 14 February 1821, p. 149; 21 June 1821, p. 175. Fritz Redlich mistakenly described this trip to Albany as the bank's first attempt to buy a new issue of securities directly from the canal commissioners. As noted above, it succeeded in doing this a year earlier in 1820. Fritz Redlich, *The Molding of American Banking*, p. 226.

Nathaniel Prime was a member of Prime, Ward & King, one of the city's leading private banking houses. The Bank for Savings' minutes show that the bank paid a premium of 6.05 percent on these bonds and that Prime refused to sell another $50,000 worth of canal bonds at the same price.

15. Minutes, Bank for Savings, vol. 1, 13 February 1822, p. 213.

16. Miller, *Enterprise*, p. 99.

17. Ibid., pp. 86-88; Minutes, Bank for Savings, vol. 1, 14 February 1821, p. 149.

18. Miller, *Enterprise*, pp. 86, 91-92.

19. Ibid., pp. 31-32; Ronald Shaw, *Erie Water West*, pp. 16, 38-40, 46.

20. Eddy, Bayard, and Cadwallader Colden would become trustees of the bank. A fourth organizer of this meeting (Clinton) was also connected with the bank. Shaw, *Erie Water*, pp. 56-57.

21. *New York State Assembly Documents*, 1834, vol. 4, no. 57, pp. 16-17.

22. Ibid., p. 16; Minutes, Bank for Savings, vol. 3, 13 April 1836, p. 1211.

23. Minutes, Bank for Savings, 1 January 1834, p. 1017.

24. *New York State Assembly Documents*, 1834, vol. 4, no. 57, pp. 16-17.

25. Miller, *Enterprise*, p. 135.

26. Ibid., pp. 115-17, 124-25, 133-34; *New York State Assembly Documents*, 1834, vol. 4, no. 57, pp. 16-17.

27. Minutes, Bank for Savings, vol. 2, 2 January 1829, p. 649. Data on New York City debt before 1830 are scarce. At the end of 1830 the Bank for Savings held over 45 percent of the city's net bonded debt of $774,556. For total New York City debt figures (1830-1896) see Edward Durand, *The Finances of New York City*, pp. 374-75.

28. The Merchants' Association of New York, *An Inquiry into the Conditions Relating to the Water Supply of the City of New York*, p. 566.

29. Minutes, Bank for Savings, vol. 3, 1 January 1836, p. 1187.

30. Pintard, *Letters*, 4: 88 and 89.

31. Allan Nevins, ed., *The Diary of Philip Hone, 1828-1851*, p. 837.

32. Merchants' Association of New York, *Water Supply*, Table 11, p. 566.

33. Minutes, Bank for Savings, vol. 3, 8 February 1837, p. 1295.

34. Miller, *Enterprise*, pp. 173, 180.

35. Emerson W. Keyes, *A History of Savings Banks in the United States*, 1: 377.

36. Harry N. Scheiber, "Enterprise and Western Development: The Case of Micajah T. Williams," *Business History Review* 37 (Winter 1963): 348-49.

37. At that time the canal commissioners of the state of New York were trying to persuade the Bank for Savings to redeem its Erie bonds, which in part may explain the legislature's willingness to grant the bank's petition.

38. Minutes, Bank for Savings, vol. 2, 13 February 1828, p. 595.

39. Leland H. Jenks, *The Migration of British Capital to 1875*, p. 361. Jenks noted that small amounts of Ohio debt first appeared on the London market in 1828.

40. Minutes, Bank for Savings, vol. 2, 4 February 1832, p. 872; figures for Ohio state debt are found in Ernest L. Bogart, *Internal Improvements and State Debt in Ohio*, pp. 242-43. Bogart's figures are for the end of each year.

41. Scheiber, *Ohio Canal Era*, p. 374.

42. Minutes, Bank for Savings, vols. 2 and 3, 1832 to 1837.

43. An indication of the extent to which the bank's aggressive bidding in a limited bond market could have driven up bond prices is given in an article by Lance Davis dealing with the Boston financial market. Davis observed a sudden drop in the long-term interest rate from 6 percent to 3 percent in 1849. He suggested that this drop was caused by "a flood of new long-term loans made by several Massachusetts savings banks and by the Provident Institution for Savings in the Town of Boston in particular. Within the space of a few weeks these banks placed several hundred thousand dollars in additional funds into the long-term loan market, and the decline in interest rates appears to represent the market adjustment to this sudden increase in supply." Lance E. Davis, "The New England Textile Mills and the Capital Markets: A Study of Industrial Borrowing, 1840-1860," *Journal of Economic History* 20, no. 1 (March 1960): 20.

44. *Charter and By-Laws of the Bank for Savings*, 1832, p. 7. In 1832 a similar provision was added to the Seamen's charter.

45. Ibid. The latter provision of the Act of 1830, which allowed deposits in commercial banks, just sanctioned what the trustees had been doing since the first day the bank opened for business.

46. Minutes, Bank for Savings, vol. 3, 1 January 1834, p. 1017.

47. Ibid., vol. 2, 3 January 1831, p. 794; 4 February 1832, p. 872, Jenks, *Migration*, p. 361.

48. Minutes, Bank for Savings, vol. 3, 1 January 1835, p. 1085.

49. Figures for Alabama debt in 1835 are not readily available, but MacGregor shows the state had issued $2.3 million of debt by 1835. If this figure approximates the amount of debt actually outstanding, then the Bank for Savings held about 17 percent. John MacGregor, ed., *Commercial Statistics of America*, p. 1073.

50. Secretary's Minutes, Seamen's Bank for Savings, vol. 1, 1829-1838; *New York State Senate Documents*, 1831, vol. 1, no. 21, pp. 1-2; 1833, vol. 2, no. 81, pp. 1-3; 1834, vol. 2, no. 53, pp. 1-2; 1834, vol. 1, no. 29, p. 5; 1835, vol. 2, no. 50, pp. 4-5; 1836, vol. 2, no. 69, p. 5; 1838, vol. 2, no. 43, pp. 3-4; *New York State Assembly Documents*, 1835, vol. 3, no. 186, pp. 1-3; 1836, vol. 3, no. 164, pp. 1-2; 1837, vol. 3, no. 180, pp. 1-3; Secretary's Minutes, Bowery Savings Bank, vol. 1, 1834-1838.

51. Peter L. Payne and Lance E. Davis, *The Savings Bank of Baltimore, 1818-1866*, p. 111; Lance E. Davis and Peter L. Payne, "From Benevolence to Business," p. 399.

52. James M. Willcox, *A History of the Philadelphia Saving Fund Society, 1816-1916*, p. 157.

53. Payne and Davis, *Baltimore*, p. 98; Davis and Payne, "From Benevolence to Business," pp. 390, 400.

54. The two exceptions to this rule were the Bank for Savings, which could make loans of amounts up to three-fourths of the value of property, and the Greenwich, which could make loans only on real estate worth at least twice the amount loaned exclusive of buildings. This restriction on the Greenwich was repealed in 1841. James H. Collins, *Ninety Years of the Greenwich Savings Bank*, p. 19.

55. The Manhattan, Broadway, and Mariners' had limits of this type ranging from $5,000 to $10,000. All of these banks successfully petitioned to be allowed to make larger loans, and by 1860 the limits were generally up to $20,000. The Irving Savings Institution could not lend more than $50,000 to one person.

56. Secretary's Minutes, Seamen's Bank for Savings, vol. 1, 4 March 1835, p. 94; 6 August 1834, p. 84; 3 September 1834, p. 86. Technically, the Bank for Savings' loans to the Public School Society in 1830 were mortgage loans. For a description of this firm's activities see Hugh G. J. Aitken, "Yates and McIntyre: Lottery Managers," *Journal of Economic History* 13, no. 1 (Winter 1953): 36-57.

57. *New York Assembly Documents*, 1837, vol. 3, no. 180, pp. 1-2.

58. Bond and Mortgage Book, Bank for Savings, no page.

59. Minutes, Bank for Savings, vol. 3, 20 January 1836, pp. 1171-72.

60. Emerson W. Keyes, *Special Report on Savings Banks*, pp. 341-43. The first of these changes appeared in 1848 in the charters of two new banks. The General Bank Act of 1853 extended the right to make these types of investments to all the older mutuals. This act also stipulated that mutuals could not purchase bonds below their par value; this applied to all bonds, not just city and county issues. This stipulation was intended to increase the market for, and to help support the price of, the debt of upstate cities. These municipal governments could adjust the interest rates, maturity date, and par price of their bonds so that they would circulate at, or above, par and thus be acceptable investments for mutuals constrained by the Act of 1853. This same act would exclude many of the outstanding bonds issued by southern and western states which were circulating below par, and thus eliminate one of the upstate cities' competitors for mutual funds. The legislature made other changes in the regulations affecting mutual investments, which were partly designed to increase the intrastate flow of capital. One such change already mentioned was to allow many of the mutuals chartered after 1848 to make real estate loans outside of the New York City area.

61. Leland Jenks maintained that if it had not been for the Erie's "sensational success," large quantities of British capital would not have flowed into other states' transport projects. Jenks, *Migration*, p. 73.

62. The one essential characteristic necessary for an institution to be classified as a "development bank" is that it specializes in supplying long-term credit. William

Diamond, *Development Banks*, pp. 1-5; David Landes, *Bankers and Pashas*, pp. 8-9.
63. Diamond, *Development Banks*, p. 23. Both Landes and Cameron have applied the term to earlier institutions established in western Europe.
64. Rondo Cameron, *France and the Economic Development of Europe, 1800-1914*, pp. 137-39.
65. Perhaps the best example of bankers' supplying entrepreneurial inputs is that of Emile and Isaac Pereire. Cameron, *France*, pp. 134-48.


CHAPTER 5
1. Davis, "The New England Textile Mills," p. 4.
2. Barbara Vatter, "Industrial Borrowing by the New England Textile Mills, 1840-1860: A Comment," *Journal of Economic History* 21, no. 2 (June 1961): 216-21.
3. Lance E. Davis, "Mrs. Vatter on Industrial Borrowing: A Reply," *Journal of Economic History* 21, no. 2 (June 1961): 225.
4. If a bank had a good experience with one type of investment it might favor it when making current decisions. Alternatively, a bank that had a large percentage of its portfolio tied up in government bonds (perhaps because of previous constraints) might avoid buying more bonds in an effort to diversify its portfolio.
5. Finally, even if we find similar investments and thus convergence, this does not constitute proof that the trustees of the various banks were in fact consciously making similar responses to market signals. At least conceivably this result could happen fortuitously, or it could reflect collusive arrangements between the banks.
6. There are no data for the Greenwich for 1837, 1843, and 1846 through 1855, and only partial data exist for the Seamen's for 1850 and 1851.
It should be emphasized that the convergence noted in Figures 6 and 7 reflects similar marginal investment made each year. For example, if one plots the yearly change in the mortgage holdings of the Bank for Savings, the Seamen's, and the Bowery, the direction of change is the same in every year from 1850 through 1861. The direction of the change in the government bond holdings of these three banks was the same in eight of the ten years from 1852 through 1861.
7. In 1842 the Seamen's trustees turned down several requests for loans with the explanation that it was "inexpedient at present . . . to loan money on real estate." Secretary's Minutes, Seamen's Bank for Savings, vol. 1, 6 April 1842.
8. The amounts cited are all par values. In 1835 the bank bought $300,000 (par) of Alabama 4 percent bonds at an average price of 93 percent of par. In 1849 these bonds sold at 75 percent of par. In 1835 the bank purchased $100,000 (par) of Indiana 5 percent bonds at an average price of 94 percent of par. In 1848 these bonds were quoted at approximately 50 percent of par. In 1849 the bank held about $270,000 of Pennsylvania 5 percent bonds, which was part of a series of purchases made between 1831 and 1834 for which the bank paid a premium of several percent. In 1848 this type of bond was quoted at about 74 percent; in 1849 the price rose to about 90 percent of par. Minutes, Bank for Savings, vol. 3, 4 February 1832, p. 872; 1 January 1833, p. 940; 1 January 1834, p. 1017; 1 January 1835, p. 1088; 1 January 1836, p. 1187; 13 April 1836, p. 1121; *Banker's Magazine and State Financial Register* 3 (1849): 573; 4 (1849-1850): 82, 496, 762-63, 1053.
Ohio debt had returned to par or above by the late 1840s, but in the early 1840s this state's debt was selling for about 70 percent of par. See Ernest L. Bogart, *Internal Improvements and State Debt in Ohio*, pp. 174-77.
9. Conversations with Professor Donald Hester, summer, 1969.
10. The comparison with present-day behavior supplies at best a relative indication of nineteenth-century mutual efficiency. Perhaps a more relevant comparison would be with contemporary intermediaries (e.g., insurance companies, commercial banks, etc.). In any case, the mere fact that the banks faced less binding legal constraints over time and thus could and did invest in a broader market is enough to suggest that their assets were probably being allocated more efficiently as time passed.
11. "The Usury Laws," *Banker's Magazine and Statistical Register* 4 (February 1850): 585. Also see *Banker's Magazine* 7 (December 1857): 500.
12. In some cases more than two sets of books containing the same information

still exist. In these instances one set was a rough copy, obviously written on the spot; the other set was a a final draft copied from the rough copy and meant to be preserved. The rough copies never reported a different rate of interest than found in the "official copies."

13. This conclusion is particularly important since Davis made extensive use of records from borrowers as well as lenders. Davis, "The New England Textile Mills," pp. 3-4.

14. Ogden was elected to the board in 1843. By 1845, as a result of his enthusiasm, he was elected to the position of secretary. He held this time-consuming post until 1861, when he took over the daily management of the bank, being elected to the newly created office of comptroller.

15. "The Usury Laws," *Banker's Magazine*, p. 584.

16. This conclusion need not follow from Ogden's statement because under varying assumptions it is possible that a profiteering trustee could favor or oppose repeal of the usury law. The assumption implicitly made above (as well as in Vatter's "Comment") is that a profiteer would favor retaining the usury law because it offered the opportunity to discriminate in favor of friends and still remain within moral and legal bounds. An alternative formulation is that a profiteering trustee might favor repeal if he were an efficient price discriminator. He could then charge higher interest rates to outsiders when the equilibrium interest rate exceeded 7 percent; this would allow him to lend to insiders at interest rates even lower than 7 percent and still cover costs. But if the latter formulation prevailed, we would expect to find mutuals violating the usury law (as did other lenders) when they lent to outsiders; there is no evidence of such violations.

There is a second possible reason for doubting the argument put forth in the text. Since the usury law worked to reduce the total assets of savings banks relative to what they would have been in its absence, its repeal would mean the trustees could allocate more assets—either for unselfish *or for selfish purposes*. But the evidence detailed in chap. 3 suggests that Ogden was not arguing for repeal of the usury law to increase his bank's assets. During the pre-Civil War era the Bank for Saving's trustees turned away several million dollars in deposits by enforcing policies designed to restrict wealthy persons from the bank's clientele.

17. From this perspective the usury law, as it operated in antebellum New York, was a perfectly rational instrument of state policy in that it created a more favorable market for the state's debt. In doing so the law served a purpose similar to the state's Free Banking Act requirements that member banks hold government bonds as reserves. Richard Sylla has analyzed the effects of similar legislation at the federal level in "Federal Policy, Banking Market Structure, and Capital Mobilization in the United States, 1863-1913," *Journal of Economic History* 29 (December 1969): 657-86.

18. For "arbitrage" to occur the interest rates in other markets would have to rise "sufficiently" above 7 percent to cover transaction costs, brokers' fees, and the risk of later capital loss.

19. Walter B. Smith and Arthur H. Cole, *Fluctuations in American Business, 1790-1860*, p. 125. For a discussion of interest rates in 1848 see: Alan L. Olmstead, "Davis and Bigelow Revisited: Antebellum American Interest Rates," *Journal of Economic History* 34, no. 2 (June 1974): 483-91.

20. Smith and Cole, *Fluctuations*, chart 47, p. 137.

21. Although it was argued above that the Bank for Savings was still locked into part of its portfolio, it still held many issues (New York and United States) that were selling at par or above.

22. Mortgage Loans of the Seamen's Bank for Savings, Ledger A (1829-1877), no page; Moses Beach, *The Wealth and Biography of the Wealthy Citizens of the City of New York*, pp. 13, 21, 23-25. Edward Pessen's newer listings do not significantly change my conclusions. Edward Pessen, "The Wealthiest New Yorkers of the Jacksonian Era: A New List," *New York Historical Society Quarterly* 54, no. 1 (January 1970): 145-72.

23. Mortgage Loans of the Seamen's Bank for Savings, Ledger A (1829-1877), no page.

24. This is implicit from Payne and Davis's discussion of the Savings Bank of

Baltimore: "One striking feature of the Bank's policy . . . was the almost unchanged rate of interest (6 per cent) charged on all loans—regardless of to whom they were made, for what period they were made, or with what collateral they were secured. That the rate did not rise above 6 per cent is explained by the fact that this was the maximum permitted under the Maryland Usury Law. . . ." Peter L. Payne and Lance E. Davis, *The Savings Bank of Baltimore, 1818-1866*, pp. 119-20; and Davis, "The New England Textile Mills," p. 3.

25. Davis and Payne, "From Benevolence to Business," p. 398. This difference continued long after the legal constraints on investments became similar.

26. Ibid.

27. Payne and Davis, *Baltimore*, p. 171.

28. Davis, "Mrs. Vatter on Industrial Borrowing," p. 225.

29. Davis and Payne, "From Benevolence to Business," p. 404.

CHAPTER 6

1. This does not take into consideration possible differences in transaction costs.

2. The bank's original charter made no provision for cash reserves, nor for a surplus. Since the bank was operating out of a basement room in the Old Alms House with no safe of its own, this was an impossible constraint, and the trustees simply ignored it. The right to make such deposits was included in all the charters of banks formed after 1830. There is no evidence in the bank's minutes that any trustees ever suggested that the policy of depositing in commercial banks violated the bank's charter.

3. Secretary's Minutes, Seamen's Bank for Savings, vol. 1, 3 June 1829, p. 16; 5 September 1838, p. 138; *Annual Reports*, Bank for Savings, 1820-1836.

4. Davis R. Dewey, *State Banking Before the Civil War*, pp. 215-16; Fritz Redlich, *The Molding of American Banking*, pt. 1, p. 53.

5. Redlich, *Molding*, p. 53.

6. In January 1828 eight New York City banks reported holding a total of only $500,000 in deposits from other banks (i.e., bankers' balances). At this time the Bank for Savings' account in the Mechanics' Bank exceeded $134,000. Commercial banks may have listed savings bank accounts under "due depositors" rather than under "due Banks" in their reports to the bank commissioners. *New York State Assembly Journal*, January 1828, pp. 646-57.

7. Ernest L. Bogart, *Internal Improvements and State Debt in Ohio*, p. 163. Bogart does not give a specific date for the reduction of the rate from 5 to 4 percent.

8. A deposit of $100,000 was made in the Bank of America in July 1833. It remained untouched until July 1835, when the entire amount was withdrawn. The account of the Bank of New York was opened in June 1833 with a deposit of $300,000. This account was closed with three withdrawals of $100,000 each in April, May, and June of 1836. *Annual Reports*, Bank for Savings, 1 February 1835, p. 5; 1836, p. 6; 1837, p. 6.

9. This crisis resulted from the recent Fire of 1835, which bankrupted many of the city's insurance companies. It was aggravated by the withdrawal of capital and deposits from the New York branch of the Second Bank of the United States. Henry W. Domett, *A History of the Bank of New York, 1784-1884*, pp. 83-85; Nathan Miller, *The Enterprise of a Free People*, pp. 188-91.

10. At this time note issues by Safety-Fund Banks were restricted to twice the paid-up capital stock, and loans and discounts were limited to two-and-one-half times a bank's capital. Robert Chaddock, *The Safety-Fund Banking System in New York, 1829-1866*, p. 262; and Miller, *Enterprise*, p. 188.

11. The loan the Bank of New York received from the canal fund was on relatively favorable terms. The commissioners of the canal fund did not extract as high a rate on their time deposits as they could have during the year following the fire—they were admittedly subsidizing financial institutions.

12. Each of the bank's three $100,000 withdrawals in April, May, and June of 1836 was accompanied by a $100,000 purchase of newly issued New York City bonds. *Annual Report of Bank for Savings* in *New York State Senate Documents*, vol. 1, no. 31, 14 February 1837, pp. 8-11.

13. For a list of the Union Bank's directors in 1835 see *New-York As It Is In 1835*, p. 103.

14. A possible exception might have been the Seamen's in 1838.

15. Francis Cooper, Gabriel Furman, George Arcularius, and Andrew Morris were all directors of the Mechanics' Bank; John Oothout, the Bank for Savings' treasurer, was a director of the Bank of New York and would be elected its president in 1843; Thomas Buckley, Jonathan Goodhue, Benjamin L. Swan, and John B. Lawrence were all directors of the Bank of America. This list was compiled from New York City directories for only a few sample years and may be incomplete. Many other Bank for Savings' trustees, although not officers of these commercial banks, probably were stockholders.

16. Secretary's Minutes, Seamen's Bank for Savings, vol. 1, 3 June 1829, p. 16; 5 September 1838, p. 138; 3 October 1838, p. 139.

17. Ibid., 3 July 1839, p. 150.

18. Ibid., 4 December 1844, no page. This citation implies that the bank received a higher rate on its deposits prior to January 1845, but there is no mention what that rate might have been.

19. At this time the Seamen's was reducing the interest rate it charged many of its customers for outstanding mortgage loans from 7 to 6 percent.

20. Secretary's Minutes, Seamen's Bank for Savings, vol. 1, 10 July 1850, no page.

21. For the names of the trustees and officers of the Greenwich Savings Bank, see James H. Collins, *Ninety Years of the Greenwich Savings Bank*, pp. 65-70; all the Greenwich Bank's stockholders for 1832 are listed in *New York Assembly Documents*, 1833, vol. 2, no. 86, pp. 62-64; the officers and directors of the Greenwich Bank in 1835 are listed in *New-York As It Is*, pp. 97-98.

22. Collins, *Ninety Years*, p. 29.

23. Henry A. Schenck, comp. *Manual of the Bowery Savings Bank*, pp. 206-208; *New York Assembly Documents*, 1833, vol. 2, no. 86, pp. 56-59; *New-York As It Is*, pp. 95-96. Ten of the Butchers' and Drovers' fourteen directors and officers were trustees of the mutual.

24. Secretary's Minutes, Bowery Savings Bank, vol. 1, 11 June 1834, p. 5; 18 July 1835, p. 18. This announcement came at a time when the other three mutuals were getting 5 percent on their accounts.

25. Ibid., 18 July 1835, p. 18.

26. Ibid., 8 February 1844, p. 156.

27. This figure is based on an average of the Bowery's monthly balances from February 1844 through April 1846. The actual yearly interest rates calculated are 1.2 for February through December of 1844, 1.4 for 1845, and 1.1 for January through April of 1846. Ibid., Secretary's Reports for 1844, 1845, and 1846.

28. Ibid., 8 April 1846, p. 202; 11 February 1846, p. 199; 11 March 1846, pp. 200-201.

29. The calculated rates on the average monthly balances were 2.2 percent for May to December 1846; 2.0 percent for 1847; 1.9 percent for 1848; 1.7 percent for 1849; and 1.1 percent for 1850. The Bowery's average balances rose over time, which accounts for the declining actual rate of interest on its account.

30. Secretary's Minutes, Bowery Savings Bank, vol. 1, 10 November 1847, p. 225; 8 December 1847, p. 227.

31. Ibid., 8 January 1851, p. 294; report dated 1 February 1851, no page; 9 July 1851, pp. 308-309.

32. Ibid., 11 February 1857, p. 497; 11 March 1857, p. 500; H. Wilson, comp., *Trow's New-York City Directory*, for the years 1853-1860.

33. Secretary's Minutes, Bowery Savings Bank, vol. 1, 10 February 1858, p. 541; 9 December 1857, p. 531.

34. The bank's minutes suggest that by May 1859 (and maybe earlier) it was receiving interest on its accounts. Ibid., 14 May 1859, p. 613.

35. There is, of course, no index as to how much constitutes a "large" or a "small" sum to use to evaluate these results.

36. The Butchers' and Drovers' capital stock was $500,000 throughout the period from 1836 to 1851.

37. A preferable measure would be to take the subsidy as a percentage of the commercial bank's total profits instead of its declared dividends, but unfortunately there is little reliable information on profits.

38. In 1832 the Butchers' and Drovers' Bank had about 150 stockholders, only three of whom held more than $10,000. *New York Assembly Documents*, 1833, vol. 2, no. 89, pp. 56-59.

39. Margaret Myers, *The New York Money Market*, p. 121.

40. Secretary's Minutes, Bowery Savings Bank, Reports for 1847-1849.

41. Secretary's Minutes, Manhattan Savings Institution, vol. 1, 8 January 1856, p. 189; 12 February 1856, p. 193; Minutes of the Finance Committee, Manhattan Savings Institution, 12 February 1856, no page. The one bank willing to pay 5 percent was probably the Bank of North America.

42. Six of the Manhattan's trustees were directors of the Bowery Bank and three were directors of the Citizen's Bank.

43. Minutes of the Finance Committee, Manhattan Savings Institution, 23 December 1856; 19 January 1858; 2 March 1858; Secretary's Minutes, Manhattan Savings Institution, vol. 1, 18 January 1857, p. 211; 12 January 1858, p. 233; 9 March 1858, p. 236.

44. Secretary's Minutes, Dry Dock Savings Institution, vol. 1, 20 December 1848, no page.

45. Myers, *Money Market*, p. 122.

46. Secretary's Minutes, Dry Dock Savings Institution, vol. 1, 17 April 1850.

47. Allan Nevins, ed., *The Diary of Philip Hone, 1828-1851*, p. 257. The following day, 10 May 1837, the Bank for Savings joined the city's commercial banks in suspending specie payments.

48. Minutes, Bank for Savings, vol. 4, 12 April 1837, p. 1315; 13 April 1837, p. 1315; 27 April 1837, p. 1316; 14 February 1838, p. 1394; *Annual Report*, 1838, pp. 10-11.

49. Secretary's Minutes, Seamen's Bank for Savings, vol. 1, 1 May 1837, pp. 119-20. The Bowery maintained liquidity only with the help of the Bank for Savings. The Bowery exchanged $40,000 of its best 7 percent "bonds and mortgages" for an equal amount (par value) of the Bank for Savings' New York City bonds. The Bowery was then able to obtain a loan of $35,000 using the city bonds as collateral. The Greenwich Savings Bank asked for a similar exchange, but the Bank for Savings trustees, fearful of their own bank's safety, rejected the request. To piece this story together see Minutes, Bank for Savings, vol. 4, 27 April 1837, p. 1316; 17 May 1837, p. 1328; Secretary's Minutes, Bowery Savings Bank, vol. 1, 15 May, p. 58; 14 June, p. 60; Bayard Tuckerman, ed., *The Diary of Philip Hone, 1828-1851*, 1: 252.

50. Tuckerman, *Philip Hone*, 1: 251.

51. Secretary's Minutes, Bowery Savings Bank, vol. 1, 15 December 1854, no page; 28 September 1857, p. 517.

52. Myers, *Money Market*, p. 190.

53. Minutes, Bank for Savings, vol. 7, 30 September 1857, p. 83.

54. Myers, *Money Market*, p. 94.

55. Emphasis added. Roger H. Hinderliter and Hugh Rockoff, "The Management of Reserves by Banks in Ante-bellum Eastern Financial Centers," *Explorations in Economic History* 11 (Fall 1973):41.

56. Chaddock, *Safety-Fund*, p. 339.

57. For example, if total assets were $100,000, a mutual could hold the entire amount in its "available fund"; if total assets were $900,000, it could hold $300,000 in its available fund.

58. In most cases the size of the available fund was the same as that described for the Emigrant Industrial. The exceptions were the Sixpenny, which was limited to $50,000 or one-third of of deposits, Bloomingdale and Union Dime, whose charters simply called for up to one-third of deposits, and the German, whose charter allowed up to one-fifth of deposits.

59. The wording in the charters on this subject is confusing and maybe purposely so. The above interpretation was offered by Emerson W. Keyes in *A History of Savings*

*Banks in the United States,* 1: 387-93.

60. Ibid., p. 406.

61. Secretary's Minutes, Bowery Savings Bank, vol. 1, 9 November 1853, p. 378; 10 May 1853, p. 398; 9 December 1857, p. 531. Many, if not most, of these loans were secured by New York City bonds, and the bank may have actually made some loans directly to the city at 7 percent.

62. Some banks could lend an amount up to 75 percent of the value. A mutual could easily evade this restriction by over-appraising property.

63. Dewey, *State Banking,* p. 15; also see pp. 5-22.

64. Chaddock, *Safety-Fund,* p. 291. The literature is not as explicit as it should be, but it seems that this latter proposal was never passed into law.

65. *New York Times,* 1851-1860; *New York Evening Post,* 1855-1857; *New York Herald,* 1852-1855; Domett, *Bank of New York,* pp. 108-109.

66. Wilson, *Trow's New York City Directory for 1853-1854,* p. 14 of Appendix.

67. Keyes was Deputy Superintendent of the New York State Banking Department at the time of his investigation. He was an ardent admirer and defender of savings banks, and thus his criticisms of this institution are particularly noteworthy. Emerson W. Keyes, *Special Report on Savings Banks,* pp. 110-11.

68. Keyes's data are inconsistent; see the note to this effect on Table 18.

69. Although Keyes implied that this mutual did not have any government securities, and none are listed in Table 18, the bank probably would have sold whatever holdings of this type (if any) it had in its fight to remain liquid. Ibid., p. 111.

70. Ibid.

71. *The Charter of the Broadway Savings Institution* in *New York State Laws of 1851,* chap. 245, p. 462, section 1; John Doggett, Jr., *Doggett's New York City Directory for 1850-1851,* pp. 10-11 of Appendix.

72. Doggett, *Directory 1850-1851,* p. 10; Trustees' Minutes, Broadway Savings Institution, vol. 1, 8 September 1851, no page; Wilson, *Trow's Directory, 1853-1854,* p. 16.

73. Trustee's Minutes, Broadway Savings Institution, vol. 1, 13 October 1858, no page.

74. This is the only period for which complete call-loan information is available.

75. The Broadway Savings Institution Ledgers (unmarked) for period covering 1 January 1853 to 6 April 1855, no pages; Doggett, *Directory,* 1850-1851; Wilson, *Trow's Directory,* 1853-1861. This bank's ledgers were not identified by name or by number.

76. This number is larger than thirty-five because many loans were secured by a number of different issues, and because one person often made several separate loans.

77. The largest loans were made to the private banking firm of Jacob Little and Company. Between January 1851 and April 1851 Little took out four loans: one of $19,000 and three of $20,000. His maximum balance was $60,000. Little borrowed from other mutuals besides the Broadway. In March 1858 he received a call loan of $40,000 from the Manhattan Savings Institution. Treasurer's Report Book, Broadway Savings Institution, January 1851 to April 1851; Minutes of the Finance Committee, Manhattan Savings Institution, 3 March 1858, no page.

78. *The Report of the Massachusetts Bank Commissioners of 1861* as quoted in Keyes, *Savings Banks in the United States,* 1: 70, 83.

79. Ibid., 1: 83-84.

CHAPTER 7

1. Secretary's Minutes, Seamen's Bank for Savings, vol. 1, 16 June 1845; 6 November 1850, no pages.

2. Trustees' Minutes, Broadway Savings Bank, vol. 1, 4 March 1852, no page.

3. Minutes, Bank for Savings, vol. 6, 12 December 1854, p. 2785.

4. Secretary's Minutes, Bowery Savings Bank, vol. 1, 11 October 1848, p. 243; 12 December 1849, p. 267; 10 March 1841, p. 121; vol. 2, 8 May 1861, p. 48.

5. Secretary's Minutes, Seamen's Bank for Savings, vol. 1, 1 May 1837, p. 119.

# Bibliography

**Bank Records**

Bank for Savings in the City of New York (deposited in the archives of the New York Bank for Savings, handwritten, except where noted):
    Account Ledgers.
    *The Annual Reports of the Trustees of the Bank for Savings in the City of New York*. New York, 1820–1866.
    Bond and Mortgage Folios. 1836–1870.
    *The Charter and By-Laws of the Bank for Savings in the City of New York*. New York, 1819, 1832, 1857.
    Deposit and New Account Books.
    Draft Ledgers.
    Files of Assorted Papers and Letters.
    Index of the Depositors.
    Minutes of the Trustees. 7 vols. 1816–1870.
    Original Test Book.
    Special Book on Bank Personnel.
    Taylor, Najah. "The Autobiography of Najah Taylor." New York, n.d., typed.
    Transfer Ledgers.
    Transfer Test Books.
Bowery Savings Bank (deposited in the archives of the Bowery Savings Bank, handwritten, except where noted):
    *By-Laws of the Bowery Savings Bank*. New York, 1839.
    Secretary's Minutes. 2 vols. 1834–1864.
    *Some Objectives to the Proposed Plan for Keeping the Accounts of the Bowery Savings Bank*. New York, n.d.
Broadway Savings Institution (deposited in the archives of the Broadway Savings Bank, handwritten):
    Deposit and Withdrawal Book. 1851–1861.
    Funding Committee Minutes and Report Book. 1851–1861.
    Ledgers showing Loans on Stocks and Loans on Bonds and Mortgages.
    Trustees' Minutes. 1851–1865.
Dry Dock Savings Institution (deposited in the archives of the Dry Dock Savings Bank, handwritten):
    Bond and Mortgage Folios. 1848–1866.
    Deposit and Withdrawal Ledger. 1848–1861.
    Funding Committee Minutes. 1848–1860.
    Secretary's Minutes. 1848–1864.
Emigrant Industrial Savings Bank (deposited in the archives of the Emigrant Savings Bank):

Annual Statements. 1860-1864 (typed), supplied by the Bank's Secretary, Joseph G. Reilly.

Bennett, William H. "A Chronological History of the Emigrant Industrial Savings Bank." New York, n.d., typed.

Manhattan Savings Institution (deposited in the archives of the Manhattan Savings Bank, handwritten, except where noted):

Charter and By-Laws of the Manhattan Savings Institution. New York, 1862.

Minutes of the Finance Committee. 1851-1861.

Trustees' Minutes. 1851-1864.

Mariners' Savings Institution (deposited in the archives of the Manhattan Savings Bank, handwritten):

Minutes of the Trustees. 1853-1860.

Savings Bank of New York (deposited in the archives of the New York Bank for Savings, handwritten):

Minutes of the Directors, 1 vol., 1816-1817 (pp. 1-16 of vol. 1 of Minutes of the Trustees of the Bank for Savings in the City of New York).

Seamen's Bank for Savings (deposited in the archives of the Seamen's Bank for Savings, handwritten):

Deposit and Withdrawal Books.

Mortgage Loans, 1834-1877 in Ledger A.

Report Books. Nos. 2-3, containing Reports of the Funding Committee and the Attending Committee.

Secretary's Minutes. 2 vols. 1829-1865.

## Government Documents

### NEW YORK CITY

New York City. Minutes of the Common Council of the City of New York, 1784-1831. New York: M. M. Brown, 1917.

### NEW YORK STATE

Assembly. Documents of the Assembly of the State of New York. Albany, 1830-1866.

——. Journal of the Assembly of the State of New York. Albany, 1819-1830.

Census of the State of New York for the years 1845 and 1855. Albany, 1846, 1856.

Laws of the State of New York. Albany, 1817-1861.

Senate. Documents of the Senate of the State of New York. Albany, 1830-1866.

——. Journal of the Senate of the State of New York. Albany, 1819-1830.

### UNITED STATES

United States Bureau of the Census. Seventh Census of the United States, 1850. Washington, D.C., 1852.

——. Sixth Census of the United States, 1840. Washington, D.C., 1841.

——. Historical Statistics of the United States, Colonial Times to 1957 Washington, D.C., 1960.

Directories, Newspapers, and Periodicals

*Albany Argus,* 1819.

*Bankers' Magazine and Statistical Register.* Boston and New York, 1846-1866. (Also called *Bankers' Magazine and State Financial Register* for some years.)

Beach, Moses. *The Wealth and Biography of the Wealthy Citizens of the City of New York.* New York, 1846, 1849, 1855.

De Bow, J. B. D., ed. *Commercial Review of the South and West.* New Orleans, 1847-1860.

*Dictionary of American Biography.* New York: Scribner's, 1928-1937.

Doggett, John, Jr. *Doggett's New York City Directory.* Annual. New York, 1842-1851.

Hazard, Samuel. *Hazard's United States Commercial and Statistical Register.* Philadelphia, 1841.

Hunt, Freeman, ed. *Merchants' Magazine and Commercial Review.* New York, 1839-1860.

*Journal of Commerce.* 1828-1837.

Longworth, David, and Longworth, Thomas. *Longworth's American Almanac, New York Register, and City Directory.* Annual. New York, 1819-1842.

National Association of Mutual Savings Banks. *National Fact Book.* May 1969.

*New York As It Is.* Annual. New York: J. Disturnell, 1833-1835, 1837.

*New York Commercial Advertiser.* 1816, 1819.

*New York Evening Post.* 1816-1865.

*New York Herald.* 1833-1865.

*New York Times.* 1851-1865.

*New York Tribune.* 1841-1865.

Niles, Hezekiah, ed. *Niles' Weekly Register.* 1819-1849.

Richards, T. P. *New York Commercial List Containing Names and Occupations of the Principal Merchants in the City.* New York, 1853.

Rode, Charles R. *Rode's New York City Directory.* New York, 1850.

Valentine, D. T., ed. *Manual of the Corporation of the City of New York.* New York, 1841-1860.

Williams, Edwin. *New York Annual Register.* 1830-1840.

Wilson, H., comp. *Trow's New-York City Directory.* Annual. 1853-1864.


Books and Reports

Adams, Henry Carter. *Public Debts; an Essay on the Science of Finance.* New York: D. Appleton, 1887.

Albany Savings Bank. *Albany Savings Bank, 1820-1920.* Albany: Albany Savings Bank, 1920.

Albion, Robert G. *The Rise of New York Port, 1815-1860.* New York: C. Scribner's, 1939.

————. *Square-Riggers on Schedule: The New York Sailing Packets to England, France, and the Cotton Ports.* Princeton, N.J.: Princeton University Press, 1938.

Armstrong, William. *The Aristocracy of New York.* New York, 1848.

Baughman, James P. *Charles Morgan and the Development of Southern Transportation.* Nashville, Tenn.: Vanderbilt University Press, 1968.

Baumol, William J. *Business Behavior, Value and Growth*. New York: Macmillan, 1959.
———. *Economic Theory and Operations Analysis*. 2d ed. Englewood Cliffs, N.J.: Prentice-Hall, 1965.
Bennett, Frank P., Jr. *The Story of Mutual Savings Banks*. Boston: F. P. Bennett, 1924.
Berger, Mark L. *The Revolution in the New York Party Systems, 1840-1860*. Port Washington, N.Y. and London: Kennikot Press, 1973.
Berger, Meyer. *Growth of an Ideal, 1850-1950: The Story of the Manhattan Savings Bank*. New York: Manhattan Savings Bank, 1950.
Bogart, Ernest Ludlow. *Internal Improvements and State Debt in Ohio*. New York: Longmans, Green, 1924.
Bourne, W. O. *History of the Public School Society of the City of New York*. New York, 1873.
Brooklyn Savings Bank. *Old Brooklyn Heights, 1827-1927*. Brooklyn: J. C. Powers, 1927 and 1937.
Brooks, Richard A. E., ed. *Diary of Michael Floy Jr., Bowery Village, 1833-1837*. New Haven, Conn.: Yale University Press, 1941.
Brown, John Crosby. *A Hundred Years of Merchant Banking*. New York: privately printed, 1909.
Buffalo Savings Bank. *Through the Years 1846-1934*. Buffalo, N.Y., 1934.
Cameron, Rondo. *France and the Economic Development of Europe, 1800-1914*. Princeton, N.J.: Princeton University Press, 1961.
Cameron, Rondo, et al. *Banking in the Early Stages of Industrialization*. New York: Oxford University Press, 1967.
Campbell, Dorcas Elisabeth. *The First Hundred Years: The Chronicle of a Mutual Savings Bank*. New York: East River Savings Bank, 1949.
Carosso, Vincent P. *Investment Banking in America: A History*. Cambridge, Mass.: Harvard University Press, 1970.
Catterall, Ralph C. H. *The Second Bank of the United States*. Chicago: University of Chicago Press, 1903.
*Century of Service: The Poughkeepsie Savings Bank, 1831-1931*. New York: n.p., 1931.
Chaddock, Robert E. *The Safety Fund Banking System in New York, 1829-1866*. Washington, D.C.: Government Printing Office, 1910.
Chamberlain, Neil W. *Enterprise and Environment: The Firm in Time and Place*. New York: McGraw-Hill, 1968.
———. *A General Theory of Economic Process*. New York: Harper and Row, 1955.
*The Chase National Bank of the City of New York, 1817-1922*. New York: De Vinne Press, 1922.
*Citizens' Savings Bank, Its Founders, History and Homes, 1860-1913*. New York: n.p., 1924.
Clark, Victor S. *History of Manufactures in the United States*. 3 vols. Washington, D.C.: Carnegie Institution of Washington, 1916-1928, 1949.
Cochran, Thomas C. *Railroad Leaders, 1845-1890: The Business Mind in Action*. Cambridge, Mass.: Harvard University Press, 1953.
Cole, Arther H. *Business Enterprise in its Social Setting*. Cambridge, Mass.: Harvard University Press, 1959.
———. *Wholesale Commodity Prices in the United States, 1700-1861*. 2 vols. Cambridge, Mass.: Harvard University Press, 1938.
Collins, James H. *Ninety Years of the Greenwich Savings Bank*. New York: Greenwich Savings Bank, 1923.

Cyert, Richard M., and March, James G. *A Behavioral Theory of the Firm.* Englewood Cliffs, N.J.: Prentice-Hall, 1963.

Daniells, Lorna M. *Studies in Enterprise.* Cambridge, Mass.: Harvard University Press, 1957.

Davis, Lance E., Hughes, Jonathan R. T., and McDougall, Duncan M. *American Economic History.* Homewood, Ill.: Richard D. Irwin, 1961.

Dewey, Davis R. *State Banking Before the Civil War.* Washington, D.C.: Government Printing Office, 1910.

Diamond, William. *Development Banks.* Baltimore, Md.: Johns Hopkins Press, 1957.

Domett, Henry W. *A History of the Bank of New York, 1784-1884.* New York: G. P. Putnam's Sons, 1884.

Downs, Anthony. *An Economic Theory of Democracy.* New York: Harper, 1957.

Dunbar, Charles F. *Laws of the U.S. Relating to Currency, Finance, and Banking from 1789-1891.* Boston: Ginn, 1893.

Durand, Edward D. *The Finances of New York City.* New York: Macmillan, 1898.

Ernst, Robert. *Immigrant Life in New York City, 1825-1863.* New York: Kings Crown Press, 1949.

Fales, De Coursey. *Some Historical Notes of the Early Days of the Bank for Savings in the City of New York.* New York: Bank for Savings, 1944.

Fishlow, Albert. *American Railroads and the Transformation of the Ante-Bellum Economy.* Cambridge, Mass.: Harvard University Press, 1965.

Flagg, Azariah C. *Banks and Banking in the State of New York from 1777 to 1864.* Brooklyn: Rome Brothers, 1868.

Foner, Philip S. *Business and Slavery: The New York Merchants and the Irrepressible Conflict.* Chapel Hill, N.C.: University of North Carolina Press, 1941.

Friedman, Milton. *A Theory of the Consumption Function.* Princeton, N.J.: Princeton University Press, 1957.

Fromm, Gary, ed. *Transport Investment and Economic Development.* Washington, D.C.: Brookings Institution, 1965.

Gibbons, James S. *The Banks of New York and the Panic of 1857.* New York, 1858.

―――. *The Banks of New York, Their Dealers, etc.* New York, 1858.

Gilchrist, David T., ed. *The Growth of the Seaport Cities, 1790-1825.* Charlottesville, Va.: University Press of Virginia, 1967.

Goldsmith, Raymond. *Financial Intermediaries in the American Economy Since 1900.* Princeton, N.J.: Princeton University Press, 1958.

―――. *A Study of Savings in the United States.* Princeton, N.J.: Princeton University Press, 1955.

Goodrich, Carter, ed. *The Government and the Economy, 1783-1861.* New York: Bobbs-Merrill, 1967.

―――. *Government Promotion of American Canals and Railroads, 1800-1890.* New York: Columbia University Press, 1960.

Goodrich, Carter, et al. *Canals and American Economic Development.* New York: Columbia University Press, 1961.

Govan, Thomas Payne. *Nicholas Biddle: Nationalist and Public Banker, 1786-1844.* Chicago: University of Chicago Press, 1959.

Gras, N. S. B. *The Massachusetts First National Bank of Boston, 1784-1934.* Cambridge, Mass.: Harvard University Press, 1937.

Gras, N. S. B., and Larson, Henrietta M. *Casebook in American Business*

*History*. New York: F. S. Crafts, 1939.

Gurley, John G., and Shaw, Edward S. *Money in a Theory of Finance*. Washington, D.C.: Brookings Institution, 1960.

Hagen, Everett E. *On the Theory of Social Change: How Economic Growth Begins*. Homewood, Ill.: Dorsey Press, 1962.

Hammond, Bray. *Banks and Politics in America*. Princeton, N.J.: Princeton University Press, 1957.

Hammond, Jabez D. *The History of Political Parties in the State of New York: From the Ratification of the Federal Constitution to December, 1840*, vol. 1. 3d ed., rev. Cooperstown, N.Y.: H. & E. Phinney, 1845.

Hardenbrook, William Ten Eych. *Financial New York: A History of the Banking and Financial Institutions of the Metropolis*. New York and Chicago, 1897.

Hartz, Louis. *Economic Policy and Democratic Thought: Pennsylvania, 1776-1860*. Cambridge, Mass.: Harvard University Press, 1948.

Heath, Milton S. *Constructive Liberalism: The Role of the State in Economic Development in Georgia to 1860*. Cambridge, Mass.: Harvard University Press, 1954.

Hester, Donald D. *Ownership and Behavior in the Savings and Loan Industry*. A Report for the Federal Home Loan Bank Board. Washington, D.C.: Federal Home Loan Bank Board, November 1967.

———. *Stock and Mutual Associations in the Savings and Loan Industry: A Study of the Economic Implications of Conversions*. A Report for the Federal Home Loan Bank Board. Washington, D.C.: Federal Home Loan Bank Board, May 1968.

———, and Pierce, James L. *Cross-Section Analysis and Bank Dynamics*. Cowles Foundation Discussion Paper No. 231. New Haven, Conn., July 1967.

———, and Scott, Kenneth E. *Conversion of Mutual Savings and Loan Associations to Stock Form: Legal and Economic Issues*. A Report for the Federal Home Loan Bank Board. Washington, D.C.: Federal Home Loan Bank Board, December 1967.

Hicks, John R. *Value and Capital: An Inquiry into Some Fundamental Principles of Economic Theory*. Oxford, England: Clarendon Press, 1946.

Hidy, Ralph W. *The House of Baring in American Trade and Finance: English Merchant Bankers at Work, 1763-1861*. Cambridge, Mass.: Harvard University Press, 1949.

Hillhouse, Albert M. *Municipal Bonds: A Century of Experience*. New York: Prentice-Hall, 1936.

Horne, H. Oliver. *A History of Savings Banks*. London and New York: Oxford University Press, 1947.

Hower, Ralph M. *History of Macy's of New York, 1858-1919*. Cambridge, Mass.: Harvard University Press, 1943.

Hugins, Walter. *Jacksonian Democracy and the Working Class: A Study of the New York Workingmen's Movement, 1829-1837*. Stanford, Cal.: Stanford University Press, 1960.

Hunt, Freeman. *Lives of American Merchants*. New York, 1858.

Husband, Joseph. *One Hundred Years of the Greenwich Savings Bank*. New York: n.p., 1933.

Jenks, Leland H. *The Migration of British Capital to 1875*. London and New York: Alfred A. Knopf, 1927.

Johnson, Arthur M., and Supple, Barry E. *Boston Capitalists and Western Railroads: A Study in the Nineteenth-Century Railroad Investment Process*.

Cambridge, Mass.: Harvard University Press, 1967.

Kardouche, George K. *The Competition for Savings: Determinants of Deposits at Commercial Banks, Mutual Savings Banks, and Savings and Loan Associations.* New York: National Industrial Conference Board, 1969.

Kass, Alvin. *Politics in New York State, 1800–1830.* Syracuse, N.Y.: Syracuse University Press, 1965.

Keyes, Emerson W. *A History of Savings Banks in the State of New York.* Albany, 1870.

———. *A History of Savings Banks in the United States.* 2 vols. New York: Bradford Rhodes, 1876, 1878.

———. *Special Report on Savings Banks.* Albany: Van Benthuysen & Sons, 1868.

King, Charles. *Memoir of the Construction, Cost, and Capacity of the Croton Aqueduct.* New York, 1843.

Knapp, Samuel L. *The Life of Thomas Eddy.* London, 1836.

Kniffin, William H. *The Savings Bank and its Practical Work.* New York: Bankers Publishing, 1912.

Knight, Frank H. *Risk, Uncertainty and Profit.* Boston and New York: Houghton Mifflin, 1921.

Knowles, Charles E. *History of the Bank for Savings in the City of New York, 1819–1929.* 2d ed. New York: by the bank, 1936.

Knox, John Jay. *A History of Banking in the United States.* New York, 1903. Reprint, New York: Augustus M. Kelley, 1969.

Kuznets, Simon. *Modern Economic Growth; Rate, Structure, and Spread.* New Haven, Conn.: Yale University Press, 1966.

Landes, David S. *Bankers and Pashas: International Finance and Economic Imperialism in Egypt.* Cambridge, Mass.: Harvard University Press, 1958.

Lanier, Henry W. *A Century of Banking in New York, 1822–1922.* New York: Gilliss Press, 1922.

Larson, Henrietta M. *Jay Cooke: Private Banker.* Cambridge, Mass.: Harvard University Press, 1936.

Lebergott, Stanley. *Manpower in Economic Growth.* New York: McGraw-Hill, 1964.

Lewins, William. *A History of Banks of Savings in Great Britain and Ireland.* London, 1866.

Lintner, John. *Mutual Savings Banks in the Savings and Mortgage Markets.* Boston, Mass.: Graduate School of Business Administration, Harvard University, 1948.

Macatamney, Hugh. *The Cradle Days of New York.* New York: Drew and Lewis, 1909.

MacGregor, John, ed. *Commercial Statistics of America: A Digest of Her Productive Resources, Commercial Legislation, Customs, Tariffs, Shipping, Imports and Exports, Monies, Weights, and Measures.* London, 1847.

McGrane, Reginald C. *Foreign Bondholders and American State Debts.* New York: Macmillan, 1935.

———. *The Panic of 1837: Some Financial Problems of the Jacksonian Era.* Chicago: University of Chicago Press, 1924.

Manchester, Herbert. *A Century of Service, The Seamen's Bank for Savings, 1829–1929.* New York: Seamen's Bank for Savings, 1929.

———. *The Lower East Side and Citizen's Savings Bank.* New York: n.p., 1930.

Manning, James H. *Century of American Savings Banks.* New York: B. F. Buck, 1917.

Martin, William E. *Internal Improvements in Alabama*. Baltimore, Md.: Johns Hopkins Press, 1902.

Massett, Stephen C. *"Drifting About," or what "Jeems Pipes of Pipesville" Saw-and-Did*. New York: Carleton, 1868.

The Merchants' Association of New York. *An Inquiry into the Conditions Relating to the Water Supply of the City of New York*. New York: I. H. Blanchard, 1900.

Michalis, Clarence G. *"Seamen's Bank:" 125 Years in Step with New York!* New York: Newcomen Society in North America, 1954.

Miller, Douglas T. *Jacksonian Aristocracy: Class and Democracy in New York, 1830-1860*. New York: Oxford University Press, 1967.

Miller, Nathan. *The Enterprise of a Free People*. Ithaca, N.Y.: Cornell University Press, 1962.

Mills, Andrew. *That's My Bank: The Story of the Dry Dock Savings Institution, 1848-1948*. New York: Dry Dock Savings Institution, 1948.

Mohl, Raymond A. *Poverty in New York, 1783-1825*. New York: Oxford University Press, 1971.

Muscalus, John A. *Bibliography of Histories of Specific Banks, 1942*. Norristown, Pa.: by the author, 1942.

Myers, Gustavus. *History of the Great American Fortunes*. 3 vols. Chicago: C. H. Kerr, 1910.

Myers, Margaret G. *The New York Money Market*, vol. 1: *Origins and Development*. New York: Columbia University Press, 1931.

National Association of Mutual Savings Banks. *Mutual Savings Banking, Basic Characteristics and Role in the National Economy*. Englewood Cliffs, N.J.: Prentice-Hall, 1962.

*The National Bank of North America in New York*. New York: n.p., 1901.

Neu, Irene D. *Erastus Corning: Merchant and Financier, 1794-1872*. Ithaca, N.Y.: Cornell University Press, 1960.

Nevins, Allan, ed. *The Diary of Philip Hone, 1828-1851*. New York: Dodd, Mead, 1936.

————. *History of the Bank of New York and Trust Company, 1784-1934*. New York: Bank of New York and Trust Company, 1934.

Nevins, Allan, and Thomas, Milton H., eds. *The Diary of George Templeton Strong*. 4 vols. New York: Macmillan, 1952.

New York Association for Improving the Condition of the Poor. *Annual Reports*. 1845-1865.

A New York Merchant. *Remarks on the Usury Laws*. New York, 1852.

North, Douglass C. *The Economic Growth of the United States, 1790-1860*. New York: W. W. Norton, 1966.

Orcutt, William Dana. *The Miracle of Mutual Savings*. New York: Bowery Savings Bank, 1934.

Payne, Peter L., and Davis, Lance E. *The Savings Bank of Baltimore, 1818-1866: A Historical and Analytical Study*. Baltimore, Md.: Johns Hopkins Press, 1956.

Pessen, Edward. *Jacksonian America: Society, Personality and Politics*. Homewood, Ill.: Dorsey Press, 1969.

Pierce, Harry H. *Railroads of New York: A Study of Government Aid, 1826-1875*. Cambridge, Mass.: Harvard University Press, 1953.

Pintard, John. *Letters from John Pintard to His Daughter Eliza Noel Pintard*. 4 vols. in the *New-York Historical Society Collections*, vols. 70-74. New York: New York Historical Society, 1937-1940.

Pleasants, Samuel Augustus. *Fernando Wood of New York*. New York:

Columbia University Press, 1948.
Porter, Kenneth W. *John Jacob Astor, Business Man.* 2 vols. Cambridge, Mass.: Harvard University Press, 1931.
Pound, Arthur. *The Golden Earth: The Story of Manhattan's Landed Wealth.* New York: Macmillan, 1935.
Ratchford, B. U. *American State Debts.* Durham, N.C.: Duke University Press, 1941.
Rawley, James A. *Edwin D. Morgan, 1811-1883: Merchant in Politics.* New York: Columbia University Press, 1955.
Ray, R. Benson, ed. *A Chronology of the Bowery Savings Bank.* New York: Bowery Savings Bank, 1947.
Redlich, Fritz. *The Molding of American Banking, Men and Ideas.* 2 parts in *A History of American Business Leaders.* New York, 1947, 1951. Reprint (2 vols. in 1): New York: Johnson Reprint, 1968.
*Report on the Subject of Paying Interest on Current Deposits. Presented to the Banks in New York.* New York, 1858.
Ryner, Ira. *On the Crises of 1837, 1847, and 1857, in England, France, and the United States.* University of Nebraska Studies, vol. 5, no. 2. Lincoln, Neb., 1905.
Salsbury, Stephen. *The State, the Investor, and the Railroad: Boston & Albany, 1825-1867.* Cambridge, Mass.: Harvard University Press, 1967.
Sanderlin, Walter S. *The Great National Project: A History of the Chesapeake and Ohio Canal.* Baltimore, Md.: Johns Hopkins Press, 1946.
Scheiber, Harry N. *Ohio Canal Era: A Case Study of Government and the Economy, 1820-1861.* Athens, Ohio: University of Ohio Press, 1969.
Schenck, Henry A., comp., *Manual of the Bowery Savings Bank.* New York: Bowery Savings Bank, 1903.
Schneider, David M. *The History of Public Welfare in New York State, 1609-1866.* Chicago, 1938. Reprint: 2 vols., Montclair, N.J.: Patterson Smith, 1969.
Schweiger, Irving, and McGee, John S. *Chicago Banking: The Structure and Performance of Banks and Related Financial Institutions in Chicago and Other Areas.* Chicago: Graduate School of Business, University of Chicago, 1961.
Scoville, Joseph A. *The Old Merchants of New York City.* New York, 1863-1870.
Seamen's Bank for Savings. *One Hundred Fifteen Years of Service, 1829-1944.* New York: Seamen's Bank for Savings, 1944.
Sherman, Franklin J. *Modern Story of Mutual Savings Banks.* New York: J. J. Little and Ives, 1934.
Shubik, Martin. *Strategy and Market Structure.* New York: Wiley, 1959.
Simon, Herbert A. *Administrative Behavior.* New York: Macmillan, 1961.
———. *Models of Man.* New York: Wiley, 1967.
Smith, James G. *The Development of Trust Companies in the United States.* New York: Henry Hold, 1927.
Shaw, Ronald. *Erie Water West: A History of the Erie Canal, 1792-1854.* Lexington: University of Kentucky Press, 1966.
Smith, Walter B. *Economic Aspects of the Second Bank of the United States.* Cambridge, Mass.: Harvard University Press, 1953.
Smith, Walter Buckingham, and Cole, Arthur H. *Fluctuations in American Business, 1790-1860.* Cambridge, Mass.: Harvard University Press, 1935.
Society for the Prevention of Pauperism. *Documents Relative to Savings Banks, Intemperance, and Lotteries.* New York, 1819.
Sowers, Don C. *The Financial History of New York State from 1789-1912.*

New York: Columbia University Press, 1914.

Stevens, Frank W. *The Beginnings of the New York Central Railroad.* New York: G. P. Putnam's Sons, 1926.

Stigler, George J. *Capital and Rates of Return in Manufacturing Industries.* Princeton, N.J.: Princeton University Press, 1963.

Stokes, Isaac Newton Phelps. *The Iconography of Manhattan Island.* 6 vols. New York: R. H. Dodd, 1915-1928.

Studenski, Paul, and Krooss, Herman E. *Financial History of the United States.* New York: McGraw-Hill, 1952.

Taus, Esther R. *Central Banking Functions of the United States Treasury, 1789-1941.* New York: Columbia University Press, 1943.

Teck, Alan. *Mutual Savings Banks and Savings and Loan Associations: Aspects of Growth.* New York: Columbia University Press, 1968.

Temin, Peter. *The Jacksonian Economy.* New York: W. W. Norton, 1969.

Thompson, D. G. Brenton. *Ruggles of New York: A Life of Samuel B. Ruggles.* New York: Columbia University Press, 1946.

Thon, Robert W., Jr. *Mutual Savings Banks in Baltimore.* Baltimore, Md.: Johns Hopkins Press, 1935.

Tooker, Elva. *Nathan Trotter: Philadelphia Merchant, 1787-1853.* Cambridge, Mass.: Harvard University Press, 1955.

Tuckerman, Bayard, ed. *The Diary of Philip Hone, 1828-1851.* 2 vols. New York: Dodd, Mead, 1889.

Van Fenstermaker, J. *The Development of American Commercial Banking: 1782-1837.* Kent, Ohio: Kent State University, 1965.

Van Vleck, George. *The Panic of 1857: An Analytical Study.* New York: Columbia University Press, 1943.

Vose, Reuben, *The Rich Men of New York.* New York, 1862.

Weise, Arthur J. *History of the City of Albany, New York.* Albany, N.Y., 1884.

———. *History of the City of Troy.* Troy, N.Y., 1876.

Welfling, Weldon, *Mutual Savings Bank: The Evolution of a Financial Intermediary.* Cleveland, Ohio: Press of Case Western Reserve University, 1968.

———. *Savings Banking in New York State.* Durham, N.C.: Duke University Press, 1939.

White, Gerald T. *The Massachusetts Hospital Life Insurance Company.* Cambridge, Mass.: Harvard University Press, 1955.

White, Philip L. *The Beekmans of New York in Politics and Commerce.* New York: New York Historical Society, 1956.

Whitehill, Walter Muir. *The Provident Institution For Savings in the Town of Boston.* Boston: Provident Institution for Savings, 1966.

Whitford, Nobell E. *History of the Canal System of the State of New York.* 2 vols. Albany, N.Y.: Brandow Printing, 1906.

Willcox, James M. *A History of the Philadelphia Saving Fund Society, 1816-1916.* Philadelphia: J. B. Lippincott, 1916.

Williamson, Oliver E. *The Economics of Discretionary Behavior: Managerial Objectives in a Theory of the Firm.* Englewood Cliffs, N.J.: Prentice-Hall, 1964.

**Articles**

Adelman, Irma, and Morris, Cynthia T. "An Econometric Model of Socio-Economic and Political Change in Underdeveloped Countries." *American*

*Economic Review* 58 (December 1968): 1184-1218.
————. "An Econometric Model of Development: Reply." *American Economic Review* 60, no. 1 (March 1970): 236-48.
Aitken, Hugh G. J. "Yates and McIntyre: Lottery Managers." *Journal of Economic History* 13, no. 1 (Winter 1953): 36-57.
Bear, Donald V. T. "The Relationship of Savings to the Rate of Interest, Real Income and Expected Future Prices." *Review of Economics and Statistics* 43, no. 1 (February 1961): 27-35.
Berry, Sara S. "An Econometric Model of Development: Comment." *American Economic Review* 60, no. 1 (March 1970): 222-26.
Callender, Guy Stevens. "The Early Transportation and Banking Enterprises of States in Relation to the Growth of Corporations." *Quarterly Journal of Economics* 17 (November 1902): 111-62.
Chandler, Alfred D., Jr. "Patterns of American Railroad Finance, 1830-1850." *Business History Review* 28 (1954): 248-63.
Cole, Arthur H. "Cyclical and Sectional Variations in the Sale of Public Lands, 1816-1860." *Review of Economics* 9 (January 1927): 41-53.
————. "The New York Money Market of 1843 to 1862" (Part 1). *Review of Economics and Statistics* 11 (November 1929): 164-70.
————. "The New York Money Market of 1843 to 1862" (Part 2). *Review of Economics and Statistics* 12 (February 1930): 30-38.
————. "Statistical Background of the Crisis Period, 1837-1842." *Review of Economics and Statistics* 10 (November 1928): 182-95.
Cole, Arthur H., and Frickey, Edwin. "The Course of Stock Prices, 1825-1866." *Review of Economics and Statistics* 10 (August 1928): 117-39.
Cranmer, H. Jerome. "Improvements Without Public Funds: The New Jersey Canals." In Goodrich, Carter, et al., *Canals and American Economic Development*. New York: Columbia University Press, 1961.
Curtis, Benjamin R. "Debts of the States." *North American Review* 58 (1844): 109-57.
Davis, Lance E. "Capital Immobilities and Finance Capitalism: A Study of Economic Evolution in the United States, 1820-1920." *Explorations in Entrepreneurial History*, 2d ser. 1 (Fall 1963): 88-105.
————. "The Investment Market 1870-1914: The Evolution of a National Market." *Journal of Economic History* 25, no. 3 (September 1965): 355-99.
————. "Mrs. Vatter on Industrial Borrowing: A Reply." *Journal of Economic History* 21, no. 2 (June 1961): 222-26.
————. "The New England Textile Mills and the Capital Markets: A Study of Industrial Borrowing, 1840-1860." *Journal of Economic History* 20, no. 1 (March 1960): 1-30.
————. "Sources of Industrial Finance: The American Textile Industry, A Case Study." *Explorations in Entrepreneurial History*, 1st ser. 9 (April 1957): 189-203.
Davis, Lance E., and Payne, Peter L. "From Benevolence to Business: The Story of Two Savings Banks." *Business History Review* 32 (Winter 1958): 386-406.
Degler, Carl N. "The Locofocos: Urban 'Agrarians.'" *Journal of Economic History* 16 (1956): 322-33.
Downs, Anthony, and Monsen, R. J., Jr. "A Theory of Large Managerial Firms." *Journal of Political Economy* 73 (June 1965): 221-36.
Eikstein, Peter. "An Econometric Model of Development: Comment." *American Economic Review* 60, no. 1 (March 1970): 227-35.
Fand, David I. "Financial Regulation and the Allocative Efficiency of Our

Capital Markets." *National Banking Review* 3, no. 1 (September 1965): 55-63.

Fishlow, Albert. "The Trustee Savings Banks, 1817-1861." *Journal of Economic History* 21, no. 1 (March 1961): 26-40.

Frederiksen, D. M. "Mortgage Banking in America." *Journal of Political Economy* 2 (March 1894): 203-34.

Gatell, Frank Otto. "Money and Party in Jacksonian America: A Quantitative Look At New York City's Men of Quality." *Political Science Quarterly* 87 (June 1967): 235-52.

Gies, T. G., Mayer, T., and Ettin, E. C. "Portfolio Regulations and Policies of Financial Intermediaries." In *Private Financial Institutions*, pp. 167-265. Englewood Cliffs, N.J.: Prentice-Hall, 1963.

Goodman, Paul, "Ethics and Enterprise Values of a Boston Elite 1800-1860." *American Quarterly* 18, no. 3 (Fall 1966): 437-51.

Gurley, John G., and Shaw, Edward S. "The Financial Aspects of Economic Development." *American Economic Review* 45 (September 1955): 515-27.

———. "Financial Intermediaries and the Savings Investment Process." *Journal of Finance* 11 (March 1956): 257-76.

Hammond, Bray. "Free Banking and Corporations: The New York Free Banking Act of 1838." *Journal of Political Economy* 44 (February 1936): 184-209.

———. "Long and Short Term Credit in Early American Banking." *Quarterly Journal of Economics* 49 (November 1934): 79-103.

Hinderliter, Roger H., and Rockoff, Hugh. "The Management of Reserves by Banks in Ante-Bellum Eastern Financial Centers." *Explorations in Economic History* 11 (Fall 1973): 37-54.

Hofstadter, Richard. "William Leggett, Spokesman of Jacksonian Democracy." *Political Science Quarterly* 58 (December 1943): 581-94.

Krooss, Herman E. "Financial Institutions." In Gilchrist, David T., ed., *The Growth of the Seaport Cities, 1790-1825.* Charlottesville, Va.: University Press of Virginia, 1967.

Machlup, Fritz. "Theories of the Firm: Marginalist, Behavioral, Managerial." *American Economic Review* 57 (March 1967): 1-33.

Margolis, Julius. "The Analysis of the Firm: Rationalism, Conventionalism, and Behaviorism." *Journal of Business* 31 (July 1958): 187-99.

Newcomer, Lee. "A History of the Indiana Internal Improvement Bonds." *Indiana Magazine of History* 32 (June 1936): 105-15.

North, Douglass C. "International Capital Flows and the Development of the American West." *Journal of Economic History* 16 (1956): 493-505.

Nurkse, Ragner. "International Investment Today in the Light of Nineteenth Century Experience." *Economic Journal* 64 (1954): 744-58.

Olmstead, Alan L. "Davis and Bigelow Revisited: Antebellum American Interest Rates." *Journal of Economic History* 34, no. 2 (June 1974): 483-91.

———. "Investment Constraints and New York City Mutual Savings Bank Financing of Antebellum Development." *Journal of Economic History* 32, no. 4 (December 1972): 811-40.

———. "Mutual Savings Bank Depositors in New York." *Business History Review* 44, no. 3 (Autumn 1975): 287-311.

———. "New York City Mutual Savings Bank Portfolio Management and Trustee Objectives." *Journal of Economic History* 34, no. 4 (December 1974): 815-34.

Pessen, Edward. "The Egalitarian Myth and the American Social Reality: Wealth, Mobility, and Equality in the 'Era of the Common Man.'" *American*

*Historical Review* 76 (October 1971): 989-1034.

————. "Moses Beach Revisited: A Critical Examination of His Wealthy Citizens Pamphlets." *Journal of American History* 58 (September 1971): 415-26.

————. "The Wealthiest New Yorkers of the Jacksonian Era: A New List." *New York Historical Society Quarterly* 54, no. 1 (January 1970): 145-72.

Ransom, Rober L. "Interregional Canals and Economic Specialization in the Antebellum United States." *Explorations in Entrepreneurial History,* 2d ser. 5 (Fall 1967): 12-35.

Rezneck, Samuel. "Social History of An American Depression, 1837-1843." *American Historical Review* 40 (July 1935): 662-87.

————. "The Depression of 1819-1822: A Social History." *American Historical Review* 39 (October 1933): 28-47.

Rubin, Julius. "An Innovating Public Improvement: The Erie Canal." In Goodrich, Carter, et al., *Canals and American Economic Development.* New York: Columbia University Press, 1961.

Scheiber, Harry N. "Enterprise and Western Development: The Case of Micajah T. Williams." *Business History Review* 37, no. 4 (Winter 1963): 345-68.

————. "State Policy and Public Domain: The Ohio Canal Lands." *Journal of Economic History* 25 (March 1965): 86-113.

Segal, Harvey H. "Canals and Economic Development." In Goodrich, Carter, et al., *Canals and American Economic Development.* New York: Columbia University Press, 1961.

————. "Cycles of Canal Construction." In Goodrich, Carter, et al., *Canals and American Economic Development.* New York: Columbia University Press, 1961.

Shelling, Richard K. "Philadelphia and the Agitation in 1825 for the Pennsylvania Canal." *Pennsylvania Magazine of History and Biography* 62 (1938): 175-204.

Simon, Herbert A. "A Behavioral Model of Rational Choice." *Quarterly Journal of Economics* 69 (February 1955): 99-118.

————. "New Developments in the Theory of the Firm." *American Economic Review* 52, no. 2 (May 1962): 1-15.

————. "Theories of Decision-Making in Economics and Behavioral Sciences." *American Economic Review* 49, no. 3 (June 1959): 253-83.

Supple, Barry E. "A Business Elite: German-Jewish Financiers in Nineteenth Century New York." *Business History Review* 31, no. 2 (1957): 143-78.

Sylla, Richard. "Federal Policy, Banking Market Structure, and Capital Mobilization in the United States, 1863-1913." *Journal of Economic History* 29 (December 1969): 657-86.

Tobin, James, and Brainard, W. C. "Financial Intermediaries and the Effectiveness of Monetary Controls." *American Economic Review* 53 (May 1963): 383-400.

"The Usury Laws." *The Bankers' Magazine and State Financial Register* 4, no. 8 (February 1850): 584-85.

Vatter, Barbara. "Industrial Borrowing by the New England Textile Mills, 1840-1860: A Comment." *Journal of Economic History* 21, no. 2 (June 1961): 216-21.

Williamson, Oliver E. "Managerial Discretion and Business Behavior." *American Economic Review* 53 (December 1963): 1032-57.

# Index

## A

Advertising, 20, 34
  of mutual dividend rates, 40–42, 69, 70
Alabama bonds, 90, 104, 206 (n. 8)
American Exchange Bank, 26
American Seamen's Friend Society, 151
Arcularius, George, 209 ( n. 15)
Available Fund, 138

## B

Bank for Savings in the City of New York, 3–4, 7–12, 13–15, 33, 34, 35, 41–42, 78, 109, 115, 119, 132–33, 147, 148, 150
  administration and philosophy, 21–26
    board, officers, committees, 21–22
    salaried staff, 22–25
  business hours, 21–22, 30–32
  cash reserves, 121–24
  charter
    constraints on investments, 77–79
    draft vs. adopted, 7–9, 11
    constraints on depositor occupation, 59
  commercial banks
    differentiation from, 33–34, 125
    deposits in, 85, 119, 123–24, 126, 187–88
      Bank of America, 123–24, 187
      Bank of Commerce, 188
      Bank of New York, 123–24, 126, 187–88
      Manhattan Company Bank, 187–88
      Mechanics' Bank, 121–24, 187
      loan from, 82, 119
      Union Bank, 123, 187
    interest rates received from, 122–23
  depositors
    occupations, 50–52
    restricted to working class, 55, 58–65
    women, special hours for, 32
  deposits
    amount of, 157
    average balance, 53, 56, 66
    dividend rates. See Bank for Savings, deposits, interest
    rates on growth of, 104
    growth of, 104
    interest rates on, 36–37, 39–40, 65, 72, 198 (n. 34)
    large, 52–53, 58–65
      discouragement of, 58–65, 207 (n. 16)
    low interest on, 39–40, 65
    number of accounts, 157
    monthly fluctuations, 67, 70
    relation to investment policy, 35, 58, 59, 60, 62, 63, 78, 82–84, 91, 92–93, 104
    size, 52–54
      distribution, 52–54
    stable accounts encouraged, 35, 58, 63, 150–51
  investments, 99–105
    during high interest rate periods as a test of trustee objectives, 112–13, 115
    kinds
      call loans, 35, 75, 138–39
      city bonds
        Brooklyn, 94
        New York City, 75, 78, 81, 86–87, 94, 99, 123, 164
          Crotan Water Works, 86–87
          fire loan of 1836, 87
          sale of, 135
        other cities, 75, 164
      mortgage loans, 75, 78, 91–93, 99, 104
        duration of contracts, 151–52
        New York Public School Society, 75, 89
        variable interest rates on, 151–52
      state bonds
        Alabama, 90, 104
        Indiana, 90, 104
          sale of, 135
        New Jersey, 90
        New York, 7–8, 75–86, 95, 99, 164
          Erie Canal, 48, 75–86

sale of, 84-85, 135
Ohio, 75, 81, 87-90, 99
  sale of, 135
Pennsylvania, 75, 89-
  90, 104
  sale of, 135
  locked into due to
    decline in
    price, 104
U.S. Government bonds
  and Treasury notes 7,
  75, 78, 99
  as secondary reserves,
    99, 135-36
management of, 22-23, 104
similarity with other mutuals,
  90-91, 99-105, 114-15
monopoly power, used to benefit
  depositors, 148-49
opening date, 3, 16
panics, action in, 99, 134-36, 210 (n.
  49)
surplus, 40, 42-45
trustees, 22-26, 46
  duties, 21-25
  regard for Bank for Savings, 25-
    26, 147-48
  ties with commercial banks, 125
Bank of America, 9, 123, 124, 187, 209
  (n. 15)
Bank of Commerce, 125, 144, 188, 189
Bank of New York, 123, 124, 126, 187,
  188
  liquidity crises caused by Bank for
    Savings withdrawals, 123
Bank of North America, 133, 194
Bayard, William, 82, 83, 84, 88, 96
Beach, Moses, 113
Bennett, James Gordon, 34
Benthan, Jeremy, 5
Bidwell, Marshall, 22, 26
Bloomingdale Savings Bank
  assets, 180
  business hours, 31
  deposits
    amount, 160
    average balance per account, 57
    interest rates on, 38
    number of accounts, 160
  investments,
    call loans, 139, 210 (n. 58)
    similarity with other mutuals,
      105-8
  opening date, 16
Bogart, Ernest, 122
Bowery Bank, 133, 134, 191, 192, 193,
  194
Bowery Savings Bank, 4, 18, 34, 41, 42,

53, 90, 93, 94, 99, 104, 115, 150, 151,
  152, 210 (n. 49)
  administration, 27
  assets, 170-71
  business hours, 31, 32
  commercial banks
    Butchers' and Drovers', associa-
      tion with, 18, 34, 121, 126-
      33
    deposits in, 126-33, 191-92
      interest rates earned on,
        126-31, 134, 191-
        92
      subsidy to, 130-33
    other commercial banks, 127-
      28, 134, 191-92
  depositors
    occupations of, 50-52
  deposits
    amount of, 159
    average balance per account, 56
    distribution, 53, 55
    interest rates on, 36-37, 40, 41-
      42, 63, 129, 133, 198 (n. 34)
    large accounts, 63, 64, 65, 72
    monthly fluctuations in, 70-71
    number of accounts, 159
    relation to investment policy,
      63, 93, 104
    stable accounts encouraged, 35,
      63, 150-51
  investments
    during high interest rate periods
      as a test of trustee objec-
      tives, 112, 114, 115
    kinds
      call loans, 138, 139
      city bonds, 94, 151
        New York City, 99, 104,
          151
      mortgage loans, 92, 93, 99
        duration of contracts,
          152
        interest rates on, 152
      state bonds,
        New York, 99, 171
        other states, 90, 171
      U.S. Government bonds
        and Treasury notes, 99,
        104, 129, 134-36, 171
    similarity with other mutuals,
      99-105
  opening date, 16
  secondary reserves, reliance on dur-
    ing panics, 99, 104, 129, 134-36
  surplus, 40, 43, 44
Broadway Bank, 34, 134, 143-45, 191,
  192, 193, 194

Broadway Savings Institution, 34-35,
121, 143-45, 151
assets, 177
and Broadway Bank, 133, 134, 143-
45
deposits in, 133, 134, 176
business hours, 31, 32
as an indications of trustee motivation, 34-35
deposits
amount of, 160
average balance per account, 57
interest rates on, 34, 38
limit on account size, 34-35, 64
monthly fluctuations, 71
number of accounts, 160
investments
call loans, 35, 139, 143-45
mortgage loans
duration of contracts, 151
similarity with other mutuals,
105-8
opening date, 16
surplus, 44, 133
Brooklyn City debt, 94
Buckley, Thomas, 209 (n. 15)
Butchers' and Drovers' Bank, 18, 126-33,
191-92

C
Call loans, 4, 35, 75, 94, 108, 138-45
Bank for Savings critical of, 35,
95
collateral backing, 140-45
interest rates on, 112-13, 141
legal for mutuals, 74, 75, 94, 138-
39
Chamberlain, Neil, 46-47
Champlain Canal stock, 84-85, 86
Citizen's Bank, 144, 193, 194
Clinton, DeWitt, 7, 10, 13, 84
Colden, Cadwallader, 7, 21, 88, 96
Collins, Joseph B., 127
Colquhoun, Patrick, 6
Columbia College, 26
Commercial Bank, The, 190
Commercial banks, 74, 82, 85, 119
alliance with savings banks, 18, 33-
34, 46, 126-33, 134, 142-43,
143-45
deposits in savings bank, 75, 121-34
opposition to incorporation of, 9
Continental Bank, 191, 192
Cooper, Francis, 209 (n. 15)
Crash of 1929, 141
Croton Water Works, 48, 86-87, 148
Crédit Fancier, 96
Crédit Mobilier, 96

D
Davis, Lance, 4, 20, 29, 49, 65, 97, 109,
114, 115, 198 (n. 27), 204 (n. 43),
207 (n. 24)
Development banks, 95-96
role of mutuals as, 96, 148
Deposits. See Mutual savings banks,
deposits
Dividend rates, 20, 35-42, 64
announcement of changes, 39-41,
69. See also Interest rates
Dix, John A., 85
Diamond, William, 95
Domett, Henry, 123
Drew, Daniel, 3, 17
Dry Dock Savings Institution, 15
administration, 27-28
assets, 173-74
business hours, 31, 32
commercial banks
accounts in, 133-34
Bowery Bank, 133-34, 193
other commercial banks,
193
depositor sensitivity to interest differentials, 66-71
deposits
amount of, 159
average balance per account, 57
interest rates on, 37-38, 70-71
maximum account size, 64
monthly fluctuations, 68, 70-71
number of accounts, 159
investments
kinds
call loans, 139
New York City bonds, 174
New York state bonds, 174
mortgage loans, 152
U.S. Government bonds
and Treasury notes, 174
similarity with other mutuals,
105-8
opening date, 16
surplus, 44
Duncan, Reverand Henry, 6

E
East River Savings Institution, 15
administration, 27-28
assets, 172
business hours, 31, 32
depositor sensitivity to interest rate
differentials, 68, 69
deposits
amount of, 159
average balance per account, 57
interest rates on, 37-38, 39, 69

number of accounts, 159
investments
    call loans, 139
    similarity with other mutuals,
        105-8
opening date, 16
surplus, 44
Eddy, Thomas, 6, 10, 13, 84, 96, 196
    (n. 30)
Emigrant Industrial Savings Bank, 15
assets, 175
business hours, 31, 32
deposits
    amount of, 159
    average balance per account, 57
    interest rates on, 37-38
    limits on size of accounts, 64
    number of accounts, 159
investments
    call loans, 138, 139
    similarity with other mutuals,
        105-8
opening date, 16
surplus, 44
Erie Canal, 4, 48, 77, 81, 88, 95, 122
    Bank for Savings, financing of, 78,
        81-85, 89, 119
    effect on market price bonds,
        78-81
Erie Canal fund, 85
    interest rates paid by commercial
        banks to, 122

F
Felmenter, Tamer, 51
Fire of 1835, 87, 208 (n. 9)
Fishlow, Albert, 55, 200 (n. 2)
Free Banking Act of 1838, 137, 207 (n.
    17)
Fulton, Robert, 84
Fulton Bank, 124, 188, 191, 192
Furman, Gabriel, 209 (n. 15)

G
General Banking Act of 1853, 138, 205
    (n. 60)
German Savings Bank, 15
assets, 181
business hours, 31
deposits
    amount of, 161
    average balance per account, 57
    number of accounts, 161
investments
    call loans, 139, 210 (n. 58)
    similarity with other mutuals,
        105-8
opening date, 16
surplus, 44

Gilmore, Henry, 62
Goodhue, Jonathan, 209 (n. 15)
Gould, Jay, 3
Grace periods, 41-42
    as a competitive device to attract
        deposits, 69-71
Greenwich Bank, 125-26, 190
Greenwich Savings Bank, 34, 41, 42, 90,
    93, 135
assets, 168-69
business hours, 31, 32
commercial banks
    accounts in, 125-26, 190
    association with Greenwich
        Bank, 125-26
depositors, occupations and socio-
    economic status, 50, 51-52
deposits
    amount of, 158
    average balance per account, 56
    distribution by size, 53, 55
    interest rates on, 36-37, 39
    large accounts, discrimination
        against, 62
    monthly fluctuations, 70-71
    number of accounts, 158
    relation to investment policy, 93
investments
    kinds
        call loans, 138, 139
        city bonds, 94
            New York, 169
        mortgage loans, 92, 93, 135
            and trustee objectives,
                115
        state bonds, 169
            New York, 169
            Ohio, 90
            Pennsylvania, 90
        U.S. Government bonds
            and Treasury notes, 169
    similarity with other mutuals,
        99-105
opening date, 16
surplus, 44
Griscom, John, 10

H
Halstead, Caleb O., 23
Hanover Bank, 46
Hanover Insurance Co., 46
Hammond, Bray, 9
Hester, Donald, 105
Hinderliter, Roger H., 136
Hone, Philip, 23, 25-26, 87, 96, 135, 148
Hume, David, 5
Hours of business of mutuals. See Mutu-
    al saving banks, hours of business

**I**
Importers' and Traders' Bank, 194
Indiana bonds, 90, 104, 135, 206 (n. 18)
Institution for the Savings of Merchants'
    Clerks
  assets, 175
  business hours, 31, 32
  investments
    call loans, 139
    similarity with other mutuals,
        105-8
  deposits,
    amount of, 159
    average balance per account, 57
  interest rates on, 37-38
  number of accounts, 159
  opening date, 16
  surplus, 44
Interest rates
  on call loans, 112-13, 141
  on commercial bank stock, 141
  on deposits in commercial banks,
      120, 121-28, 130-34
  on deposits in mutual savings banks
    advertisement of, 40-42, 69, 70
    calculation of, 35, 39, 64, 70, 198
        (n. 34)
      causing a peak-load prob-
          lem, 70
    convergence of, 38-40
    differentials between mutuals,
        66, 69
    not guaranteed in advance, 39
    stability of, 39
  on deposits in English trustee sav-
      ings banks, 56
  on insurance company stock, 141
  on mortgage loans, 92-93, 110-11,
      113, 151-52
  usury law, effect on, 108-11, 114
  *See also* Dividend rates
Investments
  constraints channeling, 17, 74-81,
      86, 87-88, 89, 91, 95
  origin of strict constraints in New
      York state, 7-11
  evaluation of efficiency of, 116, 117
  during high interest rate periods as
      a test of trustee objectives, 112-
      15
  liquidity of, 92-93, 99, 104, 113, 119,
      134-36, 142-43
  similarity between mutuals, 98-108
  *See also* by bank and by type
Irving Savings Institution
  assets, 178
  business hours, 31
  deposits
    amount of, 160

  average balance per account, 57
    interest rates on, 38
    number of accounts, 160
  investments
    call loans, 139
    similarity with other mutuals,
        105-8
  opening date, 16
  surplus, 44

**J**
Jay, Peter A., 7, 21
Jeremiah, Thomas, 18, 27

**K**
Kennedy, Robert Lenox, 26
Keyes, Emerson, 9, 11, 18, 48-49, 88,
    142, 211 (n. 67)
Knickerbocker Bank, 142-43, 144
Knickerbocker Savings Institution
  business hours, 31, 32
  investments
    call loans, 139, 142-43
    liquity of, 142-43
    failure in Panic of 1954, 142
  opening date, 16

**L**
Lawrence, Cornelius, 87
Lawrence, John B., 209 (n. 15)
Legal environment in New York state,
    7-11
Liquidity of assets. *See* Investments, li-
    quidity of
Leather Manufacturers' Bank, 124, 188-
    89
LeRoy, Bayard & Co., 83
Lewis, Zachariah, 10
Little, Jacob, 17, 211 (n. 77)
Livingston, Brockholst, 7, 10, 83
Lord, Daniel, 26

**M**
Malthus, Thomas, 5
Manhattan Company Bank, 9, 122, 168,
    173
Manhattan Savings Institution, 174
  administration, 27, 28
  assets, 176
  business hours, 31, 32
  commercial accounts
    Bank of North America, 123, 194
    St. Nicholas Bank, 123, 194
    Shoe and Leathers' Bank, 123,
        194
    others, 194
  deposits
    amount of, 160
    average balance per account, 57

interest rates on, 38, 40
limit on size of account, 64
number of accounts, 160
investments
call loans, 139
mortgage loans, 152
similarity with other mutuals,
105-8
opening date, 16
surplus, 44
Manufacturers' and Merchants' Bank,
194
Marine Merchants' Association, 15
Mariner's Savings Institution
administration, 27, 28
employee salaries, 46
trustee participation minimal,
45-46
assets, 179
business hours, 31
deposits
amount of, 160
average balance per account, 57
interest rates on, 38
limit on account size, 64
number of accounts, 160
investments
call loans, 139
similarity with other mutuals,
105-8
opening date, 16
salaries of employees determined by
deposit growth, 46
surplus, 44
Market Bank, 192
Massett, Stephen C., 24-25
McCarthy, Dennis, 10
Mechanics' and Traders' Bank, 192
Mechanics' and Traders' Savings Institution
assets, 178
business hours, 31
deposits
amount of, 160
average balance per account, 57
interest rates on, 38
number of accounts, 160
investments
call loans, 139
similarities with other mutuals,
105-8
opening date, 16
surplus, 44
Mechanics' Bank, 119, 121, 123, 124, 187,
188, 196 (n. 3), 209 (n. 15)
loan to Bank for Savings, 82
stock pledged as security for loans
from, 140

Mercantile Bank, 191
Merchants' Exchange, meeting to repeal
usury law, 109
Miller, Nathan, 76, 83, 122
Mills, Andrew, 29
Mills, James, 27
Morris, Andrew, 209 (n. 15)
Mortgage loans, 4, 75, 91, 92, 93, 94,
101, 103, 104, 105, 106, 107, 110,
111, 112, 113
as an inducement to organize a mutual, 12
Bank for Savings, application denied, 78
contract duration, 151-52
illiquidity during financial panics,
93, 99, 135, 210 (n. 49)
interest rates on
effect of usury law, 108-11, 114
relative to government bonds,
92-93, 110-11, 113
variable, 151-52
legal for mutuals, 7, 75
to New York Public School Society, 75, 89
Murry, John, 84
Mutual savings banks
accounts. See Mutual savings banks,
deposits
administration, 20-30
changes to insure competent and
professional management,
29, 197 (n. 15), 199 (n. 58)
competitive attitude
less on part of older institutions, 41-42, 199 (n. 43)
reasons for increase, 45-47
evaluation in structure, 20
effect of Civil War on, 147
new policies indicate less philanthropic attitude, 30
older institutions maintain original structure longer, 27
shift in management to professional administrators associated with longer business
hours, 32-33, 198 (n. 27)
trustees
composition of board re-
flecting business atti-
tude, 46-47
death and retirement of,
occasion for structural
change in bank, 23-24,
27
depositor's view of, 24-25
duties, 18-19
encourage the founding of

new mutuals, 15, 42
large accounts, policy
    toward, 55-66, 71-72
personal investments, 83
profit motive. *See* Mutual
    savings banks, profit
    motive
part-time operations
    through donation of
    time, 20, 21, 197 (n. 15)
assets, 184-86
charter stipulations, 7-8, 43, 59, 62,
    75-81, 91, 94, 138, 198 (n. 28),
    199 (n. 49), 205 (n. 54), 205 (n.
    55), 205 (n. 60), 210 (n. 59)
depositors
    number in New York City, 4,
        182-83
    occupation and socioeconomic
        status, 49, 50-52, 71-73,
        155-56
deposits
    accounts, 56-57, 157-61, 182-83
    fluctuations, 66-71, 203 (n. 46)
        monthly, 70-71
        in size, 66
    techniques to limit size, 59
development banks, as, 95-96, 148
hours of business, 3, 22, 30-35
    from part-time to full-time,
        30-31
    of newer mutuals, 32-33

investments. *See* by types and by
    banks
legal constraints on, 7-8, 59, 75-81
managers
    ascent to power, 45
    salaries dependent on deposits,
        45-46
New York City. *See*
    Bank for Savings in the City of
        New York
    Bloomingdale Savings Bank
    Bowery Savings Bank
    Broadway Savings Institution
    Dry Dock Savings Institution
    East River Savings Institution
    Emigrant Industrial Savings
        Bank
    German Savings Bank
    Greenwich Savings Bank
    Institution for the Savings of
        Merchants' Clerks
    Irving Savings Institution
    Knickerbocker Savings Institu-
        tion
    Manhattan Savings Institution

Mariners' Savings Institution
Mechanics' and Traders' Sav-
    ings Institution
Rose Hill Savings Bank
Seamen's Bank for Savings
Sixpenny Savings Bank
Union Dime Savings Institution
origins in Europe, 5
organization in New York, 6
pauperism, mutuals as a solution to,
    5-6, 10, 13-15
philanthropic purposes, 5, 11-
    14
politicians abuse of, 18
profit motive, 17-18, 97-98, 108-16,
    117, 130-33, 136-46, 147, 199
    (n. 47)
Myers, Gustavus, 17
Myers, Margaret, 132, 134, 136

N
National Banking Act, 129
New Jersey state debt, 90
New York Board of Health, 87
New York City
    center of mutual savings banking
        activity, 4
    debt, 89, 94, 99, 123, 135, 164, 169,
        171, 174, 186
        Bank for Savings' investments
            in, 78, 94
            before legal to do so, 78
            impact on market price, 78-
                81, 86-87
                Croton Water Works,
                    86-87
                fire loan of 1836, 87
            legal for mutuals, 75
            liquidity of, 99, 135
*New York Herald,* 34
New York Historical Society, 14
New York Interest Bank, 9
New York Life and Trust Company, 127
New York state
    canals
        Bank for Savings financing of,
            75-86, 95, 100
    debt, 89, 99, 135, 164, 167, 169, 171,
        174, 186
        legal constraints on mutuals
            benefits from, 75, 76, 77-81,
                110
        legal for mutual, 7-8, 75
        liquidity of, 99, 134.
        *See also* Erie Canal

O
Ogden, James De Peyster, 24, 26, 109,
    110, 207 (n. 14)

Ohio state
 canals
  Bank for Savings financing of,
   4, 87–89
   effect on market price, 78–
    81, 88–89
   extension of New York system,
    88
  debt, 89, 90
   legal for mutuals, 75
   first investment outside New
    York state, 87–88
  liquidity of, 99, 135
  interest rate paid on account with
   Manhattan Company Bank, 122
Old Alms House, 208 (n. 2)
 original home of Bank for Savings,
  3
Oothout, John, 209 (n. 15)
Oriental Bank, 175

P
Pacific Bank, 191, 192, 193
Palmer, Francis A., 143
Panics
 1825, 134
 1834, 135
 1837, 33, 62, 77, 90, 91, 125–26, 134,
  135, 152
 1839, 99
 1854, 142, 134, 135
 1857, 129, 134, 135, 136
 1861, 134
 1873, 153
Park Bank, 192
Payne, Peter L., 4, 20, 29, 49, 65, 114,
 115, 198 (n. 27), 207 (n. 24)
Pennsylvania state debt, 75, 85, 89, 90,
 104, 135, 206 (n. 8)
Philadelphia Saving Fund Society, 7, 8,
 90–91
 and out-of-state debt, 90–91
Pintard, John, 6, 10, 11, 13, 14, 21, 22,
 42, 51, 59, 60, 61, 62, 66, 82, 84,
 86–87, 96, 148, 196 (n. 32), 196 (n.
 3), 200 (n. 8)
Portfolios. See Investments
Prime, Nathaniel, 83, 121, 203 (n. 14)
Provident Institution for Savings in the
 Town of Boston, 8, 20, 49, 204 (n.
 43)
 administration, 29–30
 average balance per account, 56
 investments
  during high interest rate
   periods, as a test of trustee
   objectives, 114–15
  out-of-state bonds, 90

Public School Society of New York, 75,
 89

R
Real estate loans. See Mortgage loans
Redlich, Fritz, 49, 66, 200 (n. 2)
Ricardo, David, 5
Rockoff, Hugh, 136
Rose Hill Savings Bank
 assets, 180
 business hours, 31, 32
 deposits
  amount of, 160
  average balance per account, 57
  number of accounts, 160
 investments
  call loans, 139
  similarity with other mutuals,
   105–8
 opening date, 16
 surplus, 44

S
Safety Fund Act of 1829, 140
St. Nicholas Bank, 133, 176
Savings Association, proposed in 1809,
 6
Savings Bank of Baltimore, 4, 7, 8, 13,
 20, 49, 100–101, 207 (n. 24)
 administration, 29–30
 average balance per account, 53, 56,
  65–66
 investments
  as indication of trustee objectives, 114–15
  government debt, 114–15
  out-of-state, 90
Savings Bank of the City of New York,
 7–9
 Act of Incorporation, 8–9
Savings Bank of New York, 7–9
Scheiber, Harry, 76, 88, 89
Schoals, Francis P., 143
Schuyler, George W., 65
Seamen's Bank for Savings, 4, 15, 23,
 40–41, 46, 94, 132, 147
 administration, 27–28, 147
 assets, 165–67
 business hours, 31, 32
 commercial banks
  accounts in
   Bank of Commerce, 125,
    189
   Fulton Bank, 124, 188
   Leather Manufacturers'
    Bank, 124, 188–89
   Mechanics' Bank, 124, 188

interest rates received
    from, 123
avoidance of identity with, 33,
    125
deposits
    amount of, 158
    average balance per account, 53,
        56, 66
    growth, 104
        rapid due to high interest
            rates, 66, 69
    interest rates on, 36-37, 39, 41-
        42, 66, 69
    monthly fluctuations, 66, 67,
        70-71
    number of accounts, 158
    relation to investment policy,
        104
    size of accounts
        by depositors, 53, 62-63
        limit on size, 58
investments
    during periods of high interest
        rates as a test of trustee ob-
        jectives, 112-14, 115
    kinds
        call loans, 138-39
        city bonds, 94, 99
            New York City, 167
        mortgage loans, 91-92, 99,
            104, 113
            to American Seamen's
                Friend Society,
                151
            to Yates and MacIntyre,
                92
        state bonds
            New York, 99, 167
            Ohio, 89, 90, 99
            Pennsylvania, 90
        U.S. Government bonds
            and Treasury notes, 99
        secondary reserves, reliance on,
            99, 104, 113, 135
    opening date, 16
    surplus, 43-44
Seamen's Fund and Retreat, 15
Second Bank of the United States, 121
Shoe and Leathers' Bank, 133, 193, 194
Sixpenny Savings Bank
    assets, 179
    business hours, 31
    deposits
        amount of, 160
        average balance per account, 57,
            64
        interest rates on, 38, 64
        number of accounts, 160

size, 64
investments
    call loans, 139
    similarity with other mutuals,
        105-8
    opening date, 16
    surplus, 44
Slocum, William H., 29
Smith, Edward, 60
Society for the Encouragement of Faith-
    ful Domestic Servants in New York,
    51
Society for the Prevention of Pauperism,
    10-11, 14
    campaign for savings banks, 10
    treatise on pauperism, 10
Society for Promotion of the Gospel
    among Seamen in the Port of New
    York, 15
Split-dividend policy, 35-39, 59, 66, 69,
    72. See also Bank for Savings, de-
    posits, interest rates on; Bowery
    Savings Bank, deposits, interest rates
    on
Strong, Benjamin, 27
Strong, Charles, E., 26
Strong, George T., 23, 24, 26, 148
Strong, George W., 22
Surplus accounts, 17, 42-45, 93, 105
    legislation to limit, 40
    newer banks, difficulty in acquiring,
        44-45
    older banks, difficulty in maintain-
        ing, 44-45
Swan, Benjamin, 209 (n. 15)
Suydam, James, 26

T
Taylor, Najah, 23, 26
Tradesmens' Bank, 191, 192
Treasury notes. See U.S. government
    bonds and Treasury notes
Torrens, Robert, 5
Tylee, Daniel C., 42
Trustees. See Mutual savings banks, ad-
    ministration, trustees

U
Union Bank, 123, 187
Union Dime Savings Institution
    assets, 181
    business hours, 31
    deposits
        amount of, 161
        average balance per account, 57
        interest rate on, 38
        number of accounts, 161
    investments

call loans, 139, 210 (n. 58)
similarity with other mutuals, 105-8
opening date, 16
surplus, 44
U.S. government bonds and Treasury notes, 115, 164, 167, 169, 171, 174, 186
legal for mutuals, 7, 75, 78
provide liquidity and secondary reserves, 99, 104, 113, 129, 134-36
Usury law, 76, 97, 108-11, 112, 152
allocative effects on mutual investments, 110-11
in Maryland, 114
in Massachusetts, 97, 114
New York state, benefits from, 110

V
Varick, Richard, 7
Vatter, Barbara, 97, 109

W
Wage rates, as an indication of account ownership, 54-55
Washington Insurance Company, 123
Western Inland Lock and Navigation Co., 84
Williams, Micajah T., 88
Women, special hours and windows in mutuals for, 32

Y
Yates and McIntyre, 92